THE COMPLETE PRACTICAL GUIDE TO
CAMPING, HIKING &
WILDERNESS SKILLS

D1428409

THE COMPLETE PRACTICAL GUIDE TO
CAMPING HIKING & WILDERNESS SKILLS

How to enjoy the great outdoors in complete comfort and safety –
everything from simple tents and outside vacationing to navigation,
wilderness problem-solving and coping with extreme weather

PETER G. DRAKE

HERMES
HOUSE

Dedication: To my parents, who gave me my first chance to travel to wild places; to Kate who has helped me so much to continue travelling over the last 30 years, and to Neil and Colin who have made some of the expeditions special because they were there with me.

This edition is published by Hermes House

Hermes House is an imprint of Anness Publishing Ltd
Hermes House, 88–89 Blackfriars Road, London SE1 8HA
tel. 020 7401 2077; fax 020 7633 9499; info@anness.com

A CIP catalogue record for this book is available from the British Library.

Publisher: Joanna Lorenz
Editorial Director: Helen Sudell
Senior Editor: Sarah Ainley
Photographer: Martyn Milner
Designer: Nigel Partridge
Illustrator: Peter Bull Art Studio
Editorial Reader: Jay Thundercliffe
Production Controller: Steve Lang

1 3 5 7 9 10 8 6 4 2

DISCLAIMER

The author and publisher wish to stress that they strongly advise the use of a helmet and flotation aid in all paddling situations, a close-fitting cycle helmet when cycling, and a secure safety helmet when riding a horse. Travelling and living in the wilderness are all about taking responsibility for your own decisions, actions and personal safety. Although the advice and information in this book are believed to be accurate and true at the time of going to press, neither the author nor the publisher can accept any legal responsibility or liability for any errors or omissions that may be made, nor for any inaccuracies nor for any harm or injury that comes about from following instructions or advice in this book.

CONTENTS

INTRODUCTION

As little as fifty or so years ago, the wilderness areas of the world were places that few people, except the indigenous inhabitants, had any means of exploring. They were virtually the exclusive reserve of a small group of explorers, scientists and travellers, who needed either the backing of large commercial companies or research organizations, or had private means. Today all this has changed. There are now many companies offering adventure holidays, and the relatively low cost of air travel has brought the remotest parts of the world within the reach of many more travellers. The huge number of travel programmes on television have made such places seem familiar, while newspaper articles and guidebooks deliver detailed information on almost every country of the world.

The democratization of travel has meant that the pressure on sometimes fragile environments has increased a hundredfold, so that enthusiastic travellers are in danger of destroying

▼ *Mountain regions offer the adventurous traveller some of the hardest challenges, but also some of the greatest rewards.*

the very places they have set out to see. In some cases national authorities have been forced to impose rules and regulations on people wishing to go to these wilderness areas. In some ways this defeats the wish of people to get back to the simpler, more natural life of the wilderness, but it is a balancing act that must be achieved in order to protect the natural world.

As an example of this, we only need to visit the base camp area of Mount Everest, where once two or possibly three national expeditions camped each year. Now there are commercial companies taking tens of people up the mountain at a time, and producing large amounts of rubbish and waste in what was once a pristine environment.

In the 1960s you could still visit Mount Kenya or Kilimanjaro, hire your own porter and simply set off up the mountain, so long as you gave your name to the local authority or national park. Now you have to buy into a package that provides you with accommodation, guides, porters and food, taking away much of the fun of planning your own expedition. But because of the number who wish to

▲ *Travelling on horseback gives you the freedom to roam, and to appreciate all the sounds, smells and sights of the landscape.*

climb these mountains, there has to be some sort of control or the very wilderness that everybody is seeking would soon disappear.

The era of fast, cheap world travel has, ironically, brought its own set of problems for the adventure traveller. You can leave London or New York and be in the African bush or on the Arctic tundra within 24 hours, but you may not always be prepared either physically or mentally for the environment you find yourself in. This was not the case in the past, when travel was slower and gave one time to adjust to new environments and acclimatize to the cold, heat or altitude. However, there is much that you can do before you travel in terms of training and planning to allow you to make the most of your trip, whether you are travelling on foot, by boat, with animals or in a vehicle.

In writing this book, I have tried to highlight some of the skills you need to plan your visit to the wilderness, to stay there comfortably and safely and to enjoy these unique environments. There is practical advice on training before you leave, on equipping your expedition and on skills such as navigation, fieldcraft and campcraft.

▲ *Carrying all your camping equipment on your back allows you to travel along remote and beautiful paths and stop where you like.*

▼ *The leisurely pace of river travel by kayak or canoe offers a unique approach to a region and a close-up view of nature.*

You must also remember that even the best planned expeditions can go wrong, so you should always have a back-up plan. Be realistic about the risks associated with your trip, and always think ahead.

All of the wilderness areas of the world are very special and, in many cases, a shrinking asset, so look after them and try to be able to say, when you come back, that you left it no worse and, if possible, a little better than you found it.

To sum up why we want to go to wilderness areas, I cannot do better than repeat here the reasons given by a traveller in East Africa in the 1930s:

Why do I travel? I get hot, exhausted, burnt about the face, frightfully thin. I get covered in fleas, and all the sand flies and mosquitoes in the district come and graze on me. I eat the most awful food and drink the most awful tea. If I lie down in the shade, the sun goes swiftly round the tree until it is shining right on me.

But I see views, people and places I never imagined existed. I learn new customs and hear old history. Sometimes I am wonderfully lucky and see something very few other people have seen before. I make friends with all sorts of people in remote villages. I get hard and strong, my mind opens out and becomes more receptive and for a short time I'm not only independent but completely responsible for my own safety. I shed the aura of civilization and become quite a different person.

I hope the skills outlined in this book will help to set you on a sure path to adventure, and give you the confidence to find your way safely through the wilderness and to enjoy these wonderful places.
PETER G. DRAKE

PLANNING & PREPARATION

Good planning is the key to a successful trip and anticipation is a big part
of the pleasure of travelling. Careful preparations mean that everything
should run smoothly and problems can be coped with rather than turning
into crises. Don't make your plans so rigid that you can't enjoy the
unforeseen: be prepared to take a different path or follow up an exciting
opportunity that presents itself during your trip.

Planning your Trip

Some degree of planning is necessary for any kind of trip. The complexity of your planning will depend on factors such as the remoteness of the area, the size of the group, and the length of the trip, but there are several decisions that have to be made in advance for even the most straightforward of outings.

Start the planning by thinking of the type of trip you want to take. When you have decided what this is, you can start to think about the destination, the people who will be going with you, the route, the means of travel, and the length of time you will be away.

You may not be able to make final decisions without doing some research, using maps, guidebooks or the internet, and you may need to adapt or change your plans as you gather information about what is involved. This is why planning is so important. The more thoroughly you think through your ideas and construct your plan, the less chance you have of encountering unexpected problems during your trip.

DOMESTIC TRIPS

If you are going on a walking week somewhere in your own country, then choosing your destination and your travelling companions, finding out train times or planning a car journey, calling the local tourist information office for information about campsites and buying suitable maps are the key tasks. You will have to consider what type of clothing and equipment you are likely to need, and if you do not own some of the items already, you may have to borrow or buy them. It is important for safety and comfort that your clothing and equipment are suitable for the climate, and some research into the kind of weather you can expect will prove invaluable.

Depending on the activities you are planning, you may need to buy additional insurance or brush up your skills with some training. Health concerns may need to be addressed, and you should familiarize yourself with basic first aid skills.

▲ *A day's kayaking can give you a new perspective on an area, so check out the range of activities available at your destination.*

◀ *Find out about the terrain and expected weather conditions – how you cope with these is central to the success of your trip.*

FOREIGN TRIPS

If you are going further afield, your planning may involve booking trains, ferries or planes, obtaining permits to walk or climb, hiring transport or obtaining paperwork for your vehicle, as well as obtaining visas, vaccinations and an international driving licence – all in addition to the things you need for a domestic trip.

If you are hoping to travel part of your route by cycle, horse or canoe, some practice sessions are a good idea to ensure that potential problems are identified and sorted out before you are out in the field. A cycle touring trip, where the bike is loaded with heavy gear, is very different from a day's cycling in the countryside; and even if you can already ride a horse, if you are planning an expedition on horseback, you need to know how to feed and

PLANNING AND PREPARATION CHECKLIST

12 months ahead
- Decide on the destination, route and aims of the trip.
- Decide on the group members.
- Think about transport options.
- Think about the activities to be undertaken.
- Carry out your risk assessment.
- Seek permission from countries or places to be visited.
- Produce an outline budget.
- Produce an information sheet on the area to be visited.

10–12 months ahead
- Hold the first meeting for the group.
- Finalize the dates of the trips.
- Check that all members have passed any medical examinations required
- Finalize the details of any activities to be undertaken.
- Agree the dates of any training sessions.
- Have a camping weekend with all the people going on your trip.

8–10 months ahead
- Finalize the list of equipment needed.
- Draw up a personal equipment list.
- Arrange insurance (medical, personal, third party indemnity, and so on).
- Draw up an outline menu and food requirements.
- Book any ferry crossings, flights, rail tickets, campsites or hotels.
- Appoint a home contact.

4 months ahead
- Obtain any visas required.
- Start any vaccination programme required.
- Finalize food and menus.
- Finalize the itinerary for the trip.

1 month ahead
- Obtain any additional paperwork.
- Pack all non-perishable food.
- Gather together, check and pack all equipment.
- Check and make ready any vehicles you will be using.
- Send any freight ahead.

- Change money and buy travellers' cheques, if using.

1 week ahead
- Complete all vaccination programmes; start to take malaria tablets, if appropriate.
- Check all equipment and food against lists.
- Check all passports and other travel documentation.
- Go through the complete itinerary with the home contact.

1 day ahead
- Check your tickets.
- Check your kit and make sure you have packed everything.
- Check with the airport, ferry port or train station that there has been no change or delay to your transport plans.
- Make sure your hand luggage does not have anything in it that will cause you problems at airport security checks.

care for the horses at night. If you are travelling to a remote area and will be a long way from professional medical services, your first aid preparations need to be substantial. You may have to follow a vaccination programme before you travel, and you will need to take considerably more with you in your first-aid kit. In terms of first aid skills, a wider knowledge is invaluable for expeditions to remote areas or involving higher-risk activities, such as mountaineering: in the event of an accident, your chances of survival are far greater if you know what to do.

For such an expedition, planning should start at least 12 months before the trip. The checklist shown above is one that you may find useful. It is only a starting point, and you may find that you can leave some of the items out and/or add some of your own.

▶ *An off-road cycling trip can be hard going, and a programme of fitness training may be necessary for several months before you travel.*

First Thoughts

There are many different aspects to consider when organizing a trip in the wilderness, and numerous detailed plans need to be made. The enormity of the project can seem very daunting when you first begin to think it through, but if you break the task down and deal with each aspect one by one, the planning will be easier to manage and you will soon find that you have resolved all the issues.

▼ *Children can greatly enjoy a trip to the wilderness, but make sure you make your plans for the trip with them in mind.*

THE TEAM
If you are choosing a team, think about the number of people that will work best for the activities you are planning. If it is a large group, it may be a good idea to have a designated leader. Choose your travelling companions with care and bear in mind that people react in different ways to the pressures of life in the wilderness. The group needs to be compatible, with roughly equal levels of fitness. Encourage individuals to talk about what they hope to gain from the experience: taking on board everyone's comments

and establishing objectives is the first step in the organizational strategy. If team members do not know each other in advance, plan a trial camping weekend to see how you all get along. For more information, see the section Getting your Team Together.

BUDGET
Once your plans have been drafted, you need to work out a realistic budget. It is important to do this early on so that you can amend your plans to fit the budget if the total works out to be more than you want to spend. Do not underestimate costs and include a contingency fund of at least 15 per cent of the total. For more information, see the section Planning the Budget.

INSURANCE
Never overlook insurance, and make sure you are covered for the activities you are planning, as well as for your life, health and possessions in the area you are visiting. For more information, see the section Money and Insurance.

EQUIPMENT
A list of personal and group equipment can be drawn up only once you have chosen the team and decided where you are travelling to, when you are going, and what you are going to do when you get there. For information on what you need to take with you, see the section Equipment.

**MEDICAL PROVISIONS
AND FITNESS**
If you are in doubt about whether there will be reasonable access to medical help in the area you are travelling to, you may prefer to have someone in the team with reliable first aid knowledge; discuss the most appropriate type of training with your team. Check if you need vaccinations or any particular medication, such as malaria tablets, and consider what level of fitness the team will require for the activities you have planned. For more information, see the section Medical Preparations.

PLANNING FOR A GROUP

You may be planning a trip for an existing group of people – your family, for example – and this might mean that you need to accommodate a fairly wide range of abilities and interests.

- If you're travelling with children, make sure you know their limits and don't push them too hard.
- Keep your plans flexible and be ready to compromise: tired, irritable children will wreck everyone's day. If you are crossing time zones, give children plenty of time to adapt.
- Build some rest days into your itinerary. The strongest, fittest members of the group can use these days for additional, more challenging excursions if they wish, returning to camp to meet up with the group in the evening.

TRANSPORT

Consider how best to transport the team and all of its equipment to your destination. Bear in mind that the means of travel will affect the amount of luggage you can take with you.

If your trip is being planned as a simple loop, starting and finishing in the same place, you can drive to the location and leave your car (or hire car) for when you get back, or you may be able to arrange a pick-up from a family member or friend. Depending on the size of the group, you may find it easier (particularly with a group of young people) and more enjoyable to hire a multi-seater vehicle and travel together, rather than make your own way there in individual cars.

If you are planning to travel by public transport, check that there is a connecting service all the way to the start of the route, and work out how you will get there if there isn't. If you require seat reservations – which is advisable for a larger group of people – you will need to book early. Be prepared for departure delays or cancellations, with a contingency plan and a budget in case you are faced with unexpected

accommodation costs. Check that you will be able to carry bulky equipment such as bicycles or kayaks and all the related gear. If travelling by plane, find out about the weight allowance and the penalty that you will be liable to pay if you exceed it. If you are taking a vehicle abroad, see the section Vehicle-related Paperwork.

▲ *Some team members may see the trip as a chance for relaxation, while others may be making plans for an action-packed adventure. Find out what individuals expect to gain from the trip so that you can plan accordingly.*

▼ *Travelling by plane will affect the amount of equipment you can carry, so your means of transport should be one of your first decisions.*

Getting your Team Together

Having the right people in your team will add to the enjoyment of your trip and will help to make it a more valuable experience. Suitable travelling companions are as important as the right equipment, and they need to be given just as much thought.

CHOOSING AN OBJECTIVE

Whether you are planning a trip with family members, or with friends, or as part of a team of new acquaintances, encourage people to communicate their expectations and goals for the trip before you go, and try to synchronize these goals into a common objective for the team. A shared objective is a good incentive that will encourage cohesion in the group. Spend time discussing likely situations and deal with concerns until you have a clear objective that you can all feel happy with, and one that is well within the capabilities of everyone.

CHOOSING TEAM MEMBERS

If you have an idea for a trip and are now choosing others to go with you, pick people with whom you get along and who have a level of experience similar to your own. Make sure they are compatible with each other, and seem happy with the idea of teamwork and group decision-making, and that they share your objectives for the trip.

If you need individuals with specific skills, such as first aid, be clear about their level of skill and check that their training is up to date; if it is not, ask them to take a refresher course.

A similar level of physical and mental fitness across the team is important. It may seem unkind to reject someone because of ill-health or injury, but an unfit person can slow down and even endanger the whole group. If conditions will be demanding, consider whether individuals are up to the challenge, or will turn out to be complainers.

▼ *A shared agenda, common goals and compatible personalities among the team are key features for a successful trip.*

▶ *Good communication is essential, and leaders need to talk to the group at least once a day to keep everybody informed.*

LEADERSHIP

For a trip involving a large group of people, it is a good idea to have a leader. This person can be self-appointed or chosen by the group, but he or she must command sufficient respect to be able to direct the group under good and bad conditions. The leader role is especially important with a group of children, or when travelling in unfamiliar or difficult terrain, or if the planned activities require a specific skill or experience.

With a group of adult friends, the leadership role can be informal, but for a group of above 20 people, a bigger leadership structure may be needed, and other team members can be asked to take responsibility for particular concerns, such as driving or first aid.

Communication

This is the most important skill a leader can exercise. A leader needs sound judgement and has to be able to lead discussions and communicate effectively, delegate tasks, and act as a mediator in the event of disagreement or conflict. Communication is especially important when people are in difficult conditions and possibly suffering stress and panic. If communication fails, members will at best become dissatisfied and the whole trip may become an unhappy experience. At worst, the group may come to grief.

Personality problems

A clash of personalities needs to be sorted out as soon as possible (preferably before you leave if you spot it that soon). If the group starts to break up into cliques, its common objective will become more difficult to achieve. Fun bonding activities, such as team games, can help to restore team spirit.

Always avoid showing favouritism. If it is noticed, some individuals may feel undervalued, and it could act as a spark for bad behaviour or aggression.

POSSIBLE ROLES FOR TEAM MEMBERS

The list below gives an idea of the different areas of responsibility that exist within a team. You may need only some of these in your group.

Deputy leader

To take over from the leader if anything happens to him or her before or during the trip.

Quartermaster

To be responsible for all equipment and food, and for looking after and issuing these throughout the trip.

Field treasurer

To approve the final budget, record all expenditure in the field and make sure the money lasts for the duration of the trip; may also be in charge of safeguarding funds and valuables.

Head of camp kitchen

To appoint a daily team and organize a rota to carry out food preparation, cooking, and washing-up duties, to oversee those duties and to draw up appropriate daily menus.

Medic or first aider

To treat team injuries and illnesses during the trip, and to look after the group first-aid kit; for larger groups, to keep a record of allergies or intolerances and any prescription medication being taken by anyone in the team; to record any illness or accidents that happen during the trip and the treatment given; could also be responsible for pre-expedition medical check-ups, vaccination programmes and fitness sessions.

Navigator

To look after and carry the maps and compass, to advise on the planning of the route, and to ensure that all team members follow the correct route.

Translator

To communicate on behalf of the group when travelling in a foreign country with a native language different to your own. Someone who can understand a handful of phrases and key words is enormously useful.

Planning the Budget

The first task when you are planning the finances for a trip is to work out how much money you will need. The next task is to decide how the money is going to be spent. For both of these processes you will need a budget. The budget outline here is a starting point to which you can add or subtract headings to suit your trip.

BEING REALISTIC
Make your budget realistic and err on the side of caution, so that you can be confident you will be able to pay for all aspects of the trip. If you are worrying about money while you are away, your enjoyment will suffer.

Plan your budget in advance to give you time to research the costs fully. If you cannot get confirmed prices, get as many estimates as you can. Note the best price (lowest) and the worst price (highest) and budget in between the two. Ideally, the budgeted figures will

▲ *Even a simple backpacking trip involves costs, and you need to think about every aspect of the trip to plan a useful budget.*

work out just about right or too high. If they don't, you will have to dip into your contingency fund to cover basic expenditure, such as food, transport and accommodation, and there will be less money available for an emergency that necessitates a sudden change of plan.

BANK FEES
If you need to buy foreign currency, plan for bank charges for money changing and for transferring money abroad. If you have opened a bank account for the trip, budget for the charges that apply to any account.

FOOD AND EQUIPMENT
If travelling by public transport, check that you will not exceed the baggage allowance on your ticket, as this can incur charges. Goods can be freighted, but this can be expensive, and getting through customs can be costly in terms of money and time. Find out if it would be cheaper to buy food and equipment at your destination.

CONTINGENCY
Like insurance, this is essential. Allow at least 15 per cent if your trip will include vehicle transport, as you may need to pay cash for mechanical repairs.

BUDGET OUTLINE

Administration
- Postage
- Telephone/fax/ internet charges
- Publicity
- Passports and visas

Equipment
- Buy
- Hire

Training
- Canoeing or kayaking/ horse riding/cycling/ skiing
- First aid

Transport
- Plane/ferry/train/bus/taxi
- Vehicle hire
- Animal hire

Freight
- Equipment
- Vehicles

Insurance
- Personal
- Vehicle

Bank charges
- Currency changing
- Bank transfers

Food
- Buy at home
- Buy abroad

Field expenses
- Living costs
- Hire of guides/local people
- Fuel
- Customs and port duty
- Gifts
- Miscellaneous

Post-expedition expenses
- Administration
- Photography

15% contingency fund

Money and Insurance

When planning any kind of expedition, you need to consider the safest and most convenient way of carrying money. Make sure you have adequate insurance cover for all of your planned activities.

MONEY
There are a number of ways to take the money you will need in the field. Try to pay for as much as possible in advance, so that you do not have the additional risk of carrying large sums of money with you.

Travellers' cheques
These are far less tempting to thieves because they can be used only with a passport as proof of identification. Buy travellers' cheques in the currency of your destination or, if these are not available, in the currency most acceptable there. A mixture of small and large denominations is the most useful. People and businesses in rural areas and in some developing countries do not accept travellers' cheques as payment, and it will be necessary to take cash in the local currency with you as well.

Cash restrictions
In some countries, in order to control the income generated by tourism, it is necessary to change a certain amount of money per person into the local currency, and you may not be allowed to change it back again or to take it out of the country. Find out if such rules apply at your destination before you travel, and budget accordingly.

Credit cards
You may not be able to use credit cards outside larger centres of population or international hotels, and check service charges and exchange rates before using credit cards to withdraw cash from ATMs abroad. Company credit cards are available for services such as car hire. International car hire companies issue them, and anything spent on the card is billed to you in your own currency, which makes it easier to check what has been spent.

INSURANCE
Standard holiday insurance will cover your needs for most trips, but you may need to take out specialist insurance for more adventurous activities.

Personal accident insurance
Standard holiday insurance will usually include a pay-out for personal accident claims, but ensure that it gives adequate cover for death, loss of a limb or sight.

Medical insurance
If you are going to an area with inadequate or non-existent medical services, air ambulance cover will be essential. You may also require separate rescue insurance if you plan to be in a remote or mountainous area, or if you are sea-touring in a canoe or kayak.

Baggage insurance
Most holiday insurance policies include an amount for delayed or lost baggage. Expensive items such as cameras and jewellery should be properly insured; avoid taking valuable items that are not necessary for the trip. Household insurance may cover some items, but always read the small print on your policy before you travel.

Credit card insurance
Always be insured against the loss or theft of credit cards because cards are such an obvious target for thieves.

▼ *Even if you intend to carry travellers' cheques and credit cards, you should still take some cash in small denominations.*

Note the telephone number of the lost or stolen card department of your card issuer and keep it with you in a safe place, separate from your credit card.

Hazardous pursuits insurance
Winter sports, mountaineering, boating, diving, big game hunting and other hazardous pursuits usually require specific insurance, even if you are not travelling abroad. Check the details of your standard holiday insurance policy to see what it will and will not include. As there is a greater risk of injury with these activities, insurance is essential.

Third-party insurance
It is sensible to have this in case, for any reason, you harm, or even kill, someone, or cause damage to their property. Third-party insurance is usually included in standard holiday policies, but check before you travel.

Vehicle insurance
If you are hiring a vehicle or taking your own with you, make sure you have sufficient cover for the country you will be driving in, as well as any countries you may need to drive through to get there.

Light aircraft insurance
If your plans include flying in a light aircraft, check that you are covered with your personal accident insurance. If you will be flying the aircraft yourself, it may count as a hazardous pursuit and require separate insurance.

Risk Assessment

As a member of a team, you have a responsibility to yourself and to the other members of your team. It is essential to assess the possible risks that any activity undertaken on the trip could bring, where team members might be harmed and how high the level of risk is.

WHY ASSESS RISK?

Risk assessment is the evaluation of an activity to determine what could go wrong, who could be hurt and what could be done to manage the identified problems. Accidents will happen, but efficient risk assessment will reduce the potential for accidents and enable lessons to be learned from near misses and actual incidents.

IDENTIFYING HAZARDS

Mentally step back from the activity and look at it from a fresh point of view, concentrating on those aspects that could result in serious harm. Ask people who are unfamiliar with the activity what they think, as they might identify areas not immediately obvious to a regular practitioner. Equipment manufacturers' instructions may also help you to identify hazards and risks.

You should take into account other potential hazards, too, including natural disasters, extreme weather conditions, acclimatization to high altitude, dangerous wildlife and the safety of

▼ *A good guidebook can highlight potential dangers in a region, but check foreign office websites for the latest and most reliable information.*

local drinking water. If mountain rescue services could be needed, check that they will be available. Be aware of medical/health hazards and make sure that everyone has had the necessary inoculations. A good guidebook should be able to provide this information. Your journey may take you into a politically unstable area, where civil war, guerrilla warfare, kidnapping for ransom, or terrorist activity may be a threat. Foreign office websites will usually have the most up-to-date and reliable information.

When undertaking any activity, those most obviously at risk are the participants and their instructors, but you also need to gauge the potential for harm to those waiting to take part, spectators and passers-by.

EVALUATING RISK

Having identified the separate elements of the activity, you need to assign a level of risk to each element. Grade the level of risk from high to moderate or low, and take into account the past history of the activity, which may include actual incidents as well as any near misses.

▲ *An off-road mountain biking trip seems like a low-risk activity, but the potential for injury is high, especially for novices.*

A change of operating technique, additional equipment or increased training might be all that is needed to reduce the level of risk and therefore improve safety, without eliminating the

▼ *Guerrilla warfare presents a serious risk to personal safety: it is advisable to change your plans if this appears to be a hazard.*

element of challenge. Check the small print of your insurance policies (personal, vehicle and group policies) to be sure you have a level of cover that reflects the risk involved.

RECORD KEEPING

Keep records of when equipment and facilities to be used by your team were acquired (new or used), their service history, any repairs or changes, and incidents that happen on your trip. The records should be made available to any other people who may wish to use the equipment in the future.

ASSESSMENT PROCEDURE

- Look at the hazards.
- Decide who may be harmed and how.
- Evaluate the risks arising from the hazards and decide whether existing procedures are adequate or if more should be done.
- Record your findings.
- Consult your risk assessment during your trip, and revise as necessary.
- Review your assessment after your trip and revise as necessary.

▲ *Basic training before the trip is advisable for activities such as canoeing, where some knowledge of the skills will improve safety.*

▼ *Fitness and discipline are important in mountain country or on rough terrain, where careless accidents can easily happen.*

Personal Paperwork

Paperwork may not be the most exciting part of travel, but it is vitally important. If you arrive at a border or get stopped by the police, you could be in real trouble if you do not have the correct personal documents.

PASSPORT

Make sure you have at least six months of life left on your passport if you are going to a country where you require a visa. Most visas will require at least a half page and in many cases a full page of your passport, so make sure you have sufficient pages empty in your passport.

Some countries issue passports with more than the normal number of pages in them, so if you are completing lots of international travel, especially to countries that require visas, it is worth considering getting one of these. Otherwise, if the normal one runs out of pages before it has expired, you will have to pay for another passport.

VISAS

These are a way for a country to control who gets into it and, in some cases, to make money from visitors and tourists. Visa regulations are constantly under review as immigration policies change and are revised from time to time.

You should telephone the embassy of the country you wish to visit while you are still in your own country, or contact its website on the internet, to find out if you will need a visa.

Visas for which you need to make an application can be obtained from the relevant embassy in your own country, either in person or by post. Depending on your nationality, your reason for travel and your destination, the issuing time can vary from hours to weeks. If you are sending your passport and visa application, plus the fee, by post, make sure you use a registered postal service and make a note of your passport number or photocopy the information pages of your passport before you post it. To get into some countries, you will also need to be sponsored by someone already living and working there. Always make sure you read the requirements of a visa very carefully because if you get it wrong and are refused entry, you may never be allowed a visa again.

If you are already abroad, you will usually be able to get your visa from the appropriate embassy in a neighbouring country. This can take time: in some cases, up to several weeks. Do not lose your patience with the embassy system or its staff; it will not speed up the process and it could lead to further delays, if not a refusal of the visa.

This is one instance where it pays to plan ahead. Decide if you are going to visit any country for which you need a visa while you are planning your trip. This will allow you plenty of time to apply for the visa(s) while you are still at home.

◀ *Keep your passport and other papers secure, not only while travelling but also between trips, as they have a high value on the black market.*

PAPERWORK CHECKLIST

• Passport
• Visas
• Driving licence
• International driving permit
• Record of vaccinations
• International certificate of vaccination
• International camping carnet
• Currency and valuables documents

DRIVING LICENCE

Take a photocopy of your national driving licence, even if you know that you need an international driving permit to drive abroad. A national licence with your photograph on it will be accepted by most car hire companies abroad as a form of identification and proof of your ability to drive.

INTERNATIONAL DRIVING PERMIT

This document is recognized worldwide as proof that you hold a valid driving licence in your own country. The international driving permit (IDP) does not have to be carried as a legal requirement for foreign drivers in every country, because many countries recognize each others' licences, but it is intended to help motorists driving abroad, where licence requirements can vary widely, and it can be an advantage to be able to produce it if you run into difficulties with the transport authorities. It may also be a useful form of pictured identification in the case of a lost or stolen passport.

The international driving permit is printed in 10 languages – the five official languages of the United Nations (English, French, Spanish, Russian and Chinese) plus German, Arabic, Italian, Swedish and Portuguese. It is available, on payment of a small fee, from motoring organizations in the country in which your national driving licence was issued.

RECORD OF VACCINATIONS

Medical organizations and even some airlines now issue booklets in which you can record all the vaccinations you have had and when you had them. These are a convenient reminder to keep vaccinations up to date and they may also provide some sort of proof, if they are in a semi-official booklet, to a border guard or local doctor that you have received the vaccinations. If you do not have a booklet, note the vaccinations you have had and when you had them on a piece of paper and keep it with your passport.

INTERNATIONAL CERTIFICATE OF VACCINATION

Also known as the Yellow Card, this is internationally recognized proof that you have immunization against certain diseases, including measles, mumps, rubella, typhoid, hepatitis A, yellow fever and polio – all of which are recommended if you are travelling to developing countries or to rural or undeveloped areas of developed countries. It is issued by the doctor or medical organization that gave you the vaccination. Make sure the certificate is properly filled in and date-stamped with the official stamp of the centre, otherwise it may not be accepted. In some countries, you may be asked for the certificate at the border; if you do not have it, you will usually be offered the vaccination on the spot – to be administered by non-medical staff working in poor conditions and with a risk of dirty needles – or no entry.

INTERNATIONAL CAMPING CARNET

This document is issued by camping organizations worldwide, and has your passport details added to it. At many campsites you may be able to hand it in instead of your passport, which allows you to keep your passport for changing money, cashing travellers' cheques or any other reason, including peace of mind. Campsites are not obliged to accept the carnet in place of your passport, so find out in advance what the policy is at the campsites you intend to use.

CURRENCY DECLARATION

In some countries, a declaration of foreign currency has to be filled in at the border. This covers high-value items such as cameras and jewellery as well as money. Though it won't always happen, the documents can be requested when you leave the country, to check you haven't sold the items, so fill them in correctly and do not lose them.

▲ *Visa requirements vary widely between countries, depending on your nationality. Check foreign office websites for the latest information regarding what you need.*

▼ *If you are planning to paddle on rivers or lakes, check that the water has unlimited public access and you are not trespassing on private land, particularly when you are abroad or unfamiliar with local by-laws.*

Vehicle-related Paperwork

If you are planning to take a vehicle abroad with you, you should allow time to assemble all the relevant paperwork that is needed in addition to your national and international driving licences. In some countries, you could run into serious difficulties if you are stopped by the police without the correct documentation, and a lack of adequate insurance could be disastrous in the event of a breakdown or accident.

Vehicle-related documents are usually issued by driving organizations in your own country. If you are unsure about what you will need contact one of these organizations for up-to-date advice before you travel.

REGISTRATION DOCUMENTS

These documents will be required to prove ownership of the vehicle you are driving if you are stopped by the police or if you try to cross a national border.

INSURANCE PAPERS

Always carry the original paperwork for the insurance cover you have in your own country, and make sure the policy is valid. If you are taking your vehicle abroad, international insurance is available from national motoring organizations and insurance companies.

Additional protection is provided by the Green Card, which is recognized in over 40 countries (mostly in Europe, but including Russia, Iraq and Iran) as part of a United Nations system to protect motorists abroad. The Green Card does not provide insurance cover but is proof that the requirements for third-party liability insurance in the countries for which the Green Card is valid are covered by the motorist's insurance policy in their own country. Contact motoring organizations in your own country to find out if you are eligible and for further details.

PAPERWORK CHECKLIST
• Driving licence
• International driving licence
• Registration documents
• Motor insurance
• International certificate for motor vehicles
• Letter of authority
• Customs carnet

INTERNATIONAL CERTIFICATE FOR MOTOR VEHICLES

This is a vehicle passport and is valid for one year. It gives the registration document information in a number of different languages. Although the number of countries that accept it is limited, it is worth having for its translation of the information about the vehicle – which you may find useful if you need to visit a garage for mechanical repairs and you don't speak the local language. It also provides a way of recording your vehicle entering and leaving a country.

LETTER OF AUTHORITY

If you are driving a vehicle of which you are not the owner, such as a hire car, you will require a letter from the owner or the hire company stating your registration details, that you have their permission to drive the vehicle, and in what countries you will be travelling.

CUSTOMS CARNET

In some countries, you will be required to have a customs carnet to take a vehicle from one country to another, and to avoid having to pay customs duty on the vehicle. When you arrive at the border on leaving or entering, your papers will be checked and you will be asked to put up a bond – ostensibly to cover the cost of the customs duty, although the bond can be up to several times the cost of the

◀ There are many advantages to travelling in your own vehicle, but you could run into difficulties without the correct paperwork.

vehicle – before the carnet will be issued. Contact the relevant embassy before you travel to find out if a customs carnet is needed and how much the bond will be.

COPIES OF PAPERWORK
Take photocopies of all vehicle-related paperwork and keep them separate from the originals, so that if the latter are lost or stolen, you will still have proof of your entitlement to drive the vehicle. It may also be useful to carry a few passport photographs in the vehicle, as well as photocopies of the information pages of your passport.

If you are carrying valuable, bulky or unusual equipment in your vehicle, it can be a good idea to have a list of the items to produce when crossing borders. If you can get the list stamped in advance by the embassy of the country you are entering, it can help to smooth your way through customs.

▲ *Vehicle-related documents can be kept in the car, but store them in a safe place away from other gear, and keep copies separately.*

▼ *It can be useful to carry an itemized list of valuable equipment, such as work or study equipment, to produce at border crossings.*

Medical Preparations

Part of your preparation before the trip is to find out which medical issues might affect the team and how you should protect yourselves. The medical problems you are most likely to encounter will vary depending on your destination. Follow the advice given in up-to-date guidebooks to the region you are visiting and contact specialist medical organizations for current advice and guidelines.

Your family doctor will be best placed to answer any questions relating to your current physical health and how it may be affected by, for example, changes of diet or extreme climatic conditions. A vaccination programme can guard against some of the endemic disease hazards, while specialist clothing or sleeping nets will help to protect you from the insects that carry the diseases. In other cases, you will be able to avoid ill-health or injury by knowing of potential risks and adapting your behaviour accordingly. You also need to know what medical facilities and emergency services will be available in the area you are visiting, and if you will be entitled to use them free of charge.

VACCINATIONS

Before you leave, everybody going on the trip should have all the vaccinations specifically required for the area you are travelling to, which could include

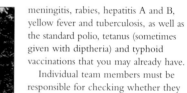

HEALTH WARNING

Some health conditions can cause serious complications while you are away. You are advised to seek medical advice about the suitability of your trip if any of the following conditions apply to you:
• Existing serious injuries
• Asthma
• Epilepsy
• Migraine
• Pregnancy
• High blood pressure
• Heart disease
• Cancer
• Contagious diseases

meningitis, rabies, hepatitis A and B, yellow fever and tuberculosis, as well as the standard polio, tetanus (sometimes given with diptheria) and typhoid vaccinations that you may already have.

Individual team members must be responsible for checking whether they need boosters of previous vaccinations, but you may need to provide the relevant information and remind them to make sure they are adequately protected. If you are travelling with children or young people, liaise with their parents or guardians to get vaccinations organized. Everyone should make sure that all the necessary vaccination certificates are in order.

Depending on your destination, malaria tablets may be necessary, and you will need to find out well in advance about when to start the course of tablets. Your family doctor or travel agent may not have this information or be fully up to date, and it may be preferable to contact a medical organization that specializes in endemic and tropical diseases, and has the latest information available for travellers. Many airline companies also offer a vaccination advisory service.

◀ *A good level of health and physical fitness will make a walking trip more enjoyable, and can help to safeguard you against injury.*

CHECK-UPS

Have a full medical check-up before you travel if you are going away for a long time, or if you are travelling to a developing country or to an undeveloped region of a developed country where the medical services may not be as good as they are at home, or if you know that medical care will be very expensive.

If a qualified doctor or medic is to accompany you on the trip, they could be asked to carry out check-ups on team members. Individuals should also be asked to fill in a questionnaire regarding their past medical history, any prescribed medication they currently take, and any drugs or foods to which they are allergic.

The parents or guardians of children or young people should be asked for this information on their children's behalf, and should sign a form giving permission for medication to be given to the child in an emergency.

Ensure that all team members have a reasonable standard of physical fitness. This will help them to acclimatize to the more difficult living conditions outdoors, and will make them less prone to injury. Anyone in doubt about an ongoing health issue should talk to their own doctor before they travel. If you feel that an individual's condition could pose a risk to the rest of the team you may need to ask them to drop out.

DENTAL CARE

Persistent toothache will spoil your trip and if you are going to be away for more than a couple of weeks neglected tooth decay could lead to an abscess, infection and even blood poisoning. Have a dental check-up before you travel if you have not visited the dentist recently, and leave enough time for any treatment that proves necessary to be completed before you travel. If you are going to a high altitude or to a very cold country, local climatic conditions can bring on severe toothache in any unfilled cavities.

▶ *Learn as much as you can about the conditions you will be living in, and think about how this will impact on your health.*

HEALTH WARNING

Your personal safety is at risk if you do not take adequate measures for existing medical conditions or against contracting disease.

▲ *If you are heading for a remote area where you know that medical services will not be available, you must make sure you take with you all that you need for any existing medical conditions, as well as an adequate stock of first aid supplies and medication for everyday ailments.*

Medical and First-aid Kits

The size and type of your first-aid or medical kits will depend on the nature of your expedition, the amount of time you will be away and the standard of your first aid or medical training.

If you will be doing a range of activities during the course of your trip, or will be travelling in different climates, you may need a greater range of first aid items or even a number of different kits to be fully prepared. Larger groups will have the capacity to carry a more comprehensive medical kit, kept in a vehicle or at the base camp, which caters for everything up to minor operations. Even so, basic first-aid kits still need to be carried by individuals, so that they can give first aid care in the field.

WHAT TO INCLUDE

When deciding on the size of the kit and what to put in it, think about the conditions in the area, the potential for risk of the activities being planned and the kind of accidents that may happen.

If you feel you need informed advice about what to include for an informal trip or with a small group, buy a standard first-aid kit and take it to your family doctor or to a specialist organization; ask them for suggestions of additional items and non-prescription drugs to include. One such item may be an emollient cream such as zinc and castor oil, which is useful for common skin conditions such as sweat rashes.

Larger groups may have a designated first aider or medically trained person, whose responsibility it will be to compile an appropriate medical kit. A standard kit will then be all that individual team members need to carry as part of their own personal equipment.

If you are travelling to a part of the world where AIDS is a major threat, or where you are not sure of the standard of medical care, include a sterile needle kit in case injections are needed. Keep the contents sealed in the case provided, so that they remain sterile and if your luggage is opened by customs officials or police you cannot be accused of using the needles for drugs.

Whatever the size of your medical or first-aid kit, make sure that all items are kept clean and are clearly labelled and easy to identify. If you need to use the kit in an emergency situation, you will want to find what you are looking for quickly.

KEY FIRST AID SKILLS

Before your trip, attend a first aid course or a refresher course to learn or brush up on procedures for the following medical conditions. (For further information see the section Emergency First Aid.)
- Resuscitation
- Recovery position
- Choking
- Shock
- Drowning
- Bites and stings
- Wounds
- Animal, reptile and insect bites
- Burns and scalds
- Sprains
- Fractures
- Effects of hot weather and cold weather

STANDARD FIRST AID ITEMS

- Plasters and adhesive dressings
- Sterile dressings
- Gauze pads
- Crêpe bandages
- Thermometer
- Small pair of scissors
- Sterile scalpel
- Safety pins
- Disposable gloves

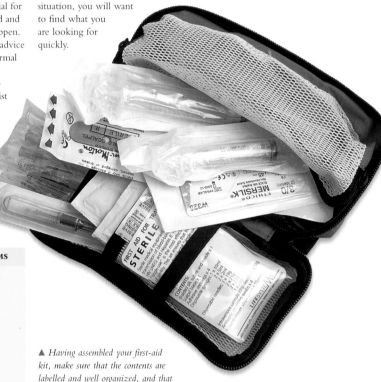

▲ *Having assembled your first-aid kit, make sure that the contents are labelled and well organized, and that the kit is always kept clean and dry.*

FIRST AID PRINCIPLES

Know your kit

It is immediately reassuring for an injury victim if you can produce a well-equipped first-aid kit when you give them treatment. It will also help you to handle the situation with confidence if you know that you have certain essential items with you. However, it is vital that you are familiar with the items in your kit. This includes knowing what they are, what to use them for, and how to use them correctly.

Practical knowledge

The casualty will feel calmer if you can dress and bandage an injury quickly and professionally, but if you become flustered and need to keep unwrapping the bandage to start again, they will start to panic.

Think on your feet

Nothing in your first-aid kit is as important as your ability to act swiftly and improvise with whatever materials you have to hand, while constantly reassuring the casualty to prevent panic.

Making contact

Communication with the outside world can be a key factor in dealing with a serious first aid situation. Focus on making the best use of whatever is available – passers-by, telephones or air and sea rescue services. Learn the international signalling codes, and be confident that you can give an accurate grid reference to locate your exact position. One day, somebody's life may depend on it.

FIRST AID TRAINING

At least one person in the team should have a good standard of up-to-date basic first aid training, but all team members can be encouraged to familiarize themselves with key first aid skills. There is no doubt that the more people in the team with first aid training, the safer the trip will be for all.

If the risk assessment has highlighted any particular areas of risk associated with your destination or activity, consider what specific training the first aider may need, such as how to treat snake bite, hypothermia, frostbite, heat stroke, dehydration or drowning. For health issues relating to specific activities, it's sensible to contact a specialist organization for advice and possible additional training.

Find out as much as possible about the medical facilities available at your destination. This kind of information is available from guidebooks, tourist information services and possibly from the relevant embassy. You will need to know the standard of local hospitals, where the nearest major towns and cities are, and the quickest way to get to them from a rural area; whether there is a 24-hour accident and

emergency facility and how good it is, and how you would go about getting an airlift rescue if someone became seriously ill or injured. The more basic and inaccessible the medical facilities, the more comprehensive your medical kit and training need to be.

▲ *Activities such as cycling introduce injury risks that can be prepared for if they have been identified in your risk assessment.*

▼ *Accidents can happen in any situation, and you need to be aware of the potential hazards in the environment you will be in.*

Physical Fitness

The level of personal fitness you should have for your trip will depend on what the trip entails. If you are planning some mountain biking or white-water canoeing, for example, you will need a more advanced level of fitness than if you are planning low-level walking, though you should still be physically fit and mentally prepared.

If you are travelling as part of a team, remember that you have a responsibility to the other team members to stay as fit and healthy as you can. One person's ill health or lack of fitness may cause problems and could endanger the rest of the group. Regular, gentle exercise every day for at least a month before the trip will help to protect you against illness and injury.

ALL-ROUND FITNESS AND PERFORMANCE

To achieve a level of all-round physical fitness appropriate for camping trips and outdoor activities, the following components are essential: endurance; strength; flexibility; speed; agility; balance; coordination; and reaction time. Of these, endurance and flexibility are the most relevant here.

◀ Cycling is good cardiovascular endurance training, and is very effective for the large powerful muscles in the thighs.

▶ Running will help to build up your stamina, but wear suitable footwear to protect yourself against impact injuries.

▲ Swimming provides an excellent workout, building stamina and promoting all-round fitness without straining any of the muscles.

ENDURANCE

This means being able to continue physical activity for a long time, and it is the most important component of fitness. The fitter the person, the greater the level of endurance. There are two different types of endurance: cardiovascular and muscular.

Cardiovascular endurance

This involves the lungs, the heart, the blood and the blood vessels. It is the ability to exercise the whole body for long periods of time without running out of breath or becoming tired.

To build up your cardiovascular performance, work out a plan to undertake a series of fairly vigorous physical exercises that will make the heart work harder. Swimming is an excellent form of fitness training because it exercises muscles throughout the body. Particularly good are the backstroke and the butterfly, as these give a good workout to the back

and shoulder muscles, which can be difficult to exercise by other means. Cycling and running are also very good for improving all-round fitness and stamina, and they are especially good for the big thigh muscles. As part of your exercise plan in the build-up period up to a month before your trip, do some regular training in the boots or other clothing you will be wearing on the expedition, in order to get used to them. Wearing a backpack that is packed with the same weight as you will carry on your trip is very useful.

Muscular endurance

This is the ability to use the same muscles repeatedly without getting tired. Different activities require skills in different areas and therefore the development of different muscles and joints. For example, a walking and climbing trip needs strength in the upper and lower parts of the legs. If you need to carry your own camping and cooking equipment in a pack on your back, the shoulder muscles will also need to be strong. A canoeing trip, by contrast, needs strength in the arms, shoulders and chest, while a cycling trip needs strong upper and lower legs and strong arms and shoulders.

▲ *Diagonal crunches, from the elbow to the knee, will help to tone the stomach muscles and increase upper-body strength.*

You can tone your muscles and improve body strength in many ways. You may find it convenient to join a fitness club, where there is professional equipment, and follow a simple but regular programme of targeted action, supplemented with regular walking carrying a backpack. Alternatively, press-ups, pull-ups and stomach crunches are good exercises to prepare you for outdoor activities, and these can be done at home without the need for fitness clubs or sports equipment.

▲ *(Top) The simple press-up is an exercise to build short, powerful muscles in the pectoral, biceps and triceps areas of the body.*

▲ *(Above) You may find that by supporting your weight with your knees, you will find it easier to do press-up repetitions.*

▼ *Pull-ups are a good way to promote arm strength. Build up the number of repetitions as your muscles get stronger.*

TESTING YOUR FITNESS

Regular exercise will improve your fitness and endurance and make you feel better and livelier in every way. You will soon notice the difference in your general health, but some simple tests can help you measure your progress and provide extra motivation to keep going.

• As aerobic exercise strengthens your heart it will pump more slowly and efficiently. To take a step test, step on and off an exercise bench or step about 30cm (12in) high. Step up with one foot, placing it fully on the step, follow with the other, then step down with one foot followed by the other. Maintain a steady pace for three minutes, then check your pulse immediately.

An average rate for a man might be between 100–110 beats per minute and between 110–120 for a woman. Compare your results over time to see how your heart rate drops as your fitness improves.

• Measure upper body strength by doing press-ups. Simply do as many repetitions as you can to the point of exhaustion. Keep a record of your total and aim to beat it.

• Measure abdominal strength by doing stomach crunches: see how many you can do in one minute.

• Measure lower body strength with squats: do as many as you can, working at a steady pace, and see how your score builds up as you work out regularly.

▶ *A gentle jog along a beach is just one way to warm up your muscles before you begin a programme of stretching exercises.*

FLEXIBILITY

Stretching and mobilizing joints and muscles is a vital way to increase your range of movement and to prevent muscle strain. Always start a stretching programme with 15 minutes of gentle warm-ups, such as a brisk walk with your arms swinging, a game of frisbee, or a jog, to prepare your body for sudden exertions and minimize the risk of muscle injury.

Practise simple stretches on their own to achieve a good all-round level of flexibility, or practise them after endurance training to increase the benefit of a workout. Start at the top of the body, with stretches for the head and neck, and work down towards the legs and feet. Never bounce to increase your range of movement, but extend yourself gently to the limit of comfort. Hold each stretch for at least 15 seconds before relaxing. The longer you stretch your muscles after a workout, the more flexibility you will attain.

▼ *Stand with your feet apart, and one hand on your hip. Raise your other arm above your head and lean slowly across to gently stretch your side. Repeat on the opposite side.*

▼ *Stand with your feet together, then bend one leg back from the knee and grasp the foot to stretch the hamstring and quadriceps. Repeat with your other leg.*

▼ *Stand with your feet together, then bend forwards, keeping your back straight, and raise your arms above your back. Join your hands together and hold for 15 seconds.*

► *Having confidence in your ability to cope with difficult challenges makes you more likely to achieve your goals.*

MENTAL FITNESS

Strength of mind comes from within and is founded on your belief in yourself to cope with any situation you find yourself in. Knowing that you have prepared well helps you to overcome mental anxiety, and feeling that you are strong and fit, and that your physical strength can see you through times of difficulty, means that you are less likely to feel anxious about living outdoors.

Preparing in advance for emergency situations is invaluable. Training will make you more able to cope with hardship and difficult conditions, both physically and mentally, and it will improve your awareness of your abilities and limitations, which will increase your confidence. In the rare event that something does go seriously wrong, it will make you less likely to panic.

MENTAL PREPARATION

Some people who are well prepared physically for a trip do not perform well when they get into the field. This is largely due to a lack of mental preparation, which leaves them unable to adjust to their new surroundings or unprepared for what they are going to see or come into contact with.

Some people find the lack of privacy in camp a problem; others are upset by the poverty or sickness they may see around them in a developing country, or the smells and sounds they will encounter. Some people find it threatening to sleep out in the open and prefer to be in a tent: if one isn't available, they may not sleep well.

Many such problems can be eased by finding out as much as possible in advance about the area and culture you are going to, and trying out new experiences before setting off, such as cooking over a wood fire for the first time, or doing a difficult climb. These things can seem strange and threatening when you first do them, but will seem less so the next time. It is usually fear of the unknown that makes us most uncomfortable, not the experience itself.

FOOD AND TEAM MORALE

Food plays a key role in team morale when you are living outdoors, where the evening meal is a welcome treat at the end of a long, tiring day in the field. A healthy appetite is a sign of a positive attitude, and if the team is eating, it is also receiving the energy supplies it needs for strenuous activity.

However, eating with gusto is not easy after several days on a diet of dehydrated food. This kind of food can cause constipation, which means discomfort, and the lack of flavour can make it very unappealing. If the team doesn't eat properly, energy levels get depleted and individuals can become lethargic and irritable; this makes team spirit sink further still, and problems can flare up as individuals become discontented.

Make sure the team knows what food rations to expect, so that they can prepare themselves mentally for any hardship. Let them try out the rations at a trial camping weekend, and consider how you can improve the food if you feel it may have a negative effect on the team's morale.

Travelling as a Group

A group expedition involves a great deal of organization to ensure that everyone has a safe and enjoyable trip. The purpose of the trip and an itinerary need to be agreed by everyone before you travel. This is important even for recreational holidays if the trip is to live up to individual expectations and you are to avoid disputes.

ORGANIZING GROUP MEMBERS

The larger the group, the greater the potential for chaos and confusion, and, not surprisingly, this is especially true with a group of children or young people. Travelling in large numbers can cause problems at ticket offices and check-in desks during the journey, where other passengers can become annoyed by the delays caused by a large group in front of them. Group leaders should remind everyone to get money, passports and tickets ready in plenty of time when approaching a border.

If your group is large, having a list of everyone's names, addresses, dates of birth and passport numbers will help when booking into accommodation or passing through borders. A list of just their names will also be useful for checking that everybody is present when you change modes of transport.

If the group is travelling by public transport, brief everyone on where they are heading and arrange a meeting point at the destination, so that if anyone does become separated, they will still be able to find the rest of the group.

You will quickly learn as the trip progresses which people take much more time to get ready than others, or never seem to have the necessary documents to hand. If they are not to hold up the others, they must be encouraged to be prompt and prepared. Other members of the group can be asked to help make sure they are at the right place at the right time.

GROUP IMPACT

If you are travelling in a group, and especially if you are acting as leader, it is important to remember that you have a responsibility not only to keep the group harmonious and happy, but to make sure that everyone respects the places and people you are visiting. Groups, especially large ones, can have a substantial impact on fragile environments, and a lack of understanding of the region's culture may cause distress and anger among local people, so good discipline is essential in camp. Before setting off, relay all the information you can about your destination to the team, and make sure everyone agrees to the standards of behaviour they will follow, to make the most of the experience for the whole group.

DISPUTES

No matter how big or small the party, and how well you know each other, disagreements and personality clashes during the trip are almost inevitable. Having a clear objective for the trip and an itinerary that has been mutually agreed by the group will help to keep these to a minimum, but deal with them quickly when they occur, before the group starts to break into factions.

CONTINGENCY PLAN

Have a fall-back plan that includes suitable accommodation should you need it at connection points on your journey, in case travel delays mean you miss a connection and are forced to make an unscheduled overnight stop. While individual travellers or a small group can usually be accommodated at short notice, a large group can run into problems if, for example, the flight arrives late, and the vehicle-hire

◄ *For the journey to run smoothly, allocate responsibilities among team members, such as looking out for particular items of kit.*

company has closed for the day. Keep phone numbers for the places you are booked into to hand, in case you need to inform them of any changes. Even if things are going to plan, it is a good idea to give your accommodation a call to make sure all is well for your arrival.

KEEPING VALUABLES SAFE

If you are staying in one place for any length of time, try to find a trustworthy individual or organization who will allow you to use their safe. The valuables of an entire group – including passports, travel tickets, expensive items such as jewellery and larger sums of money – can add up to a treasure chest for an opportunistic thief, and for peace of mind it is better to know they are stored safely under lock and key.

LOST LUGGAGE

Luggage can and does go missing when travelling, especially on public transport, and this is particularly likely with group travel because individuals tend to be less attentive of shared group equipment than they are of their own

belongings. It can help to make one or two people responsible for counting bags at each connection point, to make sure everything travels with you to your destination. If luggage is lost or delayed by an airline, you may have the complication of trying to arrange for it to be sent on to your destination.

▲ *With a large amount of gear and a big camping area, the potential for chaos at a group camp is huge. Encourage individuals to store their own kit tidily when not in use.*

▼ *Essential items of group kit, such as maps or cooking equipment, should be made the responsibility of one or two individuals.*

Travelling with Young People

For a family camping holiday with your own children, you need to think about how the children will cope with the physical demands of living outdoors and how living in the wilderness may affect their spirit. Be ready to adapt your plans if the children appear uncomfortable or unhappy with the daily routine. Otherwise, as a parent, your responsibilities will be no different to those on any other family trip.

When you take a group of children or teenagers on an organized trip, you and any other leaders are responsible for them the whole time they are away from home. Much of the advice on travelling in a group will apply here, but your position of authority and your ability to deal with young people will make this a different type of challenge.

GROUP EXPEDITIONS
There should be at least one adult to every six young people, and if your programme includes activities that are potentially hazardous, or if the group members are under 15 years old, then the ratio will have to be higher. If there are children in the group with special needs, the number of adults has to be assessed on a case-by-case basis.

LEADING YOUNG PEOPLE
The challenges of outdoor living and adventure can be particularly beneficial for children and young people, but youth leaders need to be sure that they minimize the risks inherent in such activities and fulfil any legal requirements arising from their responsibilities. Guidelines are published by national and local education authorities, as well as international youth organizations such as Young Explorers' Trust and the Scout Association.

PRE-TRIP MEETINGS
The agenda for the trip needs to be established with a series of meetings before you set off. The children's parents will want to feel informed and confident that their children are in safe hands. These meetings also allow the leaders to identify problematic issues while there is still time to amend plans.

Introductory meeting
Arrange a meeting early in the planning stage at which you can give the group and their parents or guardians detailed information about the area you will be visiting and even some training in the activities you hope to carry out there. This may also be the first time the group members meet each other. Explain the rules of behaviour for the trip and detail what will happen to any member who behaves badly.

Collect next-of-kin contact details from each person, as well as three passport photographs. If the group is travelling abroad you will need photocopies of passports and birth certificates in case any passports get lost. You will also need to talk through your insurance policy for the trip.

Ask the parents or guardians of any members under the official adult age to sign a consent form stating that you can authorize medical treatment in the event of an emergency. You also need medical information from every person, including details of any medication and any allergies to drugs or foodstuffs, as well as details of foods that they cannot eat on medical or religious grounds. If the group is travelling abroad, you will need to check that everyone has had the appropriate vaccinations.

Final meeting
Have a final meeting before you leave to run through the final risk assessment and explain what you are doing about the risks highlighted, pass on any last-minute information and answer any questions. Finally, introduce the liaison agent, who will be the point of contact between the group and the parents or guardians while you are away.

DURING THE JOURNEY
For a group of up to 12 children, have a rota so that one leader is in charge for a set time while the others relax. Larger groups of children (say, more than 20) are easier to handle if they are divided up into small units, each with its own leader, during the journey.

◀ An early morning meeting to talk about the plans for the day ahead will make everybody in the team feel involved.

If travelling by boat or train, or while waiting at an airport, and if the children are old enough to be trusted to behave sensibly on their own, they can be allowed time without adult supervision. Find a fixed point, such as a café, where a leader will be and where passports, tickets and luggage can be left, and ask each child to report in every hour. Keep a list of names to hand so that you can check everyone off as you change modes of transport.

DURING THE EXPEDITION
Start each day with a half-hour briefing session on the day's events, and give children the chance to ask questions or express concerns about any aspect of the trip. How much the children can achieve in one day will vary according to their age, physical strength and the type of activities planned. Base your schedule on past expeditions with young people of the same age, and be prepared to revise it if the group does not respond well to the challenges or if unforeseen weather conditions make the original plan untenable.

Deal with instances of bad behaviour immediately. Repeated bad behaviour may result in a child being sent home, but this is a last resort since a leader will have to accompany them, involving extra costs and the temporary lack of a leader.

▲ *Activities such as skiing should be within the capabilities of the child to avoid them becoming anxious or uncooperative.*

▼ *Allow time for rest and play to make sure young children do not overexert themselves.*

Travelling Alone

Many people love the freedom of travelling alone and relish facing new challenges and seeing new places with just themselves for company. If you hate the thought of group travel, with all the organization involved, the inevitable personality clashes and the lack of spontaneity, then it is worth considering this option.

The greatest advantage of travelling alone is that you have the flexibility of being able to change your plans as and when you want to, without having to consult anybody else. However, there are disadvantages to solo travel, and it is worth bearing in mind the following points when deciding whether or not to take a camping trip on your own.

BEING SELF-SUFFICIENT

If you are backpacking, you will have to carry everything yourself, including all of your camping and cooking equipment, so select lightweight gear and avoid taking unnecessary items. If you don't already own your equipment, try to borrow or hire as many of the expensive items as you can, or else kitting yourself out will be very costly. Make sure you know how to use all of your equipment correctly – including putting up your tent on your own – and learn how to carry out emergency repairs and maintenance.

TRAVEL COSTS

Unless you are travelling in your own vehicle and sleeping at a campsite, you may have to pay more for your trip, as ferries and organized trips will often charge a single-person supplement, especially if you want your own cabin or hotel room. If travelling on your own by train in parts of the developing world, bear in mind that a first-class ticket is worth considering from the point of view of safety and comfort.

KEEPING IN TOUCH

Make a point of phoning someone at home on a regular basis, perhaps at the same time each week, to let them know you are well and what your plans are for the days ahead (emailing is less reliable as the service is not available everywhere). If travelling in a developing country on your own, consider making your country's political representative in the country aware that you are there.

ACCOMMODATION

The thought of waking up on your own in the middle of the wilderness may seem appealing, but think very carefully about whether you want to be this isolated. Unless you are an experienced camper, a designated camping area may be a better option. Not only is there more chance of finding drinking water and washroom facilities, there will also be like-minded people nearby should you need help or advice, and it will usually be safer. If you are planning to stay in a hostel or hotel on your own, check guidebooks or ask at a tourist information office to find out about the character of the area. When travelling alone it is usually safer to choose accommodation in a better part of town.

▼ *Lone travellers have the flexibility to please themselves and change their plans at will if new opportunities arise.*

▲ *Women travelling alone are easy targets for sexual harassment. Be aware of this and make reducing the risk your top priority.*

◀ *Travelling without backup from other people makes you more vulnerable, so plan carefully to minimize the risks.*

SOLO ACTIVITIES

If you are planning a walking, cycling, horse riding or driving trip on your own, tell someone what you are doing, the route you are taking and when you expect to return. If you have an accident, they may be your only hope of help. Think very carefully about the wisdom of snow walking, climbing or mountaineering on your own, especially if there is a chance of bad weather. Some activities, such as kayaking and canoeing, should never be done solo. If you want to visit a famous site, consider joining an organized tour or getting a group of like-minded people to go together. It will be cheaper and it could be safer than going alone.

DRUG SMUGGLING

As a lone traveller, be careful whom you make friends with and never accept parcels or gifts unless you know what is in them, especially if you are passing through a national border. There are a number of people in prison around the world who carried a parcel for a "friend" that turned out to contain drugs or other contraband.

WOMEN TRAVELLERS

Observing local codes of behaviour is a matter of courtesy for all travellers, but for women it is easy to send out the wrong message, especially when travelling alone in countries where an unaccompanied female may be an unusual sight. Outside Europe, Australia and the United States, skimpy or tight clothes, including trousers, are generally inappropriate. Check the conventions before you go and always dress conservatively in loose-fitting, presentable clothes.

All lone women may face some sexual harassment. Take the same precautions you would at home: don't wander up dark alleys alone or accept drinks from strangers; find another woman to sit next to on a bus or train. If you are groped, don't get involved in an angry confrontation but get the attention of onlookers, who will probably rush to your defence. Avoid eye contact with men in public places: wearing dark glasses can help. Time your arrival in a new place during the day, so you are not wandering about late at night: travelling by night can be a good idea if it means you reach your destination in the morning.

On the plus side, local people – women particularly – will be more likely to offer you hospitality. They might assume that a male traveller can cope alone, while you need a helping hand, and they won't see a lone woman as a threat.

Be prepared for your periods to be irregular – changes in time zones, stress and exhaustion can affect them – and remember that stomach upsets can interfere with oral contraception. Sanitary protection may be hard to buy locally, and tampons with applicators are more hygienic in the absence of clean water to wash your hands. Be aware of cultural attitudes – in some countries menstruating woman are forbidden to enter religious buildings or to touch, or even go near, food, so be discreet.

BASIC EQUIPMENT

Commercial travel equipment is now so developed that it is possible to travel in the backcountry for several weeks in considerable comfort. However, some items are expensive and may be too specialist for your needs. The key to being well equipped is to take what is necessary. Do not carry more than you have to: this is especially important if you are backpacking, but even if you are transporting your gear by vehicle, it will hamper your progress if you are overloaded with luggage.

Choosing your Equipment

Having the correct basic equipment is important for your comfort and safety. When assessing what you need, you should consider the climate and terrain of the area you are visiting and the activities planned. You also need to know how you are going to carry your gear, as this will affect the amount of weight and bulk you can manage.

HOW TO ACQUIRE EQUIPMENT

Outdoor equipment suppliers sell for every possible climate and terrain, so if you are buying new items for your trip, consider what design features will serve you best to help narrow the choice. Many items are expensive, and most people build up their equipment over a number of years to spread the cost. If this is your first trip, try to borrow as much as you can from friends or a local walking or activity group. That way you will also gain from the experience of others, who will be able to tell you what is and what is not important. Have an understanding in writing with the owner on what items cost and how you will compensate them for lost, stolen or damaged items, and make sure you are sufficiently insured.

▼ *Wearing a helmet, gloves and suitable clothing and footwear is important for any cycling trip, even if the distance is short.*

CLOTHING AND FOOTWEAR

The purpose of outdoor clothing is to keep you comfortable in the weather conditions you experience on your trip. It cannot be stressed enough that clothes need to be appropriate for the climate you will be operating in. Besides this, clothes need to be durable and quick drying, lightweight and low in bulk – this is especially important if you are carrying your gear in a pack on your back. Footwear has to protect your feet from water, mud, sand and rocks, while still enabling you to carry out your activities safely. Never be tempted to compromise your safety and comfort for fashion: it will make your trip a miserable one and may even put your life in danger.

PERSONAL AND GROUP CAMP KIT

Your camp kit is the core items of equipment that you take with you on any trip to the wilderness, such as a compass, map, water bottle, wristwatch, cooking equipment and wash kit. Some items, such as a compass, are essential and you shouldn't set off without them. Other items, such as an inflatable pillow, are luxuries that you can do without if your weight/space allowance is limited. Group kit may include study materials, or catering-size cooking equipment. For more information, see the sections Personal Camp Kit and Group Camp Kit.

BASIC SURVIVAL KIT

In an emergency situation, having a few key items with you can make the difference between life and death. For information about what to include in the kit, see the section Basic Survival Kit.

TENTS

Probably the most expensive item on your list will be a tent, so be clear about what sort you need. The perfect tent is weatherproof, spacious, easy to pitch, light and compact to carry, but few tents are all of these things and you will need to decide how to compromise. For more information, see the section Choosing a Tent.

▲ *For backpacking trips you need cooking and sleeping equipment that is light in weight and designed to be packed up small.*

SLEEPING EQUIPMENT

The right sleeping gear can mean the difference between a good night's rest and a bad one. Consider where and in what conditions you will be using your sleeping bag, then buy the best one you can afford. For more information, see the section Sleeping Bags.

BACKPACKS

A backpack has to allow you to carry your equipment in comfort, and what sort of backpack you need will depend on your activities and how much you need to carry. Features such as hip belts, padding, frames or side straps can be very useful but they can also add weight and cost. For more information, see the section Backpacks.

TOOLS

When living outdoors it is very useful to have some tools with you, even if your tool kit consists of nothing more than a penknife. Check with the police to see if any of your tools are illegal. If you have a machete, large knife or flares, for example, you may be able to own them but not carry them around in public. Anything that is classed as a firearm will need an official firearms certificate. For more information, see the section Tools.

BASIC HIKING AND CAMPING EQUIPMENT CHECKLIST

The following kit list is for a walking and camping trip lasting 3–4 weeks in a temperate climate:

Clothing and footwear
Underwear
Thermal vest, long johns and long-sleeved undershirt
Cotton T-shirts
Cotton socks
Woollen socks
Short-sleeved shirts
Long-sleeved shirts
Woollen sweater or zip-up fleece
Long cotton trousers
Shorts
Lightweight waterproof jacket
Windproof jacket
Waterproof overtrousers
Walking boots
Spare boot laces
Lightweight trainers or flip-flops
Swimwear
Sturdy belt
Fleece or woollen gloves
Fleece or woollen hat
Wide-brimmed sunhat
Sunglasses
Towelling sweat rag or head scarf
Set of smart clothing plus suitable footwear
Nightwear

Personal equipment
Compass
Maps
Wristwatch
Water bottle and case
Whistle
Cotton money belt
Kitbag or backpack
Day sack
Tent
Sleeping bag
Sleeping mat
Small stuff sacks and garbage bags
Penknife
Flashlight and spare batteries
2 x plates or set of army mess tins
Mug
Knife, fork, spoon
Dishtowel
Pan scourer

Can opener
Travel wash or soap flakes
Clothes pegs (pins)
4m/13ft washline
Small folding camp chair
Walking poles

Wash kit
Towel
Soap
Toothbrush
Toothpaste
Steel mirror
Hairbrush or comb
Shampoo
Sanitary protection
Razor and shaving foam
Lipbalm
Deodorizing foot powder
Zinc and castor oil cream
Sunscreen
Insect repellent
Pocket tissues
Wet wipes
Washbasin plug

Miscellaneous items
Passport
Travel tickets
Cash, travellers' cheques, credit card
Vaccination certificate
Repair kit
Camera, spare batteries and film
Mobile (cell) phone
Binoculars
2 x spare passport photos
Photocopies of paperwork
Notebook, pen and pencil

Personal first-aid kit
Adhesive dressings (plasters), various sizes
Paracetamol tablets
Blister kit
Travel sickness tablets
Sterile dressings, various sizes
Triangular bandage
Roller bandages
Small pair of scissors
Thermometer
Tweezers
Safety pins
Disposable gloves

For more extreme weather conditions, add the following items:

Hot climate extras
Personal water purifier
Malaria tablets
Insect repellent bands and head net
Mosquito net and frame
Camp bed or hammock
Cotton liner for sleeping bag
Shade sheet
Machete
Extra water bottle

Cold climate/snow extras
Thermal underwear
Down or fleece zip-up jacket
Water- and windproof jacket and overtrousers, or fibre-pile one-piece suit
Balaclava
Inner or liner gloves
Fleece or woollen mitts
Outer mitts
Knee-length gaiters
Snow shoes or snow boots
Crampons
Climbing harness
Ice axe
Bivvy bag
Space blanket

For trips involving paddling or cycling activities, add the following items:

Kayaking or canoeing extras
Boat and paddles
Buoyancy aid or Personal flotation device (PDF)
Helmet
Thermal or cotton T-shirt
Thermal or cotton trousers
Cagoule and waterproof trousers
Technical sandals, lightweight trainers or neoprene boots
Spraydeck (spray skirt) (kayaks only)
Waterproof kit bags and containers

Cycling extras
Cycle
Helmet
Gloves
Lightweight trainers

Clothing for Temperate Climates

Temperate zones worldwide include Europe, North America and New Zealand. Average temperatures range from -14–37°C/5–100°F. This climate has warm summers with rain showers and cold, wet winters, which can turn to snow at high altitudes. Although the weather is not extreme, it is changeable, and controlling your body temperature will require you to take off or put on clothing. What to wear in winter is covered in Clothing for Cold and Wet Climates; here we deal with clothing for the spring, summer and autumn.

LAYERING SYSTEM

In a temperate climate, clothing is best worn in a layering system to give maximum flexibility. Several thin layers of clothing that trap air between them will keep you warmer than one thick garment. If you become too hot, lower your body temperature by removing layers or opening zips or buttons to allow warm air to escape and cool air to enter. If you feel cold, add a layer or refasten zips and cuffs. If it rains, put your waterproofs on straight away so that you do not get your lower layers wet, and take them off when it stops raining, so that you do not overheat.

▼ *Dress for the conditions you expect, and have with you clothing and equipment in case the weather worsens significantly.*

First layer

Cotton underwear can be worn with either a cotton vest or T-shirt in the summer. It may be cold enough to wear long johns and a long-sleeved undershirt in the spring or autumn.

Second layer

Choose a long-sleeved shirt that will allow you to roll the sleeves up or down as the weather conditions dictate. In warm weather, a cotton shirt will keep you cool, while a woollen shirt will give warmth for the cooler spring and autumn months. Trousers should be loose-fitting and made of cotton or synthetic fibres. Shorts can be worn, but take a pair of trousers with you in case the weather suddenly worsens.

Third layer

A lightweight fleece jacket or a woollen long-sleeved sweater can either be worn or carried in your rucksack, as the conditions dictate.

Outer layer

This climate will certainly be wet at times, and you will need a waterproof, windproof jacket – preferably one with cuffs inside the sleeves, a comfortable neck seal and a good hood to protect the head. Waterproof overtrousers should always be carried. It will be a great advantage if this layer is made of

▲ *A good windproof and waterproof outer layer is essential in temperate regions, where sudden rain showers can be expected.*

a breathable fabric, either synthetic or natural; non-breathable fabrics can cause you to overheat and sweat, and will be uncomfortable to wear.

ACCESSORIES

A brimmed sun hat or baseball cap will protect your head from the sun, while a woollen hat can be pulled down over your ears to keep you warm when it is cold or windy. A scarf made of towelling or wool and worn wrapped around the neck may be useful in the cooler spring or autumn. Carry a pair of woollen or fibre-pile mitts in your pack to keep your hands warm when you stop for rest breaks.

FOOTWEAR

Wear walking shoes, lightweight boots or leather walking boots, depending on the conditions. Even on a warm summer day, footpaths can be wet and muddy, and wearing short gaiters over your boots, or longer lightweight knee-length gaiters, will keep your lower legs clean and dry. Socks should be made of cotton or wool; wear one or two pairs.

◀ Lightweight cotton trousers are comfortable to wear and will dry quickly if they get wet.

◀ Wear a lightweight fleece zip-up jacket or a woollen sweater for a warm, cosy layer beneath your waterproofs.

▼ A cotton T-shirt makes a practical undergarment for any time of year.

▼ Carry woollen mitts in your rucksack to put on when you make a rest stop for any length of time.

◀ Fibre-pile gloves are water-resistant and warm, and will allow you to use your hands far better than mitts.

◀ A fleece hat is excellent head insulation and can be kept in your rucksack ready to be pulled on if the temperature drops.

▶ Gaiters attached to your boots will keep your lower legs dry and clean if conditions are wet and muddy underfoot.

▲ A woollen scarf worn around the neck and tucked inside your outer layer will effectively keep out chilly draughts.

▼ A cotton sunhat will protect the head from strong sun. Air vents in the hat will keep you cooler and reduce sweating.

▲ A folded towel worn around the neck will absorb sweat in hot temperatures.

Clothing for Hot and Dry Climates

Hot and dry environments are found in parts of the United States, Australia, Africa, and the Middle East. Typical terrain includes deserts and open plains, with a temperature range from -6–50°C/20–120°F. Local people in this climate favour loose-fitting clothing that does not constrict the airflow around the body. Rather than the flexible layering system of clothing worn in temperate climates, the key to comfort in hot, dry climates is good ventilation and protection from the sun.

Clothing should be made of strong, hard-wearing fabrics as even deserts have vegetation with thorns, and these can tear at clothing. Choose breathable natural fibres, such as cotton or wool, to encourage airflow and keep you cooler, and light colours, preferably neutrals, such as khaki or green, which do not show the dirt as much as white.

UNDERWEAR
Choose underwear made of cotton because of its breathable qualities; men may prefer to wear boxers to avoid chafing in the crotch area. A cotton T-shirt worn under the shirt will keep you warmer in the winter, when

▼ The intense sun and lack of shade can cause real problems in the desert, and your clothing is your main form of protection.

temperatures can go down to below freezing, even in the desert. At any time of year, if you are sweating a lot, wear a cotton T-shirt underneath your shirt to absorb the sweat.

SHIRT
A lightweight cotton shirt with long sleeves and buttoned cuffs will allow you to wear the sleeves rolled down to protect your arms from sunburn. A shirt with large breast pockets allows you to keep to hand items that you may need often during the day, such as a compass, camera or sunscreen.

TROUSERS
Wear lightweight cotton trousers that are loose in the crotch and long enough to be tucked into your boots. This is how you should wear them

▲ A windproof cotton gilet can be added on top of your shirt to keep out cool winds in the evenings, after the sun has gone down.

when walking on loose rocks and sand to avoid getting debris inside your socks and boots, which can cause friction against the skin and can lead to blisters. A sturdy trouser belt made of leather or heavy webbing is useful for carrying heavy items that you will need frequently, such as your water bottle. Large pockets on the trouser leg can be used to carry maps. A double thickness of material on the knee area will protect the trousers from wear.

JACKET
Take a lightweight windproof jacket for the summer and a heavier, cold-weather coat for the winter, when temperatures can drop quite severely. It does rain in the desert, and a waterproof jacket with a hood, or a waterproof poncho, will prove very useful. Some ponchos can also double up as groundsheets.

ACCESSORIES
Wear a wide-brimmed sun hat or some form of headgear at all times in extreme heat to cover your head, the back of your neck and your ears. This is especially important during the heat of the day. Deserts can be very windy

▲ *A cotton shirt with long sleeves that can be buttoned up will allow you to keep your arms covered to protect them from the sun.*

▲ *Choose loose-fitting cotton trousers in a neutral colour, and wear them tucked into your boots to prevent sand getting in.*

▲ *Carry a lightweight cotton windproof jacket in the summer, and a heavier jacket for the cooler winter months.*

places, so make sure there is a sturdy chin strap to prevent the hat blowing away. Eyelet vents around the brim give ventilation and help to keep the head cool. It is so important to keep your head covered in intense sunshine that you should carry a spare hat just in case you lose one.

Protect your eyes from the glaring sunlight with dark sunglasses that offer a good standard of protection from ultraviolet rays. If you are driving, you may prefer to wear sturdy goggles, as these will offer more protection from the blowing, gritty dust of deserts and open plains. Carry at least one spare pair of sunglasses in case you lose or damage the ones you are wearing.

A bandana, small towel or towelling sweat rag, tied loosely around your neck, is very useful for wiping sweat from your face and neck, and will help to keep the sun off the back of your neck (prolonged sun on the back of the neck can cause sunstroke.)

If you are travelling by horse, mule or camel or if you are driving, you may want to wear cotton gloves to prevent the backs of your hands getting sunburned. In the cool winter months, lightweight leather gloves are warmer.

FOOTWEAR

Wear lightweight cotton socks, and take a clean pair for every day or make provisions for washing them, as your feet will sweat and this can cause discomfort. Specially designed boots are available for deserts and extremely dry terrain. These have lightweight suede uppers, which allow feet to breathe, as well as high sides to keep out the sand, and robust soles to protect feet from the rocky terrain. Regular leather walking boots are too heavy, and the non-porous uppers will cause the feet to sweat.

▼ *This wide-brimmed cotton sun hat gives ideal protection from strong sun, with the air vents encouraging air flow to reduce sweating.*

▲ *A sturdy leather belt can be used to hang items that you need quick and easy access to, such as a water bottle, compass or map.*

▲ *Good quality sunglasses should be worn at all times when the sun is at its most intense. Attach them to a sturdy cord worn around the neck.*

▼ *Lightweight driving gloves will protect the hands from sunburn if you will be spending several hours a day driving in the sun.*

◀ *A lightweight cotton bandana worn loosely around the neck will help to absorb sweat from the neck.*

▼ *A cotton baseball cap can be worn with the brim shading the face or turned around so that the cap peak protects the back of the neck.*

Clothing for Hot and Wet Climates

High temperatures and humidity make hot and wet environments very difficult places in which to live comfortably. Hot and wet regions worldwide are found in the equatorial zones of South America, North America, Africa, Asia and parts of Australia. Average temperatures range from 20–30°C/68–86°F. Local vegetation in a hot, wet climate will usually be jungle; many plants and trees will have thorns, and some will have poisonous leaves. The important thing is to keep your body completely covered from head to toe to protect yourself from these very hostile surroundings.

Everything you wear in a hot and wet climate should be made of cotton, because as a breathable fabric it will help to keep you cool and it will dry quickly. Take two sets of clothing, so that you have one set for the day when you are working or travelling, and another clean, dry set to change into when you make camp in the evenings.

Your spare set of clothing must be kept in a waterproof bag if you are carrying all of your gear inside your rucksack during the day, otherwise the humidity alone will make it damp. Depending on the duration of your trip, you can make provision for washing your clothes while you are away to avoid having to carry huge amounts of clothing with you.

UNDERWEAR

As in a hot, dry environment, you will find that cotton underwear is the most comfortable in hot and humid weather. Choose items that fit well and avoid anything restricting that limits movement. Simple designs are best,

▲ The jungle environment is uncomfortable and dangerous, with high humidity and a range of very threatening plants and insects.

▼ Head-to-toe protection is needed at all times in a hot, wet climate; always wear your boots when crossing a jungle river.

INSECT PROTECTION

Cover your hands and neck with insect repellent, but take care not to put repellent near your eyes; do not put it on your forehead either, as sweat will wash it into your eyes. Repellent bands can be worn on your wrists, but should be reproofed every few days. You can also put insect repellent around the tops of your boots and around the eyelets of your boots and the air vents of your sun hat. Do this when you take rest stops, as the repellent will get rubbed off as you travel through the undergrowth. A head net offers good protection from insects. Put it on over your hat but only when you stop, as it cuts down visibility and can get torn as you move through dense vegetation.

▲ *A lightweight cotton shirt, with long sleeves that can be securely fastened, will offer good protection from plants and insects.*

▲ *Choose loose-fitting cotton trousers in a serviceable neutral colour. Trousers with large leg pockets are particularly useful.*

▼ *A wide-brimmed hat will protect your head from the vegetation and insects; choose a hat with air vents and a sturdy chin strap.*

▲ *Wear lightweight cotton socks inside your jungle boots, and try to change your socks every day to keep your feet comfortable.*

as the more details there are, the greater the risk of chafing. A lightweight cotton vest or T-shirt can be worn underneath your shirt to absorb sweat.

SHIRT
Choose a long-sleeved cotton shirt in a neutral colour and wear it buttoned down to the wrist to protect your arms from the vegetation and insects. You will find it useful to choose a shirt that has large breast pockets in which to keep the smaller items, such as insect repellent, that you will want easy access to throughout the day. There is no need for a jacket in a hot, wet climate, where the high temperature is constant and any kind of wind or breeze is rare.

TROUSERS
Your lower body should be well covered with loose-fitting trousers, worn tucked inside your socks and boots to protect the legs and feet from insects. Anything kept in the trouser pockets will become wet during your activities from sweat and the humidity, so keep essential maps and paperwork in waterproof pouches in order to protect them.

ACCESSORIES
Always wear a sturdy sun hat to protect your head and face from vegetation and insects. A brimmed cotton hat is ideal; air vents will encourage ventilation and reduce sweating, and a chin strap will prevent the hat getting knocked off your head by low-hanging undergrowth. A cotton bandana or towelling scarf tied loosely around your neck is useful

for wiping sweat from your face, which you will need to do almost continuously, and it will also protect your neck from sunburn. A bandana or scarf will help to prevent insects crawling inside the collar of your shirt.

FOOTWEAR
The wet, uneven surface of the jungle floor means that adequate footwear is essential to protect your feet. Jungle boots are better than walking boots because they are designed for the conditions (see the section Footwear).

▼ *Knowing what conditions to expect and equipping yourself accordingly is the secret to dressing suitably in the jungle environment.*

Clothing for Cold and Dry Climates

Cold and dry environments are found at high altitude in Europe, North America, Canada, South America, Asia and Africa, where conditions include rocky terrain as well as snow and ice. Average temperatures range from -56–18°C/ -81–65°F. In this environment your aim is to dress sufficiently well to keep warm, but not so well that you overheat.

LAYERING SYSTEM
To achieve a balanced body temperature, you will need to use the flexible layering system of clothing, which allows you to put on or take off layers depending on the conditions and your activities.

First layer
This should be a long-sleeved thermal vest and long johns, made from natural or synthetic materials, which cover the whole of the body except for the hands and feet. The garments should fit close to the skin without being tight and restrictive, and there should be a good overlap at the waist to avoid exposing the skin. Carry at least one spare set of first layer clothing.

▼ *Snow and ice are often a feature of cold, dry climates, but the sun can also get hot, and your clothing needs to give flexibility.*

Second layer
Choose either a long-sleeved button-up insulated shirt and heavy-duty trousers, or a one-piece fibre-pile suit with a high collar and elasticated cuffs to keep your neck and wrists well protected. A shirt and trousers will allow you to roll the sleeves up and down to control your body temperature; not all one-piece suits will allow you to do this, so try to find one that does. The second layer can be made of synthetic or natural materials, but the advantage of natural fabrics is that they will "breathe" and absorb moisture (in the form of sweat) from the body. Items that need to be kept at a temperature above freezing, such as your compass, should be carried in a buttoned-up pocket in this layer, where they will be easily accessible.

Third layer
If you are on a walking trip and will be able to stop to take off and put on items of clothing as and when you need to, choose a woollen sweater or a lightweight fleece jacket. However, if you are planning an activity where you are not going to be able to change your clothing easily, it will be more convenient to wear fibre-pile salopettes with a fibre-pile mountain shirt, or

a one-piece down or fibre-pile suit. These overlap at the waist to keep you warm where other clothing can be disturbed with movement, while still allowing ventilation at the chest and shoulders to reduce heat loss and discomfort through sweating.

Outer layer
This should be a zip-up waterproof jacket and a pair of overtrousers, which should be breathable, windproof and water-resistant. The jacket sleeves should come down over the wrists and upper hands so that they overlap the gloves, and it should have a large hood with a wire-structured visor, which will help to keep the front of the hood in place even in high winds. Large pockets with fasteners will be useful.

ACCESSORIES
Wear fibre-pile headgear or a woollen balaclava. Both of these will cover the head as well as all of the neck and ears. For extra protection in extremely cold conditions, you can wear a lightweight silk balaclava underneath the outer one.

Like the rest of the body, the hands should be covered with a number of layers. This can mean as many as three pairs in extreme cold conditions: first a pair of silk gloves, then woollen or fibre-pile mitts, then an outer layer of wind- and waterproof mitts, which will cover the join between the outer jacket and the second-layer under-mitts.

FOOTWEAR
Wear two pairs of woollen socks, one of which should be long enough to be pulled over the lower part of your thermal leggings to form a seal, so that no skin is exposed to the air.

Suitable footwear can mean leather mountain boots covered with insulated overboots or gaiters that come up to your knees, or plastic snow boots. Make sure that your socks and boots do not fit tightly, as this will restrict the blood circulation and can make your feet feel even colder and more susceptible to frostbite.

◀ *A lightweight fleece jacket should make up part of the third layer of clothing, and can be put on or taken off as the conditions dictate.*

▲ *Cotton trousers can be worn with a shirt tucked inside. Zip-up pockets will allow you to carry any items that you need often.*

▼ *A windproof and waterproof jacket with a hood that covers the whole of your head is your first line of defence against the cold.*

▼ *Fibre-pile mitts are waterproof and make a good outer layer to protect the hands.*

▲ *Waterproof overtrousers give protection from rain or snow showers. Take them off as soon as the showers stop to prevent sweating. Zips on the lower leg make the trousers easier to put on over boots.*

▼ *A cotton shirt can be worn as part of your second layer of clothing, and the full-length sleeves can easily be rolled up if you become too hot.*

▼ *A woollen balaclava fits snugly over the head and neck, giving good protection for the ears, and as a further advantage it will not blow off in high winds.*

▼ *Fleece gloves can be worn on their own or beneath fibre-pile mitts in cold conditions.*

Clothing for Cold and Wet Climates

Cold and wet climate zones worldwide include the polar regions, Greenland, Iceland and northern Scandinavia and Russia. Average temperatures range from -42–21°C/-34–70°F. This climate is probably the most challenging and dangerous for human beings because the moisture in the air will actively destroy the insulation properties of clothing. The effect is to rapidly reduce the body temperature, leading to a very real risk of hypothermia, which, if it isn't treated in time, can be life-threatening.

LAYERING SYSTEM

Clothing should be worn in a system of layers so that you can add on and take off items as the weather conditions dictate. It is also essential to consider which materials will offer the best insulation when wet. Clothing that is completely waterproof is not suitable for strenuous walking or climbing as it will not allow body sweat to escape. Instead, the sweat will be absorbed into your clothing, and in extremely cold temperatures it can quickly freeze.

▼ *Activities such as skiing will make you sweat, and this will cause a chill unless the moisture can be absorbed by your clothing.*

First layer

The clothing that sits next to the skin must be able to absorb sweat from the body as well as any moisture (such as rain water or melted snow) that seeps down from the outer layers of clothing, while still retaining its insulating power. A long-sleeved thermal top and thermal long johns made from wool or a fibre-pile material will offer a base layer that is both absorbent and insulating.

Second layer

This middle layer is the same as that recommended for cold and dry climates: a loose-fitting long-sleeved cotton shirt and trousers, or a one-piece fibre-pile suit with a high collar and elastic cuffs that will keep the neck and wrists protected and warm. The advantage of a one-piece suit over a shirt and trousers is that it will not become dislodged at the waist, so that no skin is exposed during strenuous activities. A woollen scarf, or even a towel, worn around your neck will stop rain or melting snow running down your neck and back, and will keep the shoulders warm. Items that need to be kept warm and dry should be carried in this layer, in a waterproof pouch inside a pocket.

▲ *Children will be very vulnerable to the conditions in a cold and wet climate, so make sure they are appropriately protected.*

Third layer

The recommendations for this layer are the same as for cold and dry climates: a woollen sweater or a lightweight fleece jacket, an all-in-one suit such as fibre-pile salopettes worn with a fibre-pile mountain shirt, or a one-piece down or fibre-pile suit with a high collar and elastic cuffs. One-piece suits should be coated in a lightweight, water-repellent fabric. Synthetic fibre pile is extremely effective in cold and wet conditions because it retains its insulation properties when wet, whereas natural down does not. Furthermore, if down is allowed to become wet frequently, it will lose its insulation properties permanently.

Outer layer

Wear a zip-up waterproof jacket and a pair of full-length overtrousers that are breathable, windproof and water-resistant. The length of the jacket will depend on the activities you are planning: a knee-length jacket will offer more warmth and protection, but a shorter, waist-length jacket is less restrictive for more strenuous walking or mountaineering.

▶ Fibre-pile long johns are warm and will quickly absorb body sweat, but they do need to be kept dry to be effective.

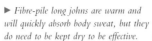

▼ Fibre-pile salopettes can be worn with a fibre-pile mountain shirt to make a highly protective and insulating third layer.

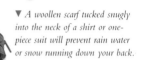

▲ A long-sleeved thermal vest top will give good insulation worn next to the skin if it is kept dry; it is less effective when wet.

ACCESSORIES

Keep your head, neck, shoulders and ears well protected with a woollen or fibre-pile balaclava. For extra insulation in conditions of extreme cold, a lighter silk balaclava can be worn beneath. Gloves should also be worn in up to three layers – first, fine silk gloves, then woollen or fibre-pile gloves, then waterproof outer mitts. It is a good idea to have your mitts attached to your jacket with a strong cord, so they cannot be lost or blown away if you take them off.

FOOTWEAR

Wear two pairs of thick woollen socks and a pair of leather mountain boots protected by insulated over-boots or heavy-duty knee-length gaiters. For very deep snow and ice conditions, you may prefer to wear plastic snow boots, which are specially designed with a thermal inner boot inside a plastic outer boot. Crampons attached to the outside of your boots will give a better grip when walking on snow and ice.

▼ A woollen scarf tucked snugly into the neck of a shirt or one-piece suit will prevent rain water or snow running down your back.

▼ A woollen balaclava gives good protection for the head and neck. Cover it with the hood of your jacket to keep it dry in a rain or snow shower.

▲ Bright sun and snow make a dazzling combination for the eyes, and good-quality sunglasses or snow goggles should be worn as much as possible when outdoors.

▼ Metal crampons can be attached to leather walking boots or snow boots to give you a surer grip underfoot in icy conditions.

▼ Knee gaiters will help to keep water and snow out of your boots and protect your legs from the cold temperatures.

▶ Plastic snow boots are better equipped than regular leather walking boots to stay waterproof and provide a good grip in snow or ice conditions.

Footwear

Your footwear is going to be one of the most important items of your kit, both for your comfort and for the protection of your feet. Boots need to fit properly, and they must be comfortable. If you have bought them new for your trip, you need to make sure they have been broken in before you use them.

BREAKING IN NEW BOOTS
Although a pair of new boots may feel comfortable in the store when you buy them, they will need to be properly broken in before use. This loosens up the uppers and moulds the insides to the shape of your feet, so as not to cause soreness. Experienced walkers say that it takes at least 160km/100 miles to break in a pair of leather walking boots, and 80km/50 miles to break in a pair of lightweight fabric boots.

SUITABILITY
A wide choice of footwear is available, but you need to make sure that what you wear on your feet is suitable for the terrain and climate and any activities involved. Boots have been designed for specific terrains, such as mountain or desert or jungle. These boots are not meant to be interchangeable, and wearing inappropriate footwear will not give your feet adequate protection and can put you at risk of injury.

PROTECTING YOUR BOOTS

Your walking boots are likely to be one of the most expensive items of your kit and as such you will want them to last for as long as possible. In order to keep them waterproof and resistant to damage, all boots should be coated in a protective waterproofing compound before you set off. Leather boots or shoes should be given two coats of oil, dubbin or a product recommended by the manufacturer. For fabric boots use a recommended silicone-based product, which can be either sprayed or rubbed on to the boot.

LIGHT WALKING
If you know you will be walking mostly on well-maintained tracks or footpaths, and you can expect the weather to be mild and dry, with dry, firm ground underfoot, you can wear leather or fabric walking shoes instead of boots. Many people find these more comfortable than boots, especially in warm weather. Walking shoes can be pulled off your feet in wet and muddy conditions and they do not offer much in the way of ankle support, but the advantage is that they dry out quickly when wet.

▲ *Do not expect the same pair of boots to be suited for every walking trip as boots are now designed to handle specific conditions.*

For low-level walking in wet or dry weather, or across open country, where you can expect the ground to be waterlogged and slippery, you can wear either lightweight fabric boots or leather walking boots. Fabric boots are a modern alternative to the leather boot. They are light and comfortable to wear, while still offering good ankle support, and the treads on the soles provide a good grip. Leather walking boots are the classic multi-purpose choice. These are more durable than fabric boots, and they have a better resistance to water if regularly reproofed.

▲ *Modern lightweight fabric boots are comfortable to wear and ideal for fine-weather walking conditions.*

▶ *Leather boots are durable and give good foot protection for cross-country walking.*

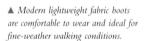

HIGH GROUND AND MOUNTAINS

If you will be walking on high ground, conditions underfoot will be unstable and you need to think carefully about your footwear. Leather walking boots or leather mountain boots, which have sturdier soles, will give good protection from the rough, often rocky, terrain. The boots should be well insulated to keep the feet warm, and they should have a sewn-in tongue to prevent water or snow getting inside.

DESERTS

Boots designed for the desert will protect you from the tough scrub and insects. The uppers are usually made of suede or light canvas, but the soles should be stout and strong, as there may be very sharp thorns on the ground. Some have smooth or ribbed soles. The pattern on the sole does not matter, unless you intend to do mountaineering or some other activity.

▲ *Heavier leather mountain boots will be needed if you are walking above the snow line.*

◀ *Desert boots have lightweight uppers and a strong sole to protect the feet and ankles from thorny plants and sharp stones and rocks.*

JUNGLE

Boots designed for jungle environments have strong rubber soles to keep out the wetness of the jungle floor, and canvas uppers that allow the feet to breathe and will dry quickly. The boots lace high above the ankle to allow the trousers to be worn inside the boot and protect the legs from leeches and other insects. Look for boots with one-way air vents, which allow water to drain out but prevent insects getting in. A sewn-in tongue will also stop insects getting to your feet. The tread pattern on the soles has wide, deep cleats to give a good grip in the wet, muddy conditions.

▲ *Gaiters will help to keep the lower legs warm and dry in cold, wet conditions.*

▶ *Jungle boots grip well, dry quickly and allow the feet to breathe, but will keep out insects.*

SNOW AND ICE

In many areas of the world you will encounter snow on high ground year-round. If the snow is deep, or if there is ice as well as snow, the ground will be extremely unstable, and your boots will have to be robust enough to take metal crampons in order for you to walk safely without sliding.

If you know you will be walking through deep snow, consider plastic snow boots. These comprise a thermal inner boot inside a plastic outer boot. The thermal inner boot gives heavy insulation for extreme cold conditions, and these boots are designed to hold the foot rigid while using crampons, allowing you to make a more stable foothold. However, like ski boots, the plastic outer boots are very inflexible and will make any kind of movement very awkward. It will often be preferable to wear snow boots when walking on snow and ice, especially if using crampons, but you should be prepared for this lack of flexibility.

One useful advantage is that the thermal inner boots can be detached and worn on their own at camp, inside the tent, if the weather is too cold to wear only socks.

▲ *Overboots are laced up over walking boots. They are useful for snow and ice conditions, and can be worn with crampons.*

▼ *Plastic snow boots consist of a thermal inner boot inside a plastic outer boot, and are excellent for use in deep snow.*

Personal Camp Kit

There are several core items of equipment that you will need to complete ordinary daily tasks while you are away. These items are known as your personal camp kit. You may feel that some of the items listed here are not relevant for your trip, and there may be other items you do need, but this list makes an excellent starting point when you first begin to pack.

COMPASS

Each person needs to have their own compass, but it is not enough just to carry it, you must also be confident that you can use it correctly. A compass is an essential aid to navigation, and if you get separated from the rest of your team it may be your only way of finding your way back to safety. Most people find the protractor compass easier to use than the prismatic type. Take good care of your compass, and keep it near to hand, either in a buttoned-up pocket, or attached to a belt or strong cord and worn around your neck. For further information see the sections The Compass and Using a Map and Compass.

MAP

A good map is essential when you are in the wilderness, but it will only be useful if you know how to read it. A planimetric map shows road systems and towns and is a useful tool when planning your transport route, but to learn about the shape of the land you need a topographic map, which is the standard map for wilderness travel. Choose a map with a scale larger than 1:100,000, because this will show land features in the amount of detail you need for accurate navigation. Take care of

▼ The compass is one of the most important items of your kit. Be sure you know how to use it properly and always keep it safe.

your map: have it neatly folded open at the right area as you travel, and keep it in a waterproof map case if the weather is wet or windy. For more information see the sections Maps, Reading a Map, and Using a Map and Compass.

WATER BOTTLE

Drinking water is essential for survival, and when travelling in the wilderness you will need to carry all the water required between water sources. Buy good quality water bottles because you risk serious problems if your bottle leaks and you lose all your supply when you are a long way from a water source.

Bottles are available in a range of sizes: quart/pint sizes are the most useful because they are not too heavy to carry when full. An attached bottle cap is best because it cannot get lost; caps that you drink through are very prone to leakages.

WATER PURIFIER

These are widely available from outdoor suppliers, and you will need to carry one if you are travelling in an area where the purity of the drinking water is in doubt. Fill the bottles with water and leave for 15 minutes, then pour the water through the bottle cap, which acts as a sterilizing filter. The filtered water will be fit to drink.

◄ Impure water is poured into the filter of this water purifier and pure water drips into the bottle below.

MONEY

While travelling keep your cash and your passport in a cotton money belt, strapped under your clothing so that it is out of view but still readily accessible. As insurance, keep an emergency fund of low denomination bills in a separate part of the belt from your main money.

Your choice of currency will depend where you are travelling to, but also remember to carry currency for any countries you will be passing through on the way to your final destination. If travelling to parts of the developing world with a minor local currency that is not available in your own country, a supply of US dollars can be extremely useful. Take around US$100 in $10 and $1 bills. US dollars are accepted in most parts of the world.

WRISTWATCH

It is tempting to do away with the trappings of urban life when in the wilderness, but you should always wear an accurate wristwatch. Besides showing the time a watch can be used as a simple check that you are on course on your route. When travelling check the time when you reach scheduled rest points to make sure you are in line with the day's plan; if you haven't reached a checkpoint by a certain time, it could be an indication that you have taken a wrong turning.

▼ Use a wristwatch set to local time to check you are where you expected to be on your route and to measure travel speeds.

▶ *Choose a flashlight that is as small as possible and waterproof as part of your kit.*

◀ *A Swiss Army penknife is compact and includes some valuable features.*

FLASHLIGHT

A small hand-held flashlight is useful for inside the tent or to read a map in dim light or darkness. If you have the space in your pack, take a head torch as well, as this will allow you to work with your hands free – if you have to put up a tent or change a cycle tyre in the dark, for example, or in an emergency situation at night.

BATTERIES

Unless you are sure you will be able to buy them while you are away, carry plenty of spare batteries for use in electrical items, such as torches and radios. Include both alkaline and lithium batteries in your kit. Alkaline batteries cost less than lithium batteries and they are more widely available, but lithium batteries run for longer and can be used in much colder temperatures. Dispose of used batteries with care. Do not burn them or bury them in the ground because the iron they contain can leach out into the earth; take them with you or dispose of them in a garbage bin.

PENKNIFE

If you do not have the space for a comprehensive tool kit, a good penknife such as the Swiss Army knife can be almost as useful. Carry it in your main kit bag before a flight (you will not be able to travel on a plane with a penknife in your hand luggage), then transfer it to your person when you arrive.

EATING EQUIPMENT

Take two plates, one of which should be a deep bowl type, or a set of army mess tins. The advantage of the latter is that you can use them for cooking as well as eating. You will also need a mug (about 300ml/½ pint capacity). Consider the pros and cons of plastic equipment versus enamel and aluminium. Plastic is light and less likely to burn you if filled with hot food or liquid, but it can melt if left too near to a direct heat source. On the other hand, enamel and aluminium are hardwearing, but they are heavier than plastic and can get very hot when filled with hot food

▲ *A set of army-style mess tins provides equipment for cooking and eating, and can still be packed away neatly after use.*

◀ *Each person will need their own mug, bowl, plate and cutlery. Sturdy plastic equipment will avoid mouth burns from hot food.*

or liquid. Your knife, fork and spoon should be made of aluminium or toughened plastic. Buy special camping cutlery if you can as it will be lighter and less bulky than kitchen cutlery.

TENT

A tent provides you with protection from the elements and a sheltered place to rest and sleep. Tents are available in a range of shapes and sizes, many with features designed for specific conditions. Choose a tent that is suitable for the climate and terrain you are visiting, and if you are backpacking, consider how heavy it will be to carry. Get used to putting up your tent before you go, and take extra tent pegs and a guy line with you. For more information, see the section Choosing a Tent.

▲ *Your sleeping bag should be stored properly when not in use and you should not allow it to get wet.*

SLEEPING BAG AND MAT

Choose a sleeping bag that is suited to the climate because otherwise you will spend your nights too warm or too cold, and in extreme conditions this could be dangerous. You can also carry an insulated sleeping mat to put underneath your sleeping bag. The bag provides your home comforts while you are living outdoors, so look after it well and do not allow it to get wet. If it does, make it a priority to dry it out as soon as you can. For more information, see the section Sleeping Bags.

▼ *Your washbag should contain everything you need for your personal hygiene regime.*

WASH KIT AND TOWEL

Besides the usual soap, toothbrush and toothpaste, facecloth and hairbrush or comb, your camp wash kit should include shampoo, a nail brush, a pair of nail scissors, and a razor and shaving foam if needed. All of this should be stored in a compact waterproof bag. If you are going to be away for more than a few weeks, have a comprehensive wash kit in your main rucksack and a smaller wash kit of essential items that you can carry around with you. Take both a bath and a hand towel. A supply of flat-packed toilet tissue may also be appreciated. You may wish to add a sunscreen, a lipbalm and some insect repellent, all of which can melt or leak and will need to be securely wrapped inside a plastic bag in the wash bag. Many women prefer to take their usual sanitary protection products with them as these can be hard – if not impossible – to find when you need them in remote areas or developing countries. Even if you do manage to find what you need they may be very expensive.

◀ *A camera and film can be included in your personal kit to give you a valuable photographic record of your trip.*

▲ *A mobile (cell) phone will help you to stay in touch with contacts at home as long as you are able to recharge the battery.*

ELECTRONIC EQUIPMENT

A radio is not an essential item but it can help to make longer trips more enjoyable. If you are travelling abroad and do not expect to have access to a television or the internet, a short-wave radio will enable you to pick up local and international radio programmes.

Other gadgets that you may want to take with you include a camera and film so that you can record your trip. A mobile (cell) phone can be useful, although it can be difficult to pick up a signal in remote or mountainous areas, and if you are travelling abroad you will need to carry a plug adaptor and charger so that you can recharge the battery while you are away.

▲ *Carry a bath towel for bathing or showering, and if your storage capacity allows it carry a hand towel as well.*

▼ *A packet of paper tissues has many uses, so keep a good supply as part of your wash kit.*

FIRST-AID KIT

Include a basic first-aid kit for your individual needs. This should contain some waterproof plasters in various sizes, some sterile gauze wound dressings, medication for diarrhoea, aspirin or paracetamol (acetaminophen), indigestion tablets and a few sachets of rehydration powder to be put in water. A small pair of scissors, a sterilized scalpel blade and a crêpe bandage are useful extras.

▲ *Include a sunscreen of at least SPF 25, especially if you will be in snow or bright sun or at high altitudes.*

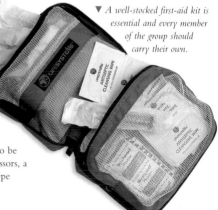

▼ *A well-stocked first-aid kit is essential and every member of the group should carry their own.*

◀ A pair of binoculars is a non-essential item but one that you will appreciate if you have the space to carry them.

▼ A repair kit that includes basic sewing items will allow you to make emergency repairs in the field.

BINOCULARS

A pair of binoculars is very useful for life in the outdoors, and as long as you are happy to accommodate the extra weight, they can add to the experience of the trip. With a pair of binoculars you can scan ahead along your route for possible hazards; watch wildlife without disturbing them; get a close-up of distant flowers or vegetation; check out a possible campsite without walking to it; or judge the best place to cross a river from a high viewpoint. Keen birdwatchers may prefer to carry a substantial pair of binoculars but for most people a pair of mini-binoculars will be adequate.

PERSONAL JOURNAL, NOTEBOOK AND WRITING MATERIALS

Paper is easily damaged if it gets damp, so carry stationery items in a waterproof pouch. It is worth keeping a travel journal to log your impressions and activities on a long trip; you will find it immensely enjoyable to read long after you have returned home. A notebook and pencil are useful for writing notes or memos for other group members.

REPAIR KITS

A mending kit can be as small as a matchbox but it should contain thread and needles and one or two spare buttons of different sizes, plus darning wool for socks and a few safety pins and a small pair of scissors. Lightweight, compact repair kits are now widely available from outdoor suppliers.

If you wear spectacles, it is worth bringing a spectacle repair kit so that you can carry out minor repairs. You can buy lightweight emergency reading glasses in a tube, which would be better than nothing if your normal glasses get broken or lost.

CLOTHES WASHING KIT

If you will be away for more than a few days and will need to wash and dry your clothes while you are away, you will need a small phial of detergent or travel wash, a washing line and some clothes pegs (pins). Roll up the washing line and pack it together with the other kit items in a plastic bag.

TRAVEL GAMES

Carrying a selection of games is a good idea to provide entertainment in the evenings or on rest days, or to fill the hours during long journeys or travel delays. If you are staying at a base camp and transporting your equipment by vehicle you will be able to fit in board games or even bat and ball games or skittles, and, if you are backpacking, a pack of playing cards can be carried without adding much weight or bulk.

Avoid carrying expensive electronic games that can be easily damaged and may be a temptation to thieves. If you are travelling with a group of young people it may be an idea to organize group games, perhaps with an educational theme; think these through before you travel and remember to include the necessary props, such as pencils, pens and notebooks.

◀ A pack of playing cards will provide entertainment at camp in the evenings and in case of travel delays.

▼ Along with a phial of detergent, carrying a washing line will mean you are equipped for washing and drying clothes.

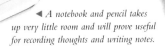

◀ A notebook and pencil takes up very little room and will prove useful for recording thoughts and writing notes.

Basic Survival Kit

If you are travelling in the wilderness it is highly advisable to carry a survival kit. The purpose of the kit is to keep you alive for 24–72 hours if you find yourself lost or injured without shelter, fire or water. It can quite literally mean the difference between life and death.

The survival kit must be carried on your person at all times to be sure it is there when you need it, so keep it small and light; attaching it to a sturdy belt around the waist is ideal. The contents should not be used for any other reason. It should be checked often and items replaced as necessary. Keep the kit in a waterproof pouch bag or in a small tin with a tight-fitting lid.

Your priority in a crisis will be to:
• Protect yourself from the elements
• Make a fire
• Carry and purify water to drink
• Signal your position
• Find your way
• Perform simple first aid

It is important to practise basic survival skills using the equipment in your kit, so that you will know what to do if a situation does arise.

MAKING A SHELTER

Your first priority in a survival situation is to construct a shelter for warmth and to give you a refuge while you take stock of your position.

Space blanket

A lightweight blanket, known as a space blanket, can be used in three ways: to keep warm, with the reflective silver material preventing body heat from escaping and deflecting it back to the body; as a horizontal shelter to reflect the sun's heat away from you; and as an A-shaped shelter to keep you dry from rain.

▲ *A space blanket helps to retain body heat and can be used to deflect the sun's rays away from you.*

◀ *The orange-coloured bivvy bag is light, packs up small and can be a lifesaver in several different ways.*

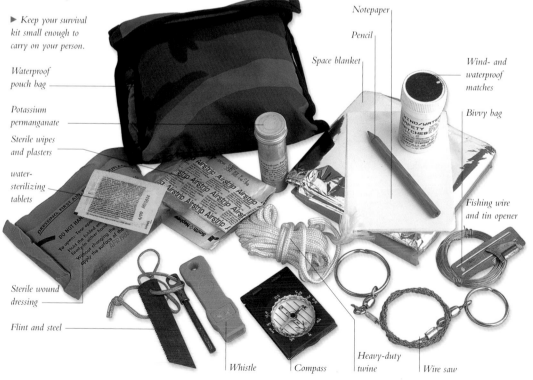

▶ *Keep your survival kit small enough to carry on your person.*

Notepaper

Pencil

Space blanket

Wind- and waterproof matches

Waterproof pouch bag

Potassium permanganate

Sterile wipes and plasters

water-sterilizing tablets

Bivvy bag

Fishing wire and tin opener

Sterile wound dressing

Flint and steel

Whistle

Compass

Heavy-duty twine

Wire saw

Bivvy bag

A large orange-coloured body-size heavy-duty plastic bag, known as a bivvy bag, has many uses yet is very light to carry. You can get into the bag as a way of keeping warm in cold and windy conditions; for a case of hypothermia, while you are waiting for help to arrive, one person can get inside the bag along with the casualty, using the body as an effective heat source to keep the casualty warm. In addition, the bivvy bag can be used as a groundsheet, or it can be used to signal to the air rescue services in an emergency situation: the bright orange colour makes it highly visible from the air, even in severe weather conditions.

▼ A length of sturdy cord should be included as part of your main kit.

Cord

If you need to construct a shelter, you will find parachute cord useful. Carry about 20m/66ft of the cord, packed inside your survival bag.

Wire saw

This packs up very small and is very effective for cutting through small to medium-size tree branches if you need to make a shelter or cut fire wood.

LIGHTING A FIRE

You can buy ready-to-use fire-making kits, or you can make your own. A flint and steel is the most effective homemade version, or you can carry a small amount of

▶ Firelighting kits, available from outdoor suppliers, contain flint and steel, tinder and matches.

cotton wool, in case you cannot find kindling, and a small magnifying lens for starting a fire from the sun, a disposable lighter and waterproofed matches (lifeboat matches, which burn in high wind and when wet, are the best). If using matches, keep the striking surface dry and carry an extra striking surface in your survival kit.

Candles

Tealight candles will take up very little room in your pack and can be used to light fires. Do not carry tallow candles as they will melt in hot weather.

CARRYING AND CLEANING WATER

Once you have found a source of water, you need a container to carry it in. A plastic bag or a condom can be used for this purpose; a condom can hold over 9 litres/2 gallons of water. Put the condom full of water into a sock or knotted trouser leg for added strength and protection. Before drinking the water, you will need to purify it using water-sterilizing tablets. Include a small phial of potassium permanganate, which can also be used to purify water (it is also an antiseptic and can be used to light a campfire). For more information, see the section Clean Water.

▶ Tealight candles burn easily and can be used to light a fire.

▲ Water sterilizing tablets are a vital part of your survival kit.

SIGNALLING

Pack a small flashlight and a heliograph, and wear a whistle on a cord around your neck. A few sheets of paper and a pencil will allow you to leave messages for rescuers trying to track you. A bivvy bag will enable you to signal your location.

FINDING YOUR WAY

Carry a spare compass in your survival kit as back-up in case you lose or damage your first compass.

FIRST-AID KIT

The survival kit should include the following first aid items:
• Adhesive dressings (plasters)
• Sterile wound dressing
• Sachets of rehydration powder
• Salt tablets
• Crêpe bandage
• Sterile scalpel blade
• Darning needle
  • Length of thread or wool

FOOD

Your body can last for up to five days without food, whereas it will last only 24 hours without water. This makes eating your least immediate need in a survival situation. Including food in your kit is not practical but if you carry a length of fishing wire and plenty of fish hooks and sinkers you will be equipped to catch fish for eating.

▶ Learn how to use fishing wire, hooks and weights for catching fish.

Group Camp Kit

If you are going away in a large group, many of the items included in the kit will belong to the group rather than to individuals. For this reason extra care must be taken to ensure that group equipment, including tents, activity or study equipment and guidebooks, is treated with care and respect. If it gets damaged or lost, everyone will suffer.

SHARING RESPONSIBILITY

Large pieces of equipment used by the whole group, such as large sleeping tents or cooking stoves, will need to be looked after by several people in order to distribute the load, if they are being carried, and to share the task of putting them up and taking them down. It can help to allocate responsibility for items to individuals for the duration of the trip. That way everybody knows who has tent A and who has tent B and so on, and there is less chance that key parts, such as tent pegs, will be lost or left behind. If there isn't enough equipment to be allocated in this way, consider working to a rotation system, which will split the responsibilities evenly between group members.

MAPS AND GUIDEBOOKS

These are essential items and as such they should be kept at a central point at the base camp and issued only when

▲ *You may be able to buy equipment such as cooking pots cheaply at local markets at your destination to save you transporting it.*

needed. One person in the group could be made responsible for ensuring the maps and guidebooks are logged out properly and returned after use.

COOKING EQUIPMENT

For group expeditions it is usually easier to handle all meal times in one session, rather than have individuals trying to set

up their own stoves in the same area of the campsite at the same time. For larger groups a campfire offers an effective and more spacious method of cooking large quantities of food, and it means you do not need to transport cumbersome stoves and fuel supplies with you. You may not feel it is worth building a campfire for just one overnight stop but it is a good idea if the group is to stay at the campsite for several days; besides, it adds a lot to the wilderness experience to eat together around an open fire.

If planning to cook over a wood fire, make sure that your cooking equipment is suitable for use over direct heat. If you try to use lightweight cooking equipment on a hot wood fire, you can melt the equipment or burn the food.

To prepare and cook food for a number of people at the same time you will need catering-size cooking equipment. If the area you are travelling to is not too remote and

▶ *So important is it that the group's map collection is well looked after that it may be worth making one person responsible for maps for the duration of the trip.*

▲ *Large-volume containers such as jerry cans will be necessary to provide water at a base camp for a big group of people.*

there will be access to local markets, you may be able to buy items such as pans, jerry cans, storage containers and utensils very cheaply. This will mean that you don't have to transport these bulky items to and from your destination, saving baggage space and possibly extra costs if you are travelling by plane and have a restricted luggage allowance. Once you have finished with the equipment you could simply give it away – to the people who run the campsite where you have been staying, for example.

FIRST-AID AND MEDICAL KITS

It is sensible to take a comprehensive first-aid kit if travelling in a large group; this should be in addition to the basic first-aid kits carried by individuals. It may be a good idea to have everyone in the group fill out a medical form that is kept with the first-aid kit; even on personal trips it is reassuring to have a list of individuals' allergies or medication to hand in case it is needed quickly.

Consider separating the group kit into clearly identified sections for emergency and non-emergency items, so that you can get to everyday treatments for blisters, cuts and

scratches or headaches without having to unpack the whole kit. This way it will be easier for group members to find what they are looking for in the kit, and medical items such as sterile dressings and bandages won't get misplaced or made dirty by being unpacked and repacked every day.

The group first-aid and medical kits should be kept in water- and dustproof containers to ensure that none of the items is found to be dirty or damaged when you need it. Make sure everybody knows where the first-aid kit is kept at camp and who is carrying it when on the move. For a large group it is a good idea to make one person responsible for the first-aid and medical kits, replenishing stock as needed and making sure the contents are kept in order. Ideally, the first-aider should have a good level of up-to-date first aid or medical training.

TOOLS

Make sure that someone in the group is responsible for any tools that the group is taking with them. Many of the tools you are likely to need, such as knives, machetes and axes, are very dangerous items and it goes without saying that this is a role for a responsible person; if the group members are children you may need to keep the tools locked up. The tool monitor can also be asked to make sure that the tools are in good working order at the end of the expedition, and that they are cleaned and stored ready for another trip.

▼ *An extensive medical kit will be necessary for a team of people; organize the kit into labelled packs so that you can find what you need easily.*

If you are going on an expedition and have bought group equipment out of expedition funds (which may include contributions from the team members as well as from sponsorship or donations) you need to decide what you are going to do with the equipment when you return home. Are you going leave it in the area you have been travelling or working in, giving it away to local people or a local organization; or will you store it for a future trip; or are the members to be allowed to buy it – perhaps it could be auctioned off for charity – when the group gets back home? Discuss as a group at your pre-trip planning meetings and make a decision before you go.

▲ *A hands-free flashlight may be needed for field or study work, and will simplify the task of putting up tents in the dark.*

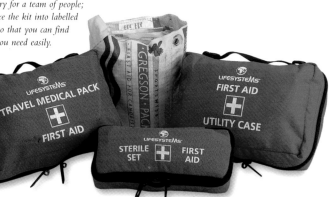

Choosing a Tent

When you choose a tent, you will be faced with a huge selection of styles, colours, weights and sizes. To help narrow down your choice, and to make sure you end up buying what you do actually need, consider where and when you are going to use the tent, how you are going to carry it, what you are going to use it for and how many people it will need to sleep.

WHERE AND WHEN ARE YOU GOING TO USE THE TENT?

Consider the climate you can expect at your destination and the environment in which you are going to camp. In the African bush your tent will need to protect you from the heat and possibly from heavy rain; on a mountainside above the Arctic Circle your priority is protection from high winds.

▲ *Small robust tents are preferable for use in exposed sites or colder climates, with the lower volume of air space retaining the heat.*

▼ *In hot, dry climates choose a larger tent with more internal space that encourages air circulation and keeps the temperature down.*

▲ *The general-purpose ridge tent is suitable for climatic conditions anywhere in the world, and is available in a range of sizes.*

▲ *Some vehicles have been adapted to take a tent on the roof to give protection from wild animals attracted to the camp at night.*

▲ *A contemporary one-person tunnel tent. The hoop pole structure offers good floor space but will not withstand high winds.*

If you are going to a hot, dry climate try to allow for as much space in your tent as possible to encourage the air to circulate and keep you cooler. If you are backpacking you will need to consider the pros and cons of an airy tent against the extra bulk to be carried. Cotton and canvas materials will stand up to and protect you from the sun far better than synthetic materials. Strong ultraviolet light in the tropics can ruin nylon materials very quickly, and the thorns on many bushes and trees can destroy lightweight material.

TENT CRITERIA

The tent is your home while you are in the wilderness. Its main function is to provide a warm and dry place for you to sleep, but you may also need to cook inside it or use it as a shelter while you sit out severe weather conditions. The following criteria are essential:
• The tent should be big enough to allow sleeping space and adequate ventilation for all users and their kit.
• There should be enough height on the inside for everyone to sit upright at the same time.
• The flooring material needs to be robust enough to give protection from the ground; if it isn't you will need to carry additional matting if you are to sleep in comfort.

If the climate is hot and wet, and you visit in the rainy season, the tent may have to withstand weeks or months of heavy rain. Natural materials such as cotton or canvas will cope better with this type of climate.

In high mountains in a cold climate, you will want a small tent that will warm up quickly with your body heat and will be able to withstand high winds. A tent made from synthetic materials will be lighter, and therefore easier to carry, than a cotton or canvas one. It will also be stronger, with a sewn-in groundsheet, made of a substantial material, suitable for pitching on snow, ice and rocks.

In very extreme cold conditions you may find that the tent doors are better fastened by some other means than a zip, such as tied or velcro fasteners, because zips can freeze if it is extremely cold .

HOW ARE YOU GOING TO CARRY THE TENT?

If you plan to transport your tent in the back of a vehicle, then weight or size will not be a major consideration. However, if you will be carrying the tent yourself, you will need to choose the lightest option possible (see the section Lightweight Camping).

▶ *The geodesic dome tent is spacious on the inside, and if the sloping wall is pitched in the direction of the wind it is very stable.*

WHAT ARE YOU GOING TO USE THE TENT FOR?

Is your tent going to be used for backpacking, where you will set it up for the night, cook, sleep, then take it down and move on? Or are you going to set up camp and use your tent as a work place, eating, sleeping and general living area, perhaps staying for several days or weeks? Think about how you will use the tent and choose accordingly.

HOW MANY PEOPLE WILL THE TENT NEED TO SLEEP?

If your tent is going to be used in a base camp, decide how many people it will need to sleep, and how much room you will allow each person. If you have a mixed-sex group, they may prefer to be separated for sleeping, using either a divided tent or separate smaller tents. How much kit each person will have must also be taken into account if the kit is going to be stored inside the tent.

RIDGE TENT

This general-purpose tent is suitable for camping anywhere, from the back garden to the desert or jungle. The ridge tent has an upright pole or an A-shaped pole assembly at each end, and, in some cases, an additional ridgepole across the top. This adds extra weight but it also stabilizes the tent, and this could be important if you are likely to experience high winds. Some ridge tents have sloping ridges to cut down on weight.

The walls of the ridge tent are created by adjustable guy lines, which stretch the inner walls outwards,

supporting the tent and allowing you to utilize the whole of the floor space without touching the sides of the tent. This is important because if the inner walls touch the outer fly sheet and the fly sheet is wet, the dampness will soak through to the inner walls, causing water to leach inside the tent. A door at each end is the preferred choice, so that if you have to cook in a doorway due to intense cold or heavy rain you can choose the door opening that offers the most shelter from the prevailing wind and the elements.

▲ *A standard ridge tent is simple to erect and maintain even for most inexperienced campers, hence its continued popularity.*

BELL OR SINGLE-POLE TENTS

Bell tents have a single pole in the middle of the tent, while single-pole tents may have either a pole or an A-shaped pole assembly. Both designs are very stable in strong winds.

▼ *Large patrol tents are ideal for basecamps but the size and weight of the canvas means they will have to be transported by vehicle.*

KEY QUESTIONS

Before making any decisions, look at the styles available and talk to a reputable tent retailer before asking yourself the following questions:

• How heavy is the tent? Pick up a packed version to feel the weight for yourself.

• Are there additional features that are of no use but add to the cost?

• Is the stitching well done and are the guying and guy line points reinforced to take the strain?

• Are the poles strong enough for the job and would they support the material in strong winds?

• If the tent gets damaged in the field, can it be repaired quickly and easily?

• If it is a dome tent can you buy spare poles for it?

• How easy is it to pitch the tent, not just on a summer's day in a local field but also on a mountain in high winds in near darkness?

• How many people are required to pitch the tent?

• Is the tent material of good quality and will it stand up well to the conditions you are going to take it into?

• Will you need a two-skin tent, i.e. an inner tent with a fly sheet, and will the fly sheet need to come right down to the ground to offer you protection in wet and windy conditions?

DOME AND GEODESIC DOME TENTS

These have a number of poles threaded into sleeves on either the inner or outer tent. The extra poles make these the most expensive types of tent to buy, and if your poles break you will need spares or splints to slide over the break.

The geodesic dome is more stable than the ordinary dome in bad weather, but it is difficult to pitch in high winds.

▼ *Large frame tents provide useful areas for study or group meetings at base camps, but several people will be needed to put them up.*

TUNNEL AND WEDGE TENTS

The tunnel tent is a cross between a ridge tent and a dome. It offers good floor space as the pole system is a series of hoops down the tent, but in high winds it can blow in and lose its shape. The wedge tent has most of the disadvantages of the tunnel and few advantages. Instability is a problem in bad weather as the large areas of material are a target for high winds.

▲ *Wedge and tunnel tents on display at an outdoor suppliers fair. The advantages of these tents are their small size and low weight, making them popular with backpackers. One disadvantage is the lack of headroom.*

▼ *Geodesic dome tents are one of the sturdiest tents available and will withstand even gale-force winds so long as the poles – which are threaded through the fabric to give the tent its shape – are not damaged.*

Sleeping Bags

A comfortable, warm sleeping bag will give you the good night's sleep you need when living outdoors. Getting enough sleep is as important to your physical health and state of mind as eating, and the right bag is important.

All sleeping bags work by trapping air in their fillings; the air is warmed by the heat from your body and retained in the filling, insulating you against the cold. The more warm air a bag traps, the greater its insulating properties.

There is a huge variety of sleeping bags available, from inexpensive but basic simple-quilted versions to quality, down-filled double-quilted ones. The criteria to look for when choosing a bag are the method of construction, what material is used, what filling is used, how it is zipped, its size and whether or not it has a hood.

CONSTRUCTION

There are basically three different types of sleeping bag construction: simple quilting or stitch-through; box-wall; and double quilting.

Simple quilting or stitch-through

This method is usually used in the cheaper sleeping bags. They are not very effective at retaining warmth because warm air will be lost where the stitching goes through the fabric. These bags have a low temperature rating, making them suitable for warm summer weather, or for two consecutive seasons: spring and summer or summer and autumn.

Box-wall

Bags with this type of construction have a high temperature rating, and they may be suitable for two to three seasons, or even three to four seasons in a temperate climate. They come in three different forms.
- Box-wall construction, where the filling is contained within "boxes" to prevent the filling from moving about.
- Slant-wall construction, with slanted layers of overlapping fibres. This improves on the box-wall version by giving the filling more room to expand, filling with air for improved insulation and, therefore, warmth.
- V-baffle construction, which improves on the slant-wall construction by making sure there is always plenty of filling throughout the bag.

Double quilting

This is effectively two simple quilting or stitch-through-type sleeping bags put together and offset to eliminate cold spots. It usually has the highest-quality filling but is heavy to carry and may not be suitable for backpacking trips.

MATERIAL

Your choice of material for the shell depends on the type of environment and what time of year you will be using the sleeping bag:
- Cotton is ideally suited to high temperatures and humidity as it is a breathable natural fabric and will absorb sweat and feel comfortable.

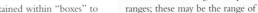

WARMTH RATINGS

Consider any kind of sleeping bag rating as a rough guide only as there is no standard rating system. Some manufacturers describe the number of seasons a bag may be suitable for. Others give temperature ranges; these may be the range of temperature in which the bag will feel comfortably warm, or it may be the temperature at which you will survive but won't feel warm.

- Nylon is better suited to cooler temperatures, where sweating is not likely to be a problem; some nylon sleeping bags have a cotton lining on the inside, which increases the comfort factor.
- Pertex is a good down-proofing material, which means that it stops the filling material from working its way through the fabric. It is also water-repellent (but not water*proof*), which makes it suitable for damp, though not wet, conditions, such as high humidity.

Military-type sleeping bags have a groundsheet sewn on to the underneath of the bag so they can be used directly on the ground, even without a tent or sleeping mat. However, these bags are often heavy and bulky and they can be difficult to clean. They are available from specialist outdoor stores that sell ex-military equipment.

▲ Simple or stitch-through quilting is found in cheaper sleeping bags that are suitable for one or two seasons of the year.

▲ Box-wall construction comes in three forms: box-wall (top and main diagram), slant-wall (centre) and V-baffle (bottom).

▲ Double-quilting construction is effectively two simple or stitch-through bags put together and offset to better retain the heat.

▶ *A basic sleeping bag for use at home or in a temperate or warm climate. This type of bag will be easy to care for and is not expensive.*

▶ *A down-filled sleeping bag will keep you comfortably warm at temperatures below freezing. Down bags need to be dry cleaned.*

▶ *A fibre-pile sleeping bag will retain the heat and keep you warm even if it gets damp. These bags are machine washable.*

▶ *A military sleeping bag with a built-in groundsheet is tough and robust and is designed to be used on its own without a tent or mat. These bags can be very heavy.*

FACTORS AFFECTING WARMTH

How warm your sleeping bag will keep you is dependent on a number of variable factors besides bag construction and filling:

- The climate, including the humidity level (high humidity makes the bag damp, and increases heat loss through conduction).
- Whether you are in a tent or shelter, or out in the open air.
- Whether you are on your own inside the sleeping bag.
- Whether or not you are using a sleeping mat underneath the bag.
- What clothes you are wearing.
- The shape of the bag, with a close-fitting bag being warmer.
- How much you have eaten, as food provides energy and heat.
- How tired you are, as it is more difficult to get warm when tired.

FILLINGS

The biggest difference between bags is in the type of filling and the thickness of it. The purpose of a sleeping bag filling is to trap air as insulation. The thicker the filling, and the more effectively it traps the air, the better the bag will be at keeping you warm.

Natural fillings

Feather-filled sleeping bags have one of three types of filling: down, feather, and down and feather mix.

Down

Pure down is the fluffy underplumage of ducks and/or geese. It is by far the lightest and warmest, weight for weight, of all bag fillings, and is comfortable over a greater temperature range. Down shapes itself around the body for a close, warm fit, unlike synthetic fillings, which tend to stand away from the body, leaving cold spots. Down is more compressible than synthetic fillings, so it packs up much smaller and won't get damaged when stuffed into a rucksack. The drawbacks of down are that it loses its insulation properties when wet, and takes a long time to dry out. It can also be damaged by damp storage. However, it is difficult to get a down bag wet in the first place, unless you drop it in water or sleep outside in the rain without shelter. This is especially so with modern shell materials, which are water-resistant and dry out quickly.

Although down bags are expensive, they can be expected to last much longer than synthetic bags – for up to 20 years if well cared for – and this makes them a more economical choice in the long term. They are most suitable for situations where warmth and space are at a premium, and are a particular favourite for cold conditions because of their comfort, weight and bulk.

Down/feather mix

A number of manufacturers mix duck or goose down and feathers together to make a cheaper filling (separating the feathers from the stalkless down plumules is very time-consuming and therefore expensive). The mixed filling has all the advantages of down: it is warm and comfortable, light to carry and easily packed up, although you do need more filling to achieve the same level of warmth. Check what proportion of down makes up the filling, as a greater amount of down means a warmer sleeping bag. There will usually be less than 50 per cent down in the mix.

▲ *A fibre-pile filling will keep you warm even if it becomes damp or wet, and this may be crucial in a cold and wet climate.*

▲ *Synthetic bag fillings are cheaper than down and although they weigh more, they will perform better when damp or wet.*

▼ *Duck or goose down is the most costly bag filling but it is also the most effective at retaining heat and it will last the longest.*

▼ *Feather filling uses poorer quality feathers than down and requires more in weight and bulk to provide the same amount of heat.*

▼ *Many people find a down and feather mix a good compromise between cost and the ability to insulate effectively.*

▲ *At good outdoor suppliers you will be faced with a huge selection of sleeping bags. Always ask for advice if you feel confused.*

Feather

These are the bigger, stiffer feathers of ducks and geese, which you will be able to feel through the bag shell. A feather filling will not have the same insulation properties as down or the down/feather mix, and you will need at least twice as much filling to achieve the same warmth, but feather bags are less expensive and they can still provide a very comfortable night's sleep.

Synthetic fillings

These fillings don't have the natural lightness of down or feather fillings, and synthetic bags at the cheaper end of the market tend to be heavy, bulky and less soft. They are also less durable, as the synthetic filling starts to lose its insulation properties after only a couple of years. However, synthetic bags are inexpensive to buy. They perform well when wet and dry out quickly, and are machine washable. They are more tolerant of careless handling and damp conditions than down bags, and are perfectly adequate for situations where warmth, low weight and bulk are not your priority.

One specialist synthetic filling is fibre pile, which is a thicker version of the material used for fleece jackets. Fibre pile will retain its insulation properties when wet, it can be hung out to dry, and is machine washable. However, it is bulkier and heavier than other synthetic-filled bags, and it may not be suitable for lightweight camping. Fibre-pile fillings can be difficult to find in stores.

SIZE AND SHAPE

Try out the bag in the store to see if it is wide and long enough for you. A bag that fits close to your body will keep you warmer than a roomy one, but check it doesn't feel too restrictive. Better quality bags have a tapered shape.

ZIPS

Most bags have a zip of some kind to allow the bag to be opened out full, which makes getting in and out easy, and allows for ventilation. It is also useful for cleaning the bag. Zips can be full-length, half-length, or down one side and across the bottom. Any zip is a potential cold spot, though a quality bag will have a protected pad of filling under the zip. If a bag does not have a zip, it will be more difficult to get into but will weigh less.

HOOD

Some 20 per cent of body heat is lost through the head, and a bag with a hood retains warmth more effectively. It also makes a comfortable resting place for your head, and can be pulled up over your head to protect you from insects, such as flies or mosquitos.

SAFETY

Never leave your sleeping bag or liner on the ground for any length of time, even when it is rolled up, but pack it away in your rucksack. In temperate or hot countries, unroll your sleeping bag only just before you get into it to avoid any insects getting in with you.

▼ *Sleeping out without a tent can be great fun but do not sleep too near the camp fire or else you could damage your sleeping bag.*

Other Sleeping Equipment

Additional items can be added to your kit for a more comfortable night's sleep. Consider the cost of buying and transporting these extra items, as well as the additional weight and bulk if you are backpacking and have to carry them.

INSULATION AND PROTECTION
You may want to insulate yourself from the ground if it will be cold, hard or wet, or if there will be ants, snakes or spiders on it.

Camp beds
These come in all shapes and sizes and are heavy, so you will want to use them only if transporting your equipment by vehicle or pack animal. However, camp beds will get you right off the ground for a very comfortable night's sleep.

If you are going to use a camp bed, you will need some insulation beneath the sleeping bag, such as a mat, as the layer of air between you and the ground will become very cold at night. If you are going to an area where there will be mosquitos, consider setting up a frame around your bed for a mosquito net. When using a camp bed, always set it up on flat ground, so that you don't tip the bed over accidentally when turning over in the night.

Air mattresses
These require inflating by mouth or with an air pump, and this makes them time-consuming to set up. Air mattresses come in different sizes, colours and thicknesses. If over-inflated, they may feel hard and uncomfortable to sleep on.

An air mattress full of air becomes cold overnight, so in anything but hot weather, you will need extra insulation underneath you, such as an insulated mat. Be careful that the mattress does not get punctured by sharp stones on the ground or carelessly pierced by a knife or penknife, and do not drag it along the ground; carry a puncture repair kit so that if necessary you can make repairs in the field.

Self-inflating sleeping mats
When you unscrew the valve on one of these mats, air will be sucked in and it will inflate itself, though you can speed up the process by giving one or two puffs of air by mouth to start off with. Check for sharp stones or thorns on the ground before laying the mat out. These mats are best carried inside the rucksack to protect them from damage.

Insulation mats
These are the lightest and cheapest type of insulation, and they come in several thicknesses. If you are going to a very cold climate, a thick foam mat will provide good insulation but it will be heavy to carry and bulky. The great advantage with these mats is that you cannot damage them, except by putting them in direct contact with something

◄ *Metal frame camp beds are bulky and heavy but they do keep you off the ground and this will greatly improve your comfort.*

▼ *Insulation mats are available in a range of thicknesses and lengths, so choose one for the conditions you will be sleeping in.*

▼ *Self-inflating mats are convenient to use, but do not over-inflate them and watch for sharp stones or rocks on the ground beneath.*

▼ *A cotton sleeping bag liner will help to keep the sleeping bag clean and is easy to wash.*

▲ *A mosquito net is essential for tropical climates. Attach it to the inside of your tent and check daily for tears.*

▶ *Self-inflating sleeping mats can be rolled up neatly and strapped on to the outside of your rucksack during transit.*

▼ *An inflatable pillow is small and light enough even for backpackers to carry, and will improve your night-time comfort.*

very hot, which will melt them. Check for stones on the ground when you unroll your mat, which could give you an uncomfortable night's sleep.

NEWSPAPER
If you are lightweight camping without a sleeping mat, and are going to have to sleep on the ground with only the tent groundsheet for insulation, you can lay sheets of newspaper under your sleeping bag. You will need at least five to ten sheets of newspaper for effective insulation, but it is better than nothing if the ground is very cold or hard.

SLEEPING BAG LINERS
Whichever material you choose for the outer shell of your sleeping bag, you might want to consider buying a separate liner. This is a thin fabric bag, usually made of cotton or silk, which fits inside the sleeping bag. It does offer a little more warmth, but its main advantage is that it protects the sleeping bag from getting dirty on the inside,

and it can be washed more easily than the bag. In hot weather, you can sleep in the liner on its own, perhaps using your sleeping bag underneath it for padding, as you would a sleeping mat.

INFLATABLE PILLOW
Although it is not strictly necessary, an inflatable pillow weighs next to nothing and will add to your comfort during the night. It can also be used to give head and neck support on long journeys. Inflate the pillow by mouth at your campsite and deflate it after use, so that it can be folded up and packed with your tent bag or tucked into your rucksack.

Backpacks and Carrying Equipment

A backpack is used to carry food and clothing while on the move. It can be used to carry camping and cooking gear if you will be living outdoors and without any other means of transporting your gear. The backpack you need for a day's walking in warm weather will be very different to the one needed for a three-week camping trip through the mountains. As with any equipment, decide how you will be using the pack before you buy one.

Many modern backpacks are covered in straps, zips, gadgets and pockets, and these additional features will often add to the price. Rather than being dazzled by the apparent complexity of these backpacks, consider if you really need the extra features. Remember, too, that most people will fill whatever size backpack they have, which can make for a very heavy load, so the smaller the sack, the less temptation there will be to take too much gear.

All backpacks are claimed to be waterproof but some fabric materials are better than others, and it is a good idea to line the main compartment with a plastic bag to keep your gear dry. (You may prefer crucial items such as your passport or first-aid kit to be wrapped in additional sturdy plastic bags as a further safeguard.)

DAY SACKS

For a day's walking in the summer, a small, light day sack with a capacity of between 20 and 35 litres containing food and water, waterproof clothing and emergency supplies will be as much as you need. If your activities will involve mountaineering, ski touring or snow hiking, choose one of the larger day sacks of around 40 litres.

Additional features

Day sacks do not need a support frame because they are not designed to carry heavy loads. Even so, comfort is always important, and because a day sack sits directly against your back, padding on the outside is advisable so that any sharp contents do not dig into you.

Main compartment

Lockable zip opening to main compartment

Smaller front compartment

Lockable zip opening to front compartment

Document pocket for quick-access items

Mesh side pockets

▲ *A day sack should be big enough to carry your waterproofs and a sweater, a survival kit, and enough food and water for the day.*

In addition, when packing make sure you place soft items such as clothing against the rear of the pack to act as an extra cushion for your back.

In hot weather or during strenuous activities, wearing the sack may cause your back to sweat. To control this, many better-designed packs have a robust cotton panel on the back to absorb sweat; a cotton panel feels more comfortable than a synthetic one. Quality modern sacks are fitted with a high-wicking padded mesh back for improved ventilation to reduce sweating.

Day sacks do not usually have pockets on the outside because the main compartment is small enough to be easily accessible. There will usually be a pocket in the top flap, which is useful for holding maps and valuables.

Larger day sacks will come with a waist strap, and if you think you are going to do a lot of scrambling or steep country work, it is advisable to have one of these, otherwise the pack can move around as you climb, and this may affect your balance.

If you are planning to walk over difficult terrain, or are mountaineering, ski touring or snow hiking, choose a larger day sack with attachment points on the outside, which will allow you to fix on your walking pole, ice axe, skis or crampons, keeping your hands free.

Other features include compressible straps, which can be pulled tight to reduce the volume of an empty sack, a key-ring attachment and a top handle.

WHAT TO LOOK FOR IN A PACK

• The pack must be sturdy and comfortable, whatever its size.
• Webbing needs to be tough, in good condition and adjustable. This is especially important on larger packs as heavy loads can quickly weaken poor webbing.
• The outer fabric should be tough and fully waterproof.
• There should be a drawstring hood inside the main sack to prevent water leaking in and contents falling out.
• Outer pockets should have zips rather than straps or drawstrings.
• A comfortable waist belt is essential on any pack bigger than a day sack.

LARGE DAY SACKS OR OVERNIGHT BACKPACKS

These will come in the 35–55 litre range, and they may have a frame or may be frameless.

As you will be carrying a heavier weight than in a smaller day sack, look closely at the waist or hip belt to see if it is strong and well padded and has a quick-release buckle in case you need to jettison the sack quickly. Also check that the shoulder straps are well padded and that the straps can be tightened or slackened quickly and easily. The webbing on all straps should be well made and strong.

This type of sack can come with external pockets, usually one or two on each side, as well as an easy-access document pocket in the top flap for maps. Side pockets are very useful for keeping water bottles, fuel and other fluids or dirty items of kit away from your main kit to prevent damage in the event of leakage. Make sure zip-up side pockets are kept securely fastened when in use, so that nothing can fall out accidentally.

Whether or not you need a pack with a frame depends on how you will be using the pack and the type of loads you will be carrying. A frame adds extra weight to the pack but it will make heavy or bulky loads more comfortable to carry, and this is very important over long distances.

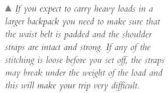

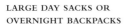

▲ *If you expect to carry heavy loads in a larger backpack you need to make sure that the waist belt is padded and the shoulder straps are intact and strong. If any of the stitching is loose before you set off, the straps may break under the weight of the load and this will make your trip very difficult.*

▲ *If fully packed a large backpack without a frame can cause sweating on the back in hot weather or during strenuous activity.*

▼ *Overnight backpacks will hold equipment for short lightweight camping trips or for day use if work or study gear is to be carried.*

Elastic holders for easy-access items

Hooded opening to main compartment

Front pocket for smaller items

Zip-fastening side pocket

Padded waist belt

Straps to carry equipment externally

EXPEDITION BACKPACKS

These packs are available in 55- to over 120-litre sizes. The smaller packs are ideal for lightweight walking, while the larger ones are for longer trips or trips to more remote areas; somewhere in between is usually enough for most people and most camping expeditions.

These packs can be expensive, so make sure the one you buy feels comfortable to wear and is suitable for the load you will be carrying.

Key features

Two or more external pockets is usual on expedition backpacks, with some packs having pockets that can be detached and used on their own as small day sacks or large belt pouches. Many modern packs have the main compartment divided so that your sleeping bag and clothes can be packed in the lower, smaller section, and the upper section can be used for general equipment. In better-quality packs, you will be able to open the zipped divider or remove it altogether to accommodate longer-length items.

Access is through the top of the pack, but zipped-front access to the divided compartments is increasingly common.

It is important that an expedition backpack is comfortable and fits well, as you could be wearing it every day for days if not weeks, travelling over difficult terrain and carrying heavy loads. The waist belt and shoulder harness must be padded and adjustable; a chest strap will hold the sack more firmly in position on your back.

External frame packs

If you have to carry boxes or oddly shaped loads into the backcountry using your backpack, tying them on to an external frame may be the best solution. The most useful frame designs will have a small step at the bottom to support the load from slipping down. If you will be walking in woodland, rainforests or jungles, where there is dense vegetation, choose a backpack with a frame that isn't too high above your head to avoid getting it caught in the tree branches and vines and making your progress more difficult.

▲ *The advantage of a frame backpack is that you can strap almost anything on to it, no matter how awkward the shape.*

CHOOSING A PACK FRAME

• A pack with an internal frame will be lighter than one with an external frame, and the pack will be less bulky for storage in transit or when not in use.
• External frames are stronger, which means they can carry a heavier load without causing damage to the backpack.
• External frames are more rigid and are especially good for awkwardly shaped and bulky items. In an emergency, a backpack with an external frame can be used as a stretcher to carry a sick or injured person to safety.
• External frames carry the load high up on your body, distributing the weight more evenly over the hip and back area.
• A good external frame is designed to allow air space between the frame and your back to minimize sweating caused by constant body contact with the pack.

Hooded opening to main compartment

Main compartment for large or heavy items

Side pockets for fuel or water bottles

External elastic straps

Padded waist belt

◀ *Modern expedition packs are designed to carry heavy loads conveniently and in comfort but they must be packed correctly.*

▲ *If carrying equipment by vehicle you can use a roofrack for bulky items to save space inside, but make sure the load is attached securely and protect it with a waterproof sheet in case of sudden showers.*

▲ *Pack animals can carry heavy loads but you must make sure that the weight is balanced on either side of the animal.*

PANNIERS

If you have to carry your gear on a bicycle, vehicle, motorbike or animal, you will need a set of panniers.

Cycle

Make sure cycle panniers are well secured and will not get in the way of the wheels or the chain of the cycle. Check that you have balanced the weight of the load as equally as possible between each side.

Vehicle or motorbike

Cars and vans can be fitted with roofracks to increase the storage space inside the vehicle. Motorbikes can be fitted with panniers that sit on either side of the bike, behind the saddle.

Animal

On animals, you will need some kind of frame or pannier bags, but these must sit comfortably on the back of the animal and not rub its back. Always check any pack animal's back at night for any signs of sore spots and treat

◀ *Panniers are essential for touring trips on a bicycle, and even then you will be very limited with the equipment you can carry.*

▲ *Equipment is loaded on a camel in a very specific way, and if you are planning to do it yourself you should ask your guide's advice.*

them immediately. Horses, mules and camels are capable of carrying heavy loads but do not overload an animal with equipment; the animal must always be able to move freely. Make it part of your routine at each rest stop to check that the load has not moved or become unsafe.

▶ *If travelling by plane and vehicle you may find conventional luggage more convenient than a backpack.*

Cooking Stoves

There are five kinds of fuel suitable for outdoor cooking stoves, and all have their advantages and disadvantages, including volatility, smell, ease of use and cost. Which fuel you choose will dictate the type of stove you can take, though multi-fuel stoves, which use more than one type, are available.

When planning your trip, consider the type of conditions you need the stove to operate in. Some gases will not perform well in extreme cold conditions and some fuels evaporate quickly in very hot conditions, so it is important to make a suitable choice. Also note that in some countries you may not be able to buy the right kind of cylinder for your stove.

◀ *The Trangia stove runs on methylated spirits. It is windproof and stable and includes its own set of cooking pans and a kettle.*

GAS
This is probably the most popular and easiest type of stove to use, though the fuel is potentially the most dangerous. There are two types of gas (liquid petroleum gas) available: butane (the more usual) and propane (which will operate in much lower temperatures).

▼ *Gas stoves are available in different sizes but the most important feature for safe use is a stable base to prevent it toppling over.*

When gas stoves are not being used, they must be turned off and kept in a well-ventilated area, away from sleeping areas. If they do leak, they can build up an invisible layer of gas that can suffocate sleeping people and explode when ignited.

METHYLATED SPIRITS
The most popular stove of this type is the Trangia stove and cooking set from Sweden, which is windproof and very stable; some models also have a small gas stove attached. These stoves come in two sizes, and each comes with its own set of cooking pans.

Methylated spirits (methyl alcohol) burn very cleanly, but the flame is almost invisible, so great care must be taken when lighting or refilling the burner. It should be carried in a specialized fuel bottle.

PARAFFIN
This burns in the form of a vapour mixed with air, and it will need to be primed or heated

▶ *A camp oven will allow you to bake fresh bread at a base camp if you are able to transport your gear by vehicle.*

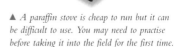

▲ *A paraffin stove is cheap to run but it can be difficult to use. You may need to practise before taking it into the field for the first time.*

▲ *A petrol stove is versatile and easy to use but can be expensive to buy.*

▲ *A windshield can be fitted around a petrol stove to protect the flame and make cooking more efficient in windy weather.*

CARRYING SPARE FUEL

Make sure you have an adequate supply of fuel for your cooking stove. If you are travelling abroad you will need to check that the fuel for your stove is available in the country you are going to. If not, you may have to change the type of stove you are using, since most airlines, including all in Europe and the United States, do not allow gas or flammable liquids to be carried on planes.

▼ *Use sturdy metal containers for carrying petrol or paraffin supplies to your destination; use plastic containers for water only.*

with another fuel to bring it to the temperature where it will vaporize. Spilt paraffin will not evaporate and will leave an unpleasant smell. Always store it in a metal fuel bottle in case of leakages.

This kind of stove is cheap to run and burns well with a hot flame, but it is also the most complicated to use and can take a while to get used to. As a further disadvantage it will blacken cooking pans and clog burner jets.

PETROL

This burns in the form of vapour under pressure and will burn cleanly unless additives are in the fuel. Unlike paraffin, it does not need a secondary fuel to heat it to the required temperature.

Petrol is very volatile and the smell is strong and unpleasant. It must be stored in a special metal fuel container in case of leakages. If spilled it will evaporate quickly, especially if the weather is hot, and it will ruin food and stain fabrics if it comes into contact with them.

SOLID FUEL

This is available in two forms: tablet (Hexamine) and alcohol jelly. This type of fuel gives off strong and unpleasant fumes, and the flame is difficult to put out (although this can be an advantage in windy conditions) and hard to regulate. Solid fuel stoves must only ever be used in a well-ventilated place.

▲ *Solid fuel stoves were first designed to be used by the army. They are for one-time use only but are useful to carry in an emergency.*

WARNING

All stoves must be treated with care. When lit they use oxygen and give out lethal carbon monoxide, and must be used in a well-ventilated place. Make sure the flame is really out before filling a stove with fuel.

▼ *Solid fuel stoves were first designed for the army. They are now available to the public and are excellent for use in windy conditions.*

Cooking Equipment

What you need in the way of cooking equipment for a backpacking trip will be minimal, since the priority is to keep your pack weight down and the meals you eat will be basic. At a base or standing camp, you may have the capacity to set up a kitchen to feed a large number of people, who may be ready for better and more varied meals than they have had out in the field. This will require the type of cooking equipment used by a catering kitchen. For anything in between, the sort of equipment you take will depend on how easily you can transport it.

LIGHTWEIGHT CAMPING

When you are carrying your equipment on your back, you cannot afford to take more than what is essential. While the food you eat is important, its primary function is as a source of energy, and it is unlikely that you will eat as well

▼ *Individuals should carry their own set of cutlery. The advantage of folding sets is that they are very convenient to pack.*

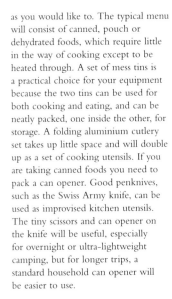

as you would like to. The typical menu will consist of canned, pouch or dehydrated foods, which require little in the way of cooking except to be heated through. A set of mess tins is a practical choice for your equipment because the two tins can be used for both cooking and eating, and can be neatly packed, one inside the other, for storage. A folding aluminium cutlery set takes up little space and will double up as a set of cooking utensils. If you are taking canned foods you need to pack a can opener. Good penknives, such as the Swiss Army knife, can be used as improvised kitchen utensils. The tiny scissors and can opener on the knife will be useful, especially for overnight or ultra-lightweight camping, but for longer trips, a standard household can opener will be easier to use.

BASE CAMPS

Much more sophisticated meals can be cooked at a base camp, which may stand for several weeks while the team completes a schedule of activities or a course of study. Because a base camp is more permanent, and is not being dismantled and moved on a daily basis, it can be better equipped, with a wider range of sturdy cooking equipment and utensils. You will need to decide the kind of heat source you will be using before choosing your equipment.

COOKING POTS

Depending on how many people you are catering for, you will need a number of pots in a range of sizes, with some big enough to boil up to 9–13.5 litres/ 2–3 gallons of water. Make sure that all pots are kept clean both inside and out and that the handles are safe and in good working order. Having lids on the pans will reduce cooking times.

◀ *Mess tins pack away neatly with one tin inside the other. They were designed for army use but are now available to the public.*

How heavy your pots will need to be will depend on whether you are using stoves or fires for cooking; lightweight metal containers can be used on stoves, but should never be used on an open fire (see the sections Cooking over a Fire and Cooking on Stoves). Frying pans, in particular, need to be heavy duty because they are used at such high temperatures.

WATER CONTAINERS

Lightweight campers cannot carry supplies of water and must source it along the route. However, if weight is not an issue because you are travelling by vehicle to a base or standing camp or to a remote area or through a dry climate, you can carry large quantities of water in dixies. These robust containers, which hold several litres of water, are made of plastic and have a screw-top lid that makes them leak-proof. The flat-sided shape of some designs makes them easy to store at camp or during transit. Fuel can be stored in metal jerry cans, but do not carry water in metal containers.

▼ *When a fire of grass or twigs is lit in the base of a volcana kettle, the heat passes up a tube in the container to heat the water.*

◀ *Camp cookware can include a range of pots of different sizes and even an egg poacher.*

▶ *If you are catering for a group you will need cooking pots that hold large quantities.*

◀ *A pair of oven gloves is invaluable to protect your hands when holding a hot pan handle or lifting the lid of a steaming pot.*

OVEN GLOVES

If you are handling hot, heavy cooking pots and pans you will need something to protect your hands, especially if you are cooking over an open fire. A couple of pairs of oven gloves should always be kept in the cooking area of the camp.

MIXING BOWLS

You will need a number of bowls in different sizes for food preparation. Bowls can be either plastic or metal; plastic is lighter to carry but must be kept away from the heat source.

▼ *Your choice of cooking utensils will depend on how much weight and bulk you can carry, and the types of food you will be cooking.*

MEASURING JUGS

These are available in all sizes, so choose the size appropriate for your needs. In a base camp kitchen catering for a number of people one large jug (pitcher) and several medium- and small-sized jugs will be the most useful.

CHOPPING BOARDS

Separate plastic boards should be used for raw and cooked vegetables, fish and meat and bread. Ideally, the boards should be colour coded so that they are used exclusively for one type of food, such as red for raw meat, blue for fish, green for vegetables, and so on. This will prevent food contamination, which could spark an outbreak of food poisoning among the group.

◀ *Do not forget to carry a can opener if you will be eating canned foods.*

OTHER USEFUL ITEMS

If you will be cooking for a large number of people from a base camp kitchen, the following items will make your task a lot easier:

- Wooden spoons in different sizes; do not use chipped wooden spoons as these can carry bacteria.
- Two or three serving spoons.
- A large slotted or draining spoon.
- Sharp knives in a range of different sizes, including some serrated knives. Make sure they are kept sharp. Knives should be kept in the camp kitchen at all times and should never be used for any other purpose.
- A fish slice or metal spatula can be used to take delicate foods, such as fried eggs, out of pans.
- Ladles in different sizes for serving soups and sauces.
- Potato peelers and mashers, which can also be used for other root vegetables, such as carrots.
- A hand-held balloon whisk for mixing powdered sauces or soups into water.
- A catering-size can opener if you need to open catering-size cans.
- Sieves for draining rice, pasta and potatoes and other vegetables.
- Salt, pepper, sugar and sauces such as ketchup and mustard.

Additional Gear

In addition to major items of gear such as backpacks, tents and cooking equipment, and personal gear such as wash kits, radios and flashlights, there are some items of kit that are not essential but may make your trip easier and more comfortable.

Lamps

A small gas lamp is a great advantage at camp when night falls. If you take one, make sure you carry extra mantles and pack the lamp well so you do not accidentally break the glass cover in transit. Like gas stoves, gas lamps cannot be carried on planes, but there are some good candle lanterns on the market and these make an effective alternative. Candle lanterns are not as bright as gas lamps, but you can transport them by plane.

▶ *A gas lamp is more convenient than a flashlight as a night-time light source.*

Never leave a lighted gas or candle lamp unattended in a tent, and do not sleep in a confined space with a gas lamp (even if it is turned off) in case it leaks.

Pillow

If you find it difficult to sleep without a pillow for your head, you could improvise by folding your dry clothing into a pillow shape to give you a more comfortable night's sleep, or you can take a cotton pillowcase with you to stuff your clothes into, so that your pillow will not disintegrate during the night. There are also small inflatable pillows and neck-rests that are quick to inflate and will pack up into almost nothing when the air is released. While these are not essential they can be worth taking for a little extra comfort that will mean the difference between a good night's sleep and an uncomfortable night.

Camp stool or chair

A stool or chair is a luxury item, but it does allow you to take a rest or eat your meals in comfort off the ground. Consider taking one only if your gear is being carried in a vehicle or on an animal; these are not suitable for lightweight camping trips. Camp stools or chairs are very useful for expeditions that will involve birdwatching or study activities that require you to sit still for lengthy periods of time.

Sitting mat

A sitting mat or a piece of foam, about 30 x 60cm/12 x 24in, such as an off-cut from an old sleeping mat, can be used to sit on when you make rest stops, protecting you from damp, wet or uncomfortably rocky ground.

◀ *A neck-rest and eye mask will make your night's sleep or plane journey much more comfortable.*

▼ *A cotton or silk sleeping bag liner will help keep the main sleeping bag clean.*

▲ *A cotton pillowcase stuffed with spare dry clothing will form a perfectly adequate pillow that will increase your comfort at night.*

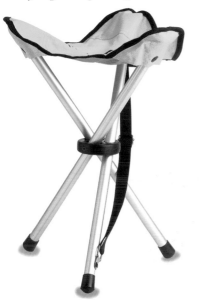

◀ *Camp stools are made from a very lightweight aluminium and can be folded up for relatively easy packing.*

▲ *Sitting mats are available from outdoor suppliers. They are light enough for day-trippers and backpackers to use.*

▼ *Pack a steel mirror in its waterproof pouch with your wash kit.*

Steel mirror

These thin pieces of shiny metal, which can be bought at most camping shops, make shaving and other toilet operations very much easier. If you can, keep the mirror in its own case or plastic envelope, so it will not get wet in your wash kit. The mirror can start to go rusty if it is wet most of the time.

Stove windshield

A number of stoves have their own small, in-built windshield, but you can buy a larger and more effective one made of cotton or aluminium. This weighs very little but it will make cooking much quicker and more efficient (you are less likely to waste fuel) and can be hugely useful if there is a chance you will need to cook outdoors in high winds.

▲ *Carry a hanging scale and use it to make sure your luggage is within your weight restriction.*

▲ *If you are a deep sleeper, you may want to carry an alarm clock to be sure you wake in time to make your daily schedule.*

▶ *Board games provide entertainment for relaxation times and can help to promote a good group spirit.*

Board games

These are impractical to carry on lightweight camping trips or where you are unable to accommodate large, bulky items, but otherwise board games can be carried to provide entertainment for evenings and rest days. If only one game is available for a group of people, divide the group into teams or even into a league table to introduce a spirit of competition and encourage team bonding. Pack any counters and dice in a secure bag because if these get lost the game will be unusable.

Alarm clock

If your wristwatch does not have an alarm setting and you think you will need an alarm call to wake you in the mornings, pack a battery-operated travel alarm clock to be sure you don't sleep right through until lunchtime.

Adaptor

If you travel abroad with electrical equipment that needs to be plugged into a mains socket, you may need to carry an adaptor. Try to find out this kind of information before you travel.

Hanging scales

If you are travelling by plane or with any weight allowance, carrying a set of hanging scales means that you can check you are not exceeding your limit and therefore avoid penalty fines.

Stretchers

These are lengths of reinforced elastic with a hook attached to each end. They can be put to any number of practical uses, from setting up a sheet as a shelter or attaching a mosquito net over your bed to securing a backpack with a broken zip. You can also use them for attaching equipment, such as a sleeping mat, to your pack.

▼ *Three- and two-pin plug adaptors will allow you to use electrical equipment in a mains socket abroad.*

▼ *Carry a good supply of stretchers: they can be rolled up small for easy packing and have a multitude of practical uses.*

Tools

Tools are usually heavy and bulky, so most will be restricted to use in a semi-permanent campsite, though some items are available in lightweight versions too. All tools should be kept dry, sharp and in good working condition, and they should always be checked before use for safety's sake.

SHOVELS

A number of long-handled shovels are essential multi-purpose tools for a base camp. If travelling by vehicle in a desert or wet environment, carry at least one shovel in case you have to dig the vehicle out if you get bogged down. One or two folding entrenching shovels are useful and take up little space. A small plastic trail trowel or shovel, which can weigh only ounces and fits easily into a backpack, will be useful for burying toilet waste.

MACHETES

These large, heavy-duty chopping knives are very useful if you need to cut a path through thick bush or jungle or clear a campsite of bush and scrub. When buying one make sure it has a good, heavy, sharp blade. You will need a sturdy leather sheath in which to store the machete safely when not in use.

▲ *Axes are dangerous tools in the wrong hands. Make sure they are stored safely.*

▼ *Check your axe is sound before you start to use it.*

▼ *A machete blade has to be kept razor-sharp for the machete to be effective.*

▼ *For safety a machete should be kept in a leather sheath when not in use.*

AXES

If your kit is to be transported by vehicle and you are going to a remote area you may want to carry a hand axe or a larger felling axe for chopping tree branches to make a camp fire or a temporary shelter.

SAWS

These are available in a range of sizes, and, for the less experienced, they are easier to use than an axe when cutting up wood. Lightweight campers can carry a small wire saw, which takes up little space and weighs next to nothing.

REPAIR KITS

Stoves and lighting equipment may need some level of maintenance while you are out in the field. Carry basic tools, such as a screwdriver, that will allow you to make repairs. Some equipment may require a specialized repair kit, so check this when you buy.

▲ *A leather mask on the axe head keeps it clean and protects the blade.*

DUCT TAPE

This is a strong adhesive tape that can be used to make temporary repairs on almost anything from tents to backpacks to vehicles. Take a large roll of tape, and store it in a lidded container or it will get covered in dust and sand.

◀ *A roll of duct tape is useful for all sorts of running repairs.*

▼ Check that the saw blade is firmly fixed in the handle before you try to use it.

▼ Sharp knives are best carried in a leather sheath for safety. If your knife does not come with its own sheath, try to buy one for it

▼ A Swiss Army penknife is as good as a tool kit, but the blades are small and relatively flimsy and need to be used with care.

▼ Folding knives are compact and safer to carry because the blade is protected by the handle.

▲ Carry a chain or wire saw in a container and oil it before and after use to keep the saw blade supple.

▼ You will need to carry a sharpening stone if you are using axes or saws.

SHARPENING STONES

These are used to keep tools in good working order. All saws, axes, knives and machetes need daily sharpening to remain effective.

PENKNIFE

A penknife, such as a Swiss Army Knife or a Leatherman, is like a pocket-size multi-tool kit. Useful features to look for include straight and serrated blades of various sizes and scissors.

▲ A multi-purpose Leatherman tool has a host of useful features, including several different blades, saws and scissors.

TENT REPAIR KITS

These are available from outdoor suppliers. A typical kit will include several nylon patches, adhesive paste, spare guy ropes and a spare tent peg. Before applying a patch to repair a tear in the tent material clean the area to remove dirt and seal the edges of the patch with adhesive paste to hold it in place.

▼ ▶ A folding shovel packs neatly away and is useful for digging trenches for camp fires or to dispose of waste.

Caring for your Equipment

Camping equipment can be expensive and your safety may depend on it, and it should be looked after if you want it to work properly. Repairs are best done when you return home at the end of a trip, while any faults or damage are still fresh in your mind. Clean, dry and repair the equipment before storing it, so that it is ready for your next trip.

TENTS

Before packing away your tent after a trip, check that the tent parts are present and in good working order. If the tent is made of a synthetic fabric and the seams are not taped, apply a sealant (available from outdoor equipment suppliers) and allow to dry before the tent is stored. If the tent has a mosquito net on the inside, check the net for holes and get these mended before you use the tent and a mosquito finds them.

STOVES

A badly maintained stove will not only be inefficient, it can also be dangerous. Never try to use a stove if you think something may be wrong with it. If you need to replace parts, use only genuine manufacturer's parts. Do not store a stove for a long period with fuel in the tank or with a partly used gas cartridge attached to it. Remove the fuel and store separately to the stove.

▼ *Remove the fuel cartridge from a cooking stove before you pack it away and store the two parts separately, preferably in the garage.*

▲ *At the end of your trip check your pack for tears or damage to the zip and seams, and make repairs before you store it away.*

▼ *Wipe your cooking stove clean after every trip, but do this in a well-ventilated place and make sure the stove is switched off first.*

COMPASSES AND EQUIPMENT WITH ELECTRICAL COMPONENTS

Keep compasses away from magnetic fields, such as an iron or radio speakers. If you have a protractor compass (which is mounted on a clear plastic base) make sure the plastic is kept clean so that the markings can be seen clearly. Batteries should be removed from battery-powered equipment that is not to be used for some time as they can leak and cause corrosion.

BACKPACKS

When in use, try not to drop or drag a loaded backpack, and do not carry it by only one strap. When you return home after a trip, empty the pack and wipe it clean inside and out with a damp cloth and check the seams for tears and holes. Make sure it is dry

▲ *Backpacks should be wiped with a damp cloth after use. Allow the pack to dry out and then store it in a well-ventilated place.*

▼ *The plastic base of a protractor compass needs to be wiped clean after use to keep the base free of dirt and the markings readable.*

before storing away. If your pack is very dirty, wash it in soap flakes and water but do not use detergents as they can destroy the waterproofing properties of the fabric. Packs should be stored in a dry, well-ventilated place.

SLEEPING BAGS

With the exception of fibre–pile bags, all sleeping bags need to be cleaned carefully and they all take a long time to dry out thoroughly. If you have your bag dry-cleaned, air it for at least half a day before you use it to get rid of the fumes from the chemicals. If you wash your bag in a washing machine dry it flat as line-drying can damage the bag's construction. If you use a bag liner, be it silk or cotton, this should be cleaned according to the manufacturer's instructions at the end of every trip.

Feather or down filling

It is safest to take a feather-filled bag to a dry-cleaners and ask them to clean it in the same way as they would a feather or down duvet. If you prefer to wash it, use a specialist product designed for the job, then dry the bag flat. While the bag is drying, break up the clumps of down. When almost dry, shake the bag to distribute the filling. When dry, store it by hanging it in a warm, dry place.

Synthetic filling

A synthetic bag should be hand-washed without detergents and dried slowly in a well-ventilated place or in a tumble drier on a low heat. Synthetic bags can also be dry-cleaned.

Fibre-pile filling

These are the easiest bags to clean. Just put them in your washing machine, using a soap-based powder rather than a detergent, and line-dry. Fibre-pile bags will dry very quickly.

FOOTWEAR

As expensive and important pieces of kit, footwear needs special care during your trip and when you return home.

During your trip

When you take off your boots at the end of each day, shake them and tap firmly together to get rid of loose dirt. Prise mud out from the treads with a penknife. Allow the boots to dry out as best you can: stuff the insides with scrunched up newspaper and leave overnight in the door of your tent or hang them outside if it isn't raining. Do not dry boots in front of a camp fire or in the hot sun because this can ruin the uppers.

At the end of the trip

Remove all traces of dirt and mud, then wash the boots in warm soapy water and allow them to dry naturally. All footwear needs to be reproofed in order to waterproof the uppers before

▲ *To dry wet walking boots, stuff the insides with sheets of newspaper or long grass and leave overnight in a dry place.*

further use; leather that isn't regularly treated with a wax or oil-based product will eventually dry out and crack. If your walking boots or shoes are made of leather give them two coats of polish, wax dubbin, oil or a recommended product before storage. If your boots are made of fabric use a recommended silicone-based product, which can be either sprayed or rubbed on.

CARING FOR WALKING BOOTS

1 With a boot on the end of each hand tap your boots together to knock off any loose pieces of mud and dirt.

2 Using a penknife or small stick, prise mud and dirt from between the treads on the underside of each boot.

3 Using a hard-bristled brush, firmly brush each boot all over to remove any remaining mud, dirt and dust.

4 Check that the laces on each boot are not frayed and replace if necessary. Wash the boots in warm soapy water.

5 Use your fingers or a soft cloth to apply an oil-based waterproofing product to leather boots or shoes.

6 Protect fabric walking boots with a silicone-based waterproofing product recommended by the manufacturer.

Preparing your Equipment

Before setting off on any trip in the outdoors, whether it is a day's walking in your local area or a month-long expedition to another country, you should check the equipment you are taking with you. Any items showing signs of wear will need to be repaired or replaced. It is far easier to carry out major repairs at home, where materials and replacements are available, rather than out in the field.

CLOTHING AND FOOTWEAR

As well as making sure your outdoor clothing is suitable for the climate and planned activities, you need to check that key items such as shirts and trousers still fit you comfortably, especially if you have not worn them for a while – you may have put on or lost weight since your last trip. Check the condition of your clothing and repair as necessary, paying particular attention to zips and buttons as these

▲ Protective sealants can be applied to the seams of clothing to strengthen the stitches and maintain the waterproofing qualities.

are likely candidates to break or fall off under the pressure of use. If you are travelling in a group with a number of other people, you may want to mark personal kit and clothing with your name or an identifying mark.

Check that your walking boots are clean and in good working order. Stitching on the seams needs to be intact; if it isn't you could take the boots to a shoe repair shop or sew the stitching yourself using a bradawl or awl and a strong needle. Intact seams should be coated with a sealant to protect the stitches.

◀ Ordinary boot polish can be used on leather boots but fabric boots will need a recommended silicone-based product.

▲ Always check the head and shaft of your axe. A head that comes loose when in use can result in a nasty, if not fatal, accident.

Small splits in the leather or fabric uppers of boots can be repaired at home with an adhesive. A shoe repair shop may be able to patch up large tears, otherwise you will need to replace the boots: large tears will let in water or sand and dirt and they will worsen with use during the trip. Replace frayed laces and take at least one spare pair of laces with you.

Check that the sole is not coming away from the main boot; if it is you may be able to get it repaired at a shoe repair shop or you may need new boots. Reproof or polish leather boots before every trip (and again when you return home) to maintain the condition of the leather, and treat fabric walking boots with a silicone-based product.

CHECKING YOUR BOOTS

1 Check boot laces for damage or early signs of fraying that may cause them to break under the pressure of hard use. Fit new laces if needed and carry spares.

2 Check that none of the D-rings is bent or broken and make sure they are free of mud or dirt from previous trips, which may make it difficult to fit laces.

3 Look closely at the stitching all the way round each boot, and organize repairs for any that is loose. Apply a sealant to waterproof the stitches.

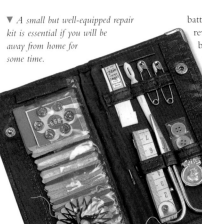

▼ *A small but well-equipped repair kit is essential if you will be away from home for some time.*

battery, once you have checked it, reverse one of the batteries so as to break the circuit, which means the equipment cannot be switched on by mistake. Carry correctly sized spare batteries for all your equipment, including lithium batteries for camera or computer equipment.

▲ *Gas stoves are awkward shapes but they can be packed into pouch bags designed for the purpose for easy storage and transit.*

CAMPING EQUIPMENT

Check that your tent has all its parts and enough pegs to put it up as well as some spare, and that everything is in working order. Look for holes or tears in the tent and groundsheet, and check that the guying points are in good condition. Check that your sleeping bag is clean and that the zip, if there is one, works properly.

▼ *Check that you have enough fuel for the trip. If you haven't used your stove for a while try it out to make sure it works.*

BATTERY-POWERED EQUIPMENT

Equipment that requires batteries should have had them removed when they were last used, as leaking batteries can cause corrosion. If this wasn't done and a battery has leaked, you may be able to remove any corrosion with an emery file or a piece of abrasive paper. (It will be a lot easier to do this now at home than in some cold field at dusk when your torch does not work.) Check all of the battery terminals for corrosion, and remove any that you find. If this is not successful the item may need to be replaced. Otherwise, put new batteries into the equipment and check that it works properly. If equipment requires more than one

COOKING EQUIPMENT

Try out your stove to make sure it is working and check you have sufficient fuel to last the duration of your trip unless you know for certain that you will be able to buy that particular type of fuel at your destination. If you are travelling by plane you will not be able to carry fuel with you, so part-used gas containers should be removed from your stove. Crockery and utensils should be clean and supplies of washing-up liquid and condiments replenished. Check that pan handles are not damaged, that pan lids fit properly, and that your water containers do not leak.

CARRYING EQUIPMENT

Your backpack should be clean, with all straps and/or zips undamaged. Repair any straps that appear to be loose or weak, paying attention to the waist belt and shoulder straps of large backpacks, which take the bulk of the weight. Apply a sealant to waterproof all of the seams.

▶ *Always make sure your first-aid kit has been properly restocked before setting out on a trip.*

▼ *Check the straps on your pack and make any repairs while you are still at home. Weak straps can break easily under pressure.*

▼ *Make sure the zips and seams on your pack are intact and apply a protective sealant to the seams to reinforce the stitches.*

Packing your Gear

When packing your equipment, the first rule is to pack as lightly as possible without omitting any essential items. The second rule is to pack carefully, so that anything that you do not want to get wet is sealed in a waterproof wrapping, and anything that might break is adequately padded.

PERSONAL EQUIPMENT

The first step is to get your equipment together, based on a well-thought-out checklist. Lay out all of the equipment on the floor and check each item against the list. When you are satisfied that you have everything you need, go through it one more time to make sure you are only taking items that are useful enough to justify the weight and bulk they will add to your pack.

When you are ready to pack, wrap up all your small items in separate stuff sacks or packing cubes, or even sturdy plastic bags, so they do not get lost in a large kit bag or holdall.

Make a list of the contents of each sack and attach to the outside, so that when you are at camp, you will not have to open every sack to find what you are looking for.

Pack your sleeping bag with care and keep it in a waterproof bag or container, so that if your kit gets wet you will still have something dry to sleep in. Down and feather sleeping bags are highly compressible, and can be rolled up into small bundles without causing damage to the filling. Synthetic bags can lose their thickness, and therefore their insulation properties, when rolled, so pack them in as large a stuff sack as you have space for, and unpack them and shake them loose as soon as you reach your destination.

GROUP EQUIPMENT

Assembling shared group equipment in one place to pack means that you are less likely to forget key items. It also gives you the chance to check that you are not over the weight allowance if travelling by plane.

◀ *Waterproof plastic bags are useful for carrying sleeping bags and tents.*

▲ *Pack your backpack with heavier items at the top to keep the centre of gravity high and prevent the pack from pulling you backwards.*

PLANE TRAVEL

Equipment that will not be with you all the time during the journey should be locked or secured, and fragile items should be well protected against rough treatment by baggage handlers. Put sharp implements, such as knives, scissors, scalpels or razor blades in your kit bag rather than your hand luggage. These items are not allowed in the cabin of the plane, and if your hand luggage is searched, they will almost certainly be removed.

▶ *Waterproof rigid storage containers can be used for storing valuable or delicate items. They are ideal for use in kayaks or canoes.*

PACKING A VEHICLE

Make sure items are packed in boxes, crates or bags, so that they will not be able to fly about if you hit a bump or drive on rough tracks. If there are lots of parcels, label each one with the contents to make items easier to locate. Do not overload your vehicle, and keep the weight as near to the axles as possible.

Pack only light, bulky items on roof-racks as a top-heavy vehicle will turn over easily on rough ground. If using a roof-rack or trailer, pack all non-water-resistant items in waterproof containers or sturdy plastic bags, or cover the load with a tarpaulin sheet.

▲ *Stuff sacks and packing pods will help you to organize your personal equipment within a bigger backpack or kit bag.*

Fragile items should be protected with padding. Filled fuel containers should be kept well away from food, clothing, medical supplies and any source of flame, electric spark or direct heat. Put padding around fuel and water containers as these can puncture if jolted continuously on a rough track.

PACKING A BACKPACK

Pack your sleeping bag first, then your tent and waterproofs last, so that they are in the correct order of need when you come to unpack. Water bottles, maps, compasses and personal items, such as lipbalm, can be kept in side or top document pockets for easy access. Carry your stove and fuel in side pockets, away from food, clothing and your sleeping bag in case of leakage.

PACKING A HOLDALL

The most user-friendly holdall is a rectangular bag in which the top can be opened to allow you to see inside. Heavy items, such as books, should be packed in a layer at the bottom, with fragile items in the middle, and soft items, such as clothes or your sleeping bag, wedged in around them.

Maps, notebook and pencil in a waterproof wallet.

Warm sweater, hat and gloves, sunglasses and wash kit.

Food, eating and cooking equipment, tent, tent poles and pegs.

Sleeping bag, clothing, length of rope, bivvy bag.

First-aid kit, stove and fuel, water bottle and waterproof overtrousers.

◄ *Try to fit all your gear inside your backpack, as outside attachments are likely to get lost or damaged.*

NAVIGATION

Knowing how to find your way in unfamilar territory is the most
important skill for wilderness travel and it is no exaggeration to say that
your life may depend on it. Learn how to use a map and compass before
the trip, and train yourself to think in navigational terms, developing an
awareness of nature and the landscape around you. This will help you
to follow your course and to correct yourself when you go wrong.

Maps

A map is a flat pictorial representation of a complex, multi-dimensional landscape. Maps range from rough artistic representations that look nice on the wall, through to very accurate, perfectly drawn masterpieces. The accuracy of maps varies dramatically from country to country, and unless you have previous knowledge of the map you are using you must always treat them as potentially suspect. You will need to use very different maps if you are planning an overland journey from one country to another than if you are planning a walking expedition in a mountain range. Good quality maps are usually dated and list revisions; always check the date when the map was last surveyed or updated, and if a map is old be prepared to make allowances in your navigation.

◄ *Choose maps carefully, making sure they are for the right area and to a scale that will give you all the information you need.*

dangerous mountain terrain. Often the scale and accuracy of the available maps of an area you are operating in are not ideal and in these circumstances you may have to modify your approach to navigation.

SCALE

The choice of scale depends entirely on what you want the map to show. If you are planning an expedition across a number of countries, then a map with a scale of 1:2,500,000 (25km to 1cm/40 miles to 1in) might be sufficient. If, however, you want a map for a walking expedition then considerable more detail is required.

MAP SCALES AND THEIR USES

Scale	Use
1:15,000	Orienteering
1:25,000	Walking (detailed)
1:50,000	Walking or climbing
1:100,000	Cycling, trekking, canoeing or kayaking
1:250,000	Motoring
1:1,000,000	Map of country

For serious cross-country navigation in difficult terrain, maps of 1:50,000 or 1:25,000 scale are desirable. The 1:50,000 scale is the most practical for longer journeys as it covers a relatively large area and lacks the intense clutter often found on 1:25,000 scale maps. The 1:25,000 scale comes into its own in very difficult conditions – for example, darkness, white-out or very

SYMBOLS

Every map will show both natural and man-made features. Waterways, roads, railways and areas of habitation will tend to dominate on larger scale maps because these are designed to show a more detailed picture of the area; do not expect to find this amount of detail on smaller scale maps.

Both natural and man-made features will be represented by a number of symbols and are usually described by a key on the map. Maps from different countries have very different symbols. Most symbols have some pictorial link to the feature they represent but always check the key, if it exists, as some symbols can be quite obscure. If something is marked on a map it is likely to exist on the ground, but many things that exist on the ground are not necessarily marked on the map

▼ *A map with a scale of 1:25,000 means that every 1km is represented by 4cm of map space, which allows a lot of detail.*

▼ *A 1:50,000 scale means that 1km is equal to 2cm, and this makes it easy to measure distances of hundreds of metres.*

▼ *Very large scale maps, such as a town plan, may be useful if you need to navigate your way through an urban area.*

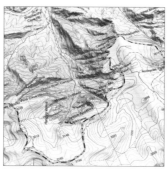

▲ *The information provided on a map enables you to build up a three-dimensional visual picture of the landscape it covers.*

RELIEF

On some maps different colours show different land heights, and on others the steep sides of hills is shaded to bring the map alive. On large scale maps contour lines are lines of equal altitude and create a picture of the terrain. Typically, contour lines on large scale maps are at 10–20m/30–60ft intervals. This interval does vary so make sure you check before making any important calculations. The ability to look at contour lines on a map and to visualize what the ground will look like is the key to accurate map-to-ground interpretation. Obviously the closer the contour lines, the steeper the country. You can quickly work out how steep the ground is by measuring the distance then counting the contour lines over that distance. You can then work out the ratio of the two in your head or draw a rough scale drawing.

GRID SYSTEMS

On many large scale maps you will find a series of numbered or lettered grid lines running north to south and east to west. Grid systems are nationally based and, usually, they bear no relation to the system of an adjacent country.

Most grid systems are based on 1-kilometre squares and allow you to name a particular square through a number system. This allows you to accurately communicate your position or the position of a feature to someone else, using a coordinate of the numbers printed on the map. To increase the accuracy of a position from 1 kilometre to 100 metres or 10 metres more numbers are added to the coordinate.

If you think you may need to use grid references during the course of your journey (and if you are using maps there is always the chance that you will need to, even if you don't plan to) then you must familiarize yourself with the system in operation in that area prior to setting off. In the absence of a grid system latitude and longitude are used, again with the position being given as a coordinate of the references.

TYPES OF MAP

The following are examples of the most common types and scales of map used for travelling. Topographical maps are usually produced by government agencies. They were originally military in origin and are the most accurate maps available. They are checked and updated on a regular basis; if you are buying a map from a map or book store, it is worth checking that it is as recent a revision as possible.

Privately produced maps must be treated with caution unless you have actually used them in the area and are experienced in how to read them. They are often produced primarily for information only, and are not as accurate or as reliable as a standard topographical map. Privately produced maps may not be drawn to scale and may be of a pictorial nature. If this is the case they are unsuitable for serious navigation and should be regarded as for interest only.

In some parts of the world, such as developing countries or in remote parts of developed countries, poor quality maps will be the only ones available and you will have to adopt a far more exploratory approach to navigation.

National maps (1:1,000,000)

These are useful for calculating the size of an undertaking or for getting an understanding of where various places are in relation to each other. They show the general outline of countries, their borders, major cities and towns, and major roads and rivers. With this very sparse level of detail, bear in mind that, depending on the country featured, a line on the map denoting a road could mean anything from a six-lane highway to a rutted dirt track.

Regional maps (1:250,000)

These are essentially road maps and are not suitable for serious off-road navigation. They can be useful for initial inspiration and planning. They will tend to feature smaller centres of population and minor roads. Sometimes they will show major areas of mountainous country and large areas of forest or jungle.

Specialized maps (1:50,000)

If available then these are the best maps for travel in wilderness terrain. They give all the information required to plan and navigate a safe route. At this scale they will normally be topographical maps based on accurate contour lines. They will show detailed geographical features, such as cliffs and rock outcrops, along with accurately mapped vegetation. They will also feature footpaths and forest tracks.

Large scale maps (1:15,000)

These are almost too accurate for the purpose of navigation and wilderness travel. They are large and difficult to handle, and they cover a very small land area in a tremendous amount of detail. It is difficult to visualize the country portrayed on the map as the contour lines have broad intervals, and this has the effect of "flattening" the land. Large scale maps can be overly cluttered with information, which makes them difficult to read and interpret for the walker or traveller. However, they are very useful in difficult conditions, such as poor visibility, when intricate detail can be extremely helpful.

Reading a Map

For thousands of years man navigated successfully all over the world over land and sea without the aid of maps. The luxury of accurate maps that we have become used to is a relatively recent development and really only goes back a couple of hundred years. The reassurance of accurate maps has made navigation as much more accurate art, but the ability to read maps well, interpret them and then apply the information gleaned from them, is still a skill that must be learned and developed for your own safety.

THE THREE NORTHS

Most national and regional maps are drawn with true north (the direction of the geographic North Pole) at the top. Large scale maps with a grid system, however, use grid north. The difference between grid north and true north occurs because a map is a flat illustration of the Earth's curved surface. In low to mid latitudes the difference between true and grid north can be disregarded, but at high latitudes it becomes significant. The third north is magnetic north. A compass needle does not point to the geographic North Pole but to the magnetic North Pole, which is currently in Hudson Bay, northern Canada, and moves slowly but continually. All quality maps will have all three norths – true, grid and magnetic north – marked on them, along with the annual rate of change of the magnetic variation.

▲ *Geographical features in the landscape can be checked off against the map to make sure you are where you should be.*

LEARNING MAP SYMBOLS

A list of symbols used on the map is usually printed on it in a key. Symbols do vary from map to map so be careful to check before making decisions regarding route choice and distance. You should make yourself familiar with the symbols on the map you are using so that you do not have to continually refer back to the key. This makes map reading fluid and allows you to really see the land as you look at the map. An understanding of and ability to interpret contours is the most important skill of map reading. It is not an easy skill and needs practice to get it right.

If you are not familiar with map reading, spend time practising before your journey until you can read the map with reasonable accuracy. Look at a map of your local area – preferably an area with height variation in the form of hills, and including some natural and man-made features. Choose a route to follow on foot, looking at the contours to assess height variation and noting the features you would expect to find. Then take your map outdoors and follow the route to see how accurate you were.

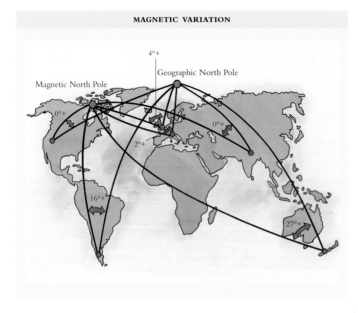

MAGNETIC VARIATION

4°+

Geographic North Pole

Magnetic North Pole

0°+

0°+

2°+

16°+

27°+

A PICTURE OF THE LANDSCAPE

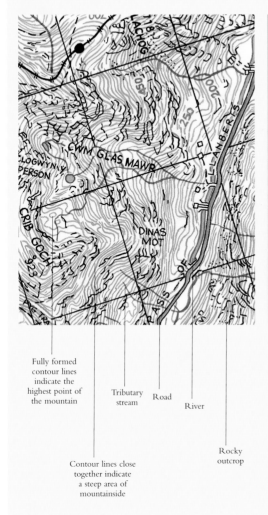

Fully formed contour lines indicate the highest point of the mountain

Tributary stream

Road

River

Contour lines close together indicate a steep area of mountainside

Rocky outcrop

The map and photograph do not bear much relation to each other at a quick glance. You must pick out and identify features in relationship to each other in order to relate the view to the map. Learning to make allowance for areas of land that are hidden from view and to get a grasp of scale are both very important. This is a simple exercise but it will help you to understand the basic principles of reading a map.

Start slowly, identifying features in the landscape and using their symbols to locate them on the map. Focus on one feature at a time, and note how the steepness of the hills is shown by the densely packed contour lines. As you progress, you will begin to see how closely the landscape in the photograph has been represented in pictorial form on the map.

FINDING YOUR LOCATION

Good navigators can always relocate quickly and accurately. It is always done by a systematic process of positively identifying and positively eliminating features in the surrounding landscape. The first thing to do is to orientate your map. This can be done visually by lining up the map with features that you can see around you, such as a forest or a lake, or by using your compass (see the section The Compass). Either way, your map will now be pointing north and mimicking the landscape. You can then set about finding features that fit with where you are and eliminating the places you could not possibly be. For example: you are standing on a steep, rocky slope that faces south, looking down on a stream with an S-bend and the stream is flowing east. This immediately eliminates all the slopes that don't face south and all streams that don't flow east. This may leave you with a few possibilities, but continue your process of elimination: how many of the other east-flowing streams have S-bends below a steep rocky south-facing slope? If you are unlucky and there are two you need only find one other distinct feature and you are sure to reduce your possible location to a single choice.

The Compass

The development and use of compasses to help maintain direction of travel goes back thousands of years. Contrary to what a lot of people imagine, a compass needle does not point to the geographic North Pole but aligns itself along the magnetic field of the earth, pointing to the magnetic North Pole, which is currently situated in Hudson Bay in northern Canada.

Compasses were traditionally a swing needle housed in a round case with the 360 degrees of the circle and the cardinal points (north, south, east and west) marked in order to give a bearing. Later, sighting prisms were added to increase the accuracy of the bearing. In order to take a bearing off a map a protractor had to be carried to measure the angle of travel in relation to the North Pole. After the Second World War the Scandinavians came up with the combined instrument that is almost universally thought of today as a compass. This is a combination of a compass, protractor and a ruler.

The protractor compass is perhaps the most popular type of modern compass. It is a versatile navigation tool which allows you do the following:
• Orientate a map.
• Measure distances on the map.
• Work out a grid reference for the location where you are or for a specified location on your route.
• Take a bearing directly from the ground in front of you.
• Take a bearing from a map, apply magnetic variation (see the section Reading a Map), and follow the bearing to your destination.

LOOKING AFTER YOUR COMPASS

A compass is a delicate instrument that could save your life. Keep your compass safe, and do not drop it or stand on it. Keeping it strapped to your wrist or worn around your neck on a cord is a sensible option. Do not allow your compass to come into contact with a magnet as this could damage it and will drastically affect its accuracy.

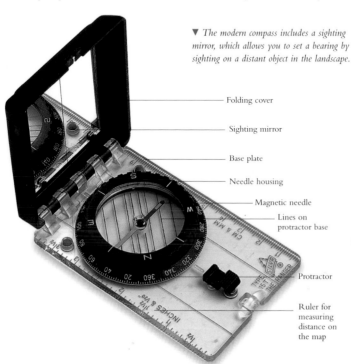

▼ The modern compass includes a sighting mirror, which allows you to set a bearing by sighting on a distant object in the landscape.

- Folding cover
- Sighting mirror
- Base plate
- Needle housing
- Magnetic needle
- Lines on protractor base
- Protractor
- Ruler for measuring distance on the map

AN IMPROVISED COMPASS

A sewing needle that is repeatedly stroked in *only* one direction against a piece of silk will become magnetized and can be suspended on a piece of string or thread so that it swings to north. Top up often to maintain the magnetism. Stroking the needle with a magnet, if you have one, would be even more effective than silk. Stroke the metal in one direction *only*.

FINDING NORTH

Hold the compass flat in your hand and make sure there is no large source of ferrous metal nearby (this may act like a magnet and attract the compass needle, thereby affecting the accuracy of the reading). The red magnetic compass needle will point towards magnetic north. In order to find true (geographic) north, you will need to know the magnetic variation for the area where you are and apply this to the protractor. Depending on where you are on the earth you may have to add or subtract the variation: your map will be able to tell you which. Line up the red magnetic needle with the lines on the base plate of the protractor; the direction of travel arrow will now be pointing at true north.

FOLLOWING A BEARING

If there is an absence of line features along your route, such as a footpath, stream or ridge that you can follow to maintain your sense of direction, a compass bearing can act as a reliable substitute, providing a continuous guide to your direction.

Having established the bearing you wish to travel on, line up the red magnetic needle with the lines on the base plate of the protractor; the direction of travel arrow will now be pointing on your bearing. The bearing then has to be laid on to the ground: in other words, you have to identify a feature on the ground, such as a tree,

◀ *The button compass features a magnetic swing needle that shows your location in relation to magnetic north.*

▼ *The protractor compass has an in-built protractor, as well as a compass and ruler, which allows you to set an accurate bearing on the map.*

that is in line with the bearing when the compass is held flat in your hand, and walk towards it. Having arrived at the feature, you will need to repeat the process in order to move further along the route. Line up the red magnetic needle with the arrow on

◀ *The prismatic compass is so-named because it contains a prism, which allows for greater accuracy when taking a bearing.*

the base plate to find your direction of travel, and choose a feature on the ground in that direction. Continue in this way until you reach your destination or are able to pick up a line feature along your route.

In poor visibility it is extremely easy to lose your way and you must avoid drifting off your bearing at all costs. You may have to use ground features that are very close to you to be absolutely safe, such as outcrops of rock or even tufts of grass. If you have other people in your group, you can send one party member ahead to the limit of visibility on your bearing, then ask them to stop and wait until the rest of the party has caught up before sending them off again. If visibility is so poor that you can barely see in front of you, it is an advantage to use a party member as a ground feature because if you call out to them, your voice acts as an indicator of direction and distance; by calling back to you they will be able to direct you to their position relatively easily.

HOW TO CARRY A COMPASS

• All types of compass are sensitive to knocks and shocks, and all must be treated with care when you are on the move. Aim to keep the compass in some form of casing at all times. For easy access, keep the cased compass in the buttoned-up breast pocket of a shirt or jacket, or strapped to your wrist, or worn on a sturdy cord around your neck.
• If travelling by plane as part of the trip, carry your compass in your hand luggage to protect it from the pressure differences of high altitude, which may affect its accuracy. It also means you will not be without your compass if your luggage is lost or delayed.

LAYING A BEARING TO GROUND

1 Hold the compass with the direction of travel arrow pointing on your bearing. Select an object in the distance that is in line with your bearing. Walk towards it.

2 When you arrive at the object, repeat the process to continue along the route. Line up the red magnetic needle with the arrow on the base plate.

3 With the direction of travel arrow pointing on your bearing, select an object that aligns with the bearing and walk towards it. Repeat as necessary.

Using a Map and Compass

The essence of navigation is to be able to establish your position anywhere on the earth's surface and then be able to plot a course to another position. Armed with a map and compass a good navigator can confidently navigate in any conditions.

To navigate accurately you need to know your starting point; your direction of travel; and the distance you have travelled. People who get lost have almost always failed to keep track of these three key points, and having done so they then panic and wander around blindly. Re-establishing your position is a matter of quiet, logical observation and slowly proving to yourself that the features you can see in the surrounding landscape fit the position on your map.

SETTING A MAP TO NORTH

The ability to orientate a map so that it points north and therefore mimics the land is an easy but important skill. If you can recognize features then you can orientate the map visually. If this is not possible you can use your compass to orientate the map. First you must apply the local magnetic variation to

▼ *If used correctly a map and compass can help you plan a route, indicate distance and locate your position in the wilderness.*

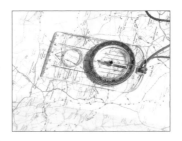

▲ *You need to orientate your map to the land before you set out on the route. Use your compass for this if visibility is poor.*

the compass, then place the compass on the map with the lines on the protractor running parallel to the grid lines on the map. Now move the map around until the red half of the compass needle is in line with the lines on the protractor and pointing north. Your map is now orientated.

MAP-TO-GROUND INTERPRETATION

Many navigators rely too much on the use of the compass. This produces a blinkered approach to navigating. The ability to navigate using the map alone gives you a much broader understanding of the landscape you are travelling through and also allows you

GLOBAL POSITIONING SYSTEM

The global positioning system (GPS) is an important development in navigational equipment. It can be used for all outdoor pursuits, and is particularly popular for those that cover large distances in remote areas, such as kayaking, cycling, horse trekking and vehicle travel.

The GPS works by picking up transmissions from orbiting satellites and it will locate your position with great accuracy. Some models include an electronic compass and altimeter, which allow you to predict weather trends and plot your route.

However, like any electronic device the GPS is prone to damage and battery failure, and it should never be carried as an alternative to a conventional map and compass.

to reassure yourself that your course is the correct one. Travelling by compass bearing alone has no second check if things go wrong. Contour line interpretation is the most important skill of navigating and you should aim to regularly "tick off" contour features as you travel. By doing so you maintain a continual check on your position, direction of travel and distance. Then if you do go wrong, you can backtrack to the last point at which you knew you were on the right path, which will not be too far away, and restart from there.

SETTING A COURSE

Walking on a compass bearing becomes necessary in poor visibility, at night or on particularly featureless terrain, such as open plains or desert.

To take a compass bearing between two points on a topographical map with grid lines, place the long edge of the protractor base plate along the line between your starting point and your destination. Make sure the direction of travel arrow on the base plate is pointing the right way. Hold the map and compass base plate firmly

together. Now turn the protractor around until the lines on the base plate are parallel to the north grid lines on the map. Take the compass off the map and read your grid bearing at the base of the direction of travel arrow. Before you set off on your course you need to apply the local magnetic variation to the bearing. Holding the compass flat in your hand, move yourself around until the red half of the needle is in line with north on the protractor base. Your course is where the direction of travel arrow is now pointing.

ADJUSTING MAGNETIC NORTH TO TRUE NORTH

The red half of the compass needle points to magnetic north. Your map is drawn to grid north or, with small-scale maps, to true north. In all but very high latitudes the difference between true north and magnetic north is known as magnetic variation. This angle varies dramatically across the globe and, of course, can be easterly or westerly, depending on where you are on earth in relation to the magnetic North Pole.

For compass bearings applied to the ground to be the same as those taken from the map the bearing must be adjusted for magnetic variation. In Europe you will need to add the variation to your grid bearing but in many parts of the world you will need to subtract it. The amount of variation, the direction and the annual change will be printed on your map.

The above information applies if you are taking a bearing off a map and laying it on to the ground (identifying a feature on the ground that falls in the direction of your bearing so that you can use it as a visual guide to your direction). Often you will want to take a bearing off the ground to apply it back to your map – perhaps to check you are on the right route or to locate your position if you have left the route. If you are doing this then the variation needs to be applied in reverse: if when applying information from map to ground you need to add the magnetic variation, then to apply information from ground to map you will need to subtract the variation, and vice versa.

▲ *Magnetic variation needs to be added to, or subtracted from, the grid bearing taken from your map before you try to follow a course using your compass.*

WILD READINGS

Whenever you are using a compass, bear in mind that the proximity of large amounts of ferrous metal will affect the accuracy of the reading, giving you what is known as a "wild reading". Far worse, it could permanently damage the compass. Keep any magnetic or iron objects, such as work equipment, well away from the compass at all times.

SETTING A BEARING USING A MAP AND COMPASS

1 First connect your start and finish points with the edge of the compass base plate. Make sure the direction of travel arrow is pointing the right way.

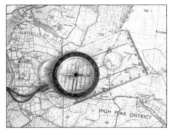

2 Turn the needle housing around until the lines on the base align with the map grid lines. The arrow on the compass base should point to north on the map.

3 Add or subtract any magnetic variation. You now have a bearing to walk on as long as the magnetic needle and the direction of travel arrow are aligned.

Navigation by the Sun, Moon and Stars

Modern man has so many distractions and gadgets that we often fail to notice all the help that nature can give us in finding our way around. There is no doubt that navigating by map and compass is efficient and accurate, but what happens if you are deprived of these tools, if you lose your map or damage your compass?

The heavenly bodies behave in predictable ways, predictions that were worked out by our ancient ancestors and have been used for navigation for centuries. In the event of lost or damaged equipment your ability to use the sun, the moon and the stars to monitor your direction could be a lifesaver, and it pays to commit a few basic principles to memory.

Practise each of the following natural navigation methods before you travel and afterwards use your map and compass to check how you did. Not only will it give you faith in the accuracy of natural signposts, it will also boost your confidence in your own abilities as a navigator. Seasoned navigators are aware of and actively read the signs provided by nature at all times, no matter how sophisticated their modern equipment. After all, the ability to navigate accurately is the most important bushcraft skill of all.

USING THE SUN

The sun rises in the east and sets in the west every day wherever you are in the world, so you may want to take note of obvious geographical features that are in line with the sunrise or sunset to give you a rough sense of direction for use throughout the day. The techniques outlined below are only useful if the sun is visible, but even with a heavy cloud cover it is usually possible to detect the lightening of the sky that happens at sunrise. This can then be noted for use later in the day.

In the northern hemisphere the sun will be due south at noon and in the southern hemisphere it will be due north. The techniques below are at their most accurate when carried out as near to local noon as possible.

INACCURATE READINGS

The nearer you are to the equator the less accurate any attempt to find a direction using the sun will be. When the sun is almost directly overhead it is extremely difficult to determine its direction.

Finding north and south using your wristwatch

To do this you will need a traditional analogue watch with two hands set at local time (without variation for summer daylight savings, which do not match real time) and held horizontally. If you are in the northern hemisphere, point the hour hand of your watch towards the sun. Imagine a line halfway between the hour hand and the 12. This line will be pointing roughly south. If you are in the southern hemisphere, point the 12 at the sun and an imaginary line between the 12 and the hour hand will give you a rough indication of north.

FINDING NORTH AND SOUTH USING A WRISTWATCH

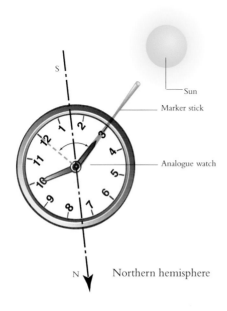

Sun

Marker stick

Analogue watch

Northern hemisphere

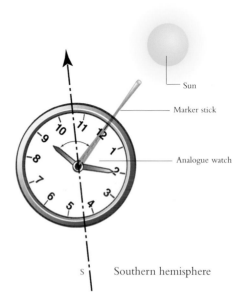

Sun

Marker stick

Analogue watch

Southern hemisphere

Finding east and west using the shadow stick method

This is a useful method if you are in open country and can afford the time to stop for a while. It works at any time of the day when there is sunshine of any strength, and at any latitude or in either hemisphere.

Select a stick about 90–120cm/3–4ft long and as upright as possible. Plant the stick into a piece of flat ground that is not overlooked by trees, vegetation or any other geological formations. Mark where the tip of the shadow falls with a pebble. Wait for 15–20 minutes and mark where the tip of the new shadow falls, then join the two points together. This line will run east–west with the first point marked being west.

If you will be in your location from the early morning and have time to wait there for almost the entire day, you can try an alternative method using a shadow stick, and the reward is that this is usually more accurate. Plant a stick

about 90–120cm/3–4ft long and as upright as possible into the flat, open ground and mark the first shadow tip in the morning. Draw a smooth arc in the ground at exactly this distance from the stick, using the stick as the centre point of the arc. As noon approaches, the shadow will shrink. During the afternoon, the shadow will start to lengthen again, and you need to mark the exact point where it touches the arc. Join up the two points to give an east–west reference, with the mark made in the morning being west.

▲ *Try to be aware of the general direction of the sunrise and sunset at all times, even when you do not need to orienteer yourself.*

SHADOW STICK METHOD

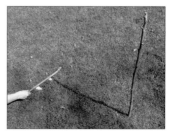

1 Plant a stick of 90–120cm/3–4ft and as straight as possible into a flat, open piece of ground. Mark the tip of the shadow that forms with a pebble.

2 Wait for about 15–20 minutes before checking the shadow. It will now have moved, so mark the tip of the new shadow with another pebble.

3 Lay a stick on the ground to connect the two pebbles. The line that it forms will give you an east–west reference, with the first pebble being west.

▶ *A moon that is not hidden behind clouds may be able to direct you to reference points for north–south and east–west.*

USING THE MOON

Unlike the sun the moon has a highly variable pattern of visibility and it is far less bright than the sun. As a result its usefulness as a navigational aid is much more limited, particularly in cloudy conditions when the moon can be almost completely obscured.

The moon reflects the light of the sun and as the moon travels around the earth we see different amounts of its sunlit face, ranging from a sliver crescent through to a full moon. When the moon lies between the sun and the earth the side of the moon facing the earth has no sunlight so we cannot see it at all: this is called a new moon. It takes 29.5 days for the moon to travel round the earth.

If the moon rises before the sun has completely set, the visible side of the moon (which is the side illuminated by the sun) will be on the west. If the moon rises after midnight, when there is no sun, the visible side of the moon will be on the east. A basic rule to remember for an east–west reference at night is that if you can see the moon rising you are facing east, and if you can see it setting you are facing west. This will apply whichever hemisphere you are in.

Finding north and south using a crescent moon

If the moon is not full, and is not obscured by cloud, you will be able to work out a simple north or south reference during the night. Looking up at the moon, imagine a line drawn through the two tips of the crescent moon and continue the line all the way down to the horizon. If the two tips of the crescent are on the left, the point where the imaginary line meets the horizon will be roughly south in the northern hemisphere and roughly north in the southern hemisphere. If the tips of the crescent are on the

right the reverse is true, and the point at which the imaginary line meets the horizon will indicate north in the northern hemisphere and south in the southern hemisphere.

▼ *The diagram below shows how to find north or south using a crescent moon. The dotted line connects the tips of the left-hand moon and meets the horizon at a point that is south in the northern hemisphere and north in the southern hemisphere. The right-hand moon shows the other way a crescent moon can appear. Here, the dotted line intersects the horizon at north in the northern hemisphere and south in the southern hemisphere.*

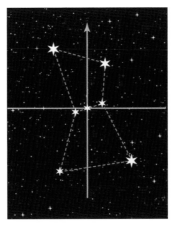

▲ *The North Star lies above the North Pole and can be found by running a line into the sky from the far side of the Plough's pan.*

▲ *An imaginary line drawn across the middle of the Orion constellation lies roughly east–west in the northern hemisphere.*

▲ *The Southern Cross will help you to find south in the southern hemisphere. Note the false cross of dimmer stars to the right.*

USING THE STARS

Because of the many and varied constellations, navigation by the stars is by far the most complex part of celestial navigation and therefore the most difficult to commit to memory. The constellations and individual stars visible from the two hemispheres differ, and this adds to the difficulty. Despite this, stars have been used for navigation for tens of thousands of years.

As the earth is constantly moving, note that the star constellations may appear upside down or sideways when compared to the above diagrams. Like the sun, star constellations always rise in the east and set in the west.

In the northern hemisphere

To find north, locate the North Star or Polaris, which lies over the North Pole. This is one of the brightest stars in the sky and the only one that appears to remain static. To locate it, first find the pan-shaped constellation known as the Plough or Big Dipper. Follow the two stars that form the far side of the pan for six times the distance between them; this will bring you to the North Star.

To find an east–west line, use the star constellation known as Orion or the Hunter. A line taken through the three stars that make up the Hunter's belt lies roughly east–west.

In the southern hemisphere

The North Star is not visible in the southern hemisphere and there is no equivalent star coveniently lying over the South Pole. Instead you can use the Southern Cross constellation. To find it, look towards the middle of the Milky Way where there is a dark area known as the Coal Sack. Straddling this area is the Southern Cross: four bright stars forming a cross plus a fifth fainter star and two bright pointer stars. (A false cross of dimmer stars lies to the right.) Follow the longest line through the cross and down four-and-a-half times its length, then look down to the horizon and that will be due south.

MARKING YOUR DIRECTION

When using the moon and stars as navigational tools, do not forget that they will not be visible the next day when the sun has risen. If you are not planning to start on your course straight away during the night, you will need to mark the direction to give yourself a reference point for the morning. Mark your course with a stick or identify it with a prominent object on the horizon, so that you will know which way to go without your guiding moon and stars.

▲ *Remember to mark the direction with a stick or a pebble before daylight breaks.*

Other Natural Signposts

Nature provides us with endless clues to help us establish direction, which we can gather from the physical, animal and plant worlds. Natural signs will only provide an approximate direction and you may soon leave behind or lose the clue that is helping you, but if all else is unavailable you may be very grateful that you took the time to digest the following points. Ideally, you should hunt for a combination of signs to determine your direction.

THE WIND

Many parts of the world have consistent wind patterns where the prevailing wind will blow in the same direction for the whole year or part of the year. If you are able to find out this information in advance, you may be able to use the wind as an aid to orientation. Beware of the effect that land formations have on wind. For example, deep valleys or steep ridges can completely change true wind direction. The only accurate way to establish true wind direction is to look at the clouds in the free air.

Trees and bushes in exposed places will lean away from and be shaped by the prevailing wind. However, in some

areas of the tropics palm trees will grow into the wind; this goes against the general rule but the palm trees will still give an indication of wind direction.

The wind also leaves clues in sand and snow. Sand and snow drifts always form downwind of any obstruction.

▼ Trees in an open landscape can help you determine the wind direction, but by far the most accurate guide is the clouds up above.

▲ Find out about the direction of prevailing winds in the area you are travelling to: local people will often be able to tell you.

▼ Never trust the wind direction in steep valleys or canyons as land formations can have a severe effect on how the wind blows.

Wind blows up the sloping side of the drift before meeting the obstruction that causes it to deposit its load of sand or snow. So, from the direction the drift faces you can deduce which way the wind was blowing when it was formed.

VEGETATION

Plants need sunlight and water to survive, and analysing where and how well they are growing can help us to establish our direction. Because of the interplay between sun and water, you may have to think about which influences are the more dominant, depending on whether you are in a hot, dry country or cold, wet country. Mosses and lichens dry out quickly, and will generally grow on the cooler, damper sides of trees or rocks, away from the sun. In cold areas, larger plants and trees will dominate the warm sides of terrain and most plants will grow more prolifically on the sunward side. Having sorted this out think about which hemisphere you are in. Some plants, such as the North Pole Plant, which grows in South Africa, will lean to the north to take advantage of the sun. Many flowers move from east to west on a daily basis, following the sun as it moves across the sky.

▼ *Moss will grow on the northern side of trees in the northern hemisphere, and on the southern side in the southern hemisphere.*

▲ *Snowfall at the base of trees can show the direction of the prevailing wind, and you may be able to use this for navigation.*

SNOWY TERRAIN

If you are in or can see snow-covered terrain you will see that the snow cover is more extensive on land sheltered from the sun. Likewise, snow will be markedly deeper on land to the lee of the prevailing wind. It will depend on where you are as to which direction you can establish from these observations. You may already know whether or not the prevailing wind blows in the same direction year-round. If so, and you can establish the wind direction, you can orienteer yourself accordingly.

ANIMAL TRACKS

In dry country, if you see animal tracks following in one direction, it is likely they will be heading for a water source. This can also be true of flocks of birds, though the distances can be far greater. In very heavy vegetation, animal tracks can help in making headway and will often lead to more open country, which may allow you more visibility to plan your subsequent route.

ANT HILLS

In Australia, ants and termites build their nests in the form of mounds or thin blade-like structures. These are always orientated north–south, so that they can take full advantage of the sun's warmth in both the morning and the afternoon in winter; in the summer months the ant hill structures offer some shade from the intense sun.

▼ *Wildlife can be a very valuable source of information. Animal tracks on the ground may be able to lead you to a water source.*

TRAVELLING

The wilderness areas of the world survive because they present a challenge
to the traveller, whether of extremes of climate, ruggedness of terrain, lack
of water or sheer distance from today's human settlements. Time moves at
a different pace in such places, and to appreciate the wonders they offer
we need to match that pace by travelling slowly – on foot, with
animals or by pedal or paddle power.

Planning your Day's Travel

Before the journey begins you will have planned your overall route and, unless you are wilderness camping, will probably be aiming for specific locations for overnight stops. However, unforeseen events, particularly changing weather conditions, often mean that you need to establish the details of the route on a daily basis.

DISTANCE

Always plan to start your trip with a relatively short day, mileage-wise, and gradually build up to longer distances each day as you get used to carrying a full pack. Factor in either an easy day or a rest day every four to six days.

When planning a long-distance walk, most people tend to overestimate how far they can go. Most fit and experienced walkers will enjoy walking 16–24km/10–15 miles a day, though much will depend on the kind of terrain you are covering, and the weather conditions you can expect. If you will be carrying your cooking and camping equipment, then you should expect to achieve no more than 16km/10 miles a day, or even 13km/ 8 miles a day to begin with.

The appropriate distance for a day's travelling can vary even more when your journey is by bicycle, kayak or

canoe, or with animals or a vehicle. As with walking, much will depend on your level of experience, and on the terrain and climate.

WATER AND FOOD

An adequate supply of drinking water should be your first consideration. Establish whether water will be available at your campsites and along the route. This does not have to be drinking water, it could be water from rivers or streams that you can purify yourself for drinking and cooking. On mountains or in polar regions snow can be melted for water. On parts of your route where water will not be available, you will have to carry your own supplies. Top up your water containers whenever you have the opportunity. As you will be active, each person in the group should expect to

▶ *Fill your water bottle before you leave camp; if you have to refill the bottle use a water purifier.*

▲ *When travelling by water, your daily route planning needs to take into account suitable landing and launch points as well as the distance you can paddle.*

drink at least 4 litres/7 pints of water per day, or as much as 8 litres/14 pints in hot weather. Don't be tempted to carry sweetened or alcoholic drinks with you: they will

REST DAYS

Don't forget to rest during your journey. If you are exploring a new area it's easy to feel that a day not travelling is a wasted day. However, if you are moving under your own steam your body will rebel if you don't give it an adequate break from time to time.

In a group, individual members' needs for rest will vary, and the timing of rest days may depend on where you are: it makes sense to organize prolonged stops at interesting sights or in beautiful surroundings where everyone will be content to linger.

▲ *In mountains, where clouds come and go, always take the opportunity of checking your route when you get a clear spell.*

simply increase your need for water and could even lead to dehydration if your water supply is limited.

A substantial breakfast and evening meal, and a high-energy snack at midday, are the best combination on days when you will be active and away from camp during the day. Apart from adding to the weight of your pack, too much food in the middle of the day will make you feel sluggish in the afternoon while you digest your lunch. Choose trail snacks carefully: unsalted nuts, raisins, chocolate and oat-based cereal bars will provide a steady release of energy that will sustain you during endurance pursuits like walking or cycling. Avoid taking any foods that are too salty as they will simply make you thirsty.

▼ *Take high-carbohydrate snacks such as cereal bars or chocolate in your pack to maintain your energy levels during the day.*

CLOTHING

Do not overdress. If you set off feeling a little cold, within 15 minutes of starting out you should be feeling just about right. If you set off feeling warm, however, you will be too hot within 15 minutes. If you are in a temperate climate, be prepared for sudden changes in the weather.

Consider the type of terrain you will be travelling through. If you will be walking or cycling through lots of scrub or thick undergrowth, or if there are biting insects in the area, wearing shorts will mean cuts and grazes to your legs and insect bites.

In hot countries you may need to change from shorts to lightweight trousers as the sun's heat increases in order to protect your legs from sunburn. A wide-brimmed sun hat will protect the back of your neck from the sun.

If you are going to be walking over loose rock or sandy soil, some short gaiters over the top of your boots will stop small stones and soil getting into your boots. If the conditions are going to be very wet under foot, you will find knee-length gaiters useful to protect your boots and feet from the mud and water.

If you will be travelling in an area where it is likely to rain, pack your waterproofs at the top of your pack so you can get them out quickly if it starts to rain very suddenly. Items such as maps, guidebooks and a compass can

▲ *When packing your bicycle, always arrange the load carefully so that it can be controlled safely.*

be carried in a large pocket in your clothing or in a plastic document wallet on a cord around your neck. If you have to stop to take them out of your pack each time you need to refer to them, you will slow down the pace or the group and, if you are walking, will find it almost impossible to get into a good rhythm.

PACKING A DAY SACK

If you day's route is part of a longer journey you will be carrying your whole pack, but for a one-day outing from an established camp you can carry a smaller pack for the day's needs. These should include some emergency supplies in case of accidents or getting lost:
• Maps, compass and guidebooks
• Small first-aid kit
• Insect repellent and high-factor sun cream and/or sunblock
• Spare socks if walking
• Water
• Trail snacks
• Waterproof clothing
• Extra layer of warm clothing such as a fleece jacket
• A mobile (cell) phone may be appropriate in some situations

Walking

Most trips will involve some walking, even if the main activity is cycling or horse riding. A short hike is within most people's capabilities, but if you are going to walk 16–19km/10–12 miles or more a day with a pack on your back, daily for several days, your feet and body will suffer if you have not prepared yourself beforehand.

PREPARATION

If you are not an experienced walker and are expecting to find your walking trip quite demanding, try to get in some training walks as part of your preparation. Start with gentle walks of 3–5km/2–3 miles a day on easy-going terrain around your home or place of work. Build this up to 16–19km/ 10–12 miles walking on local footpaths once or twice a week wearing your boots and carrying your pack.

BUYING NEW BOOTS

When you go to a store to buy a pair of walking boots, take with you the socks you will be wearing on the trip. Always try the boots on before you buy. Make sure you have plenty of room to move your toes, but not so much room that your foot slips, which can cause rubbing and blisters. If you are unsure about what you need, ask a trained sales assistant to recommend the best boot for you and the conditions you are going to.

New boots need breaking in before you wear them for long walks, so that the inside of the boot is moulded to the shape of your foot. This is particularly important for leather boots. Lightweight fabric boots need less breaking in than leather ones, but you should still wear them around the house for a few days, for half an hour at a time, before going outdoors in them. Even then, wear them on short walks at first, gradually building up the distance.

Think about your overall physical fitness if you are overweight or out of condition, or if you have been ill or are recovering from an injury. On a backpacking trip, where you will be carrying all of your camping and cooking gear, including food and water, you will be carrying considerable extra weight on your feet and legs and putting a greater strain on your body, and you need to be sure that this won't cause health problems or severe discomfort, or aggravate existing injuries.

CARE OF YOUR FEET

Never underestimate the importance of comfortable feet on a walking trip; uncomfortable or sore feet can make your trip truly miserable, so it is worth taking care of them properly.

Harden your feet before a walking trip by rubbing them with surgical spirit (rubbing alcohol) after washing and drying. Concentrate on the ball of the foot, the toes and around the heel.

During the expedition, keep your toenails cut short, so that your boots don't press on them. Keeping your feet clean will make you more comfortable and washing them every day is advisable; not only does it make good hygiene sense, but it is also hugely refreshing to wash your feet when you return to camp at the end of the day. Dry feet well after washing, and check for sores or blisters before pulling on cotton socks and lightweight trainers or flip flops to wear around camp. Dust feet with an anti-fungal foot powder if they are prone to sweating.

Deciding on footwear

The most important criteria with walking boots is that they fit you properly. Badly fitting boots can cause

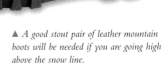

▲ *A good stout pair of leather mountain boots will be needed if you are going high above the snow line.*

discomfort and blisters, and this will be enough to ruin your day. Boots should give good ankle support, and this is especially important for mountain walking. Bear in mind that the same boots will not necessarily be suitable for every trip. For extreme conditions, such as snow and ice, jungle or desert, you will need specially designed boots, because the conditions underfoot are so harsh that your feet and lower legs need extra protection.

For a fine-weather walking trip on well-maintained paths and tracks, strong walking shoes might be just as good as walking boots. They may even be better, because they are not quite so enclosed and will allow your feet to "breathe" better, and this will improve your comfort in hot weather.

Treating blisters

Some people are more prone to blisters than others, but blisters are very likely to develop on a walking trip if your boots have not been adequately broken in, or if they are fastened too tightly, or if your socks have dirt or sand in the weave. Check your feet after your training walks or when breaking in your boots. Look for any red or pink areas where your boots might be starting to rub. If left unchecked, these could form blisters. Cover any sore areas with adhesive plasters or surgical tape before you wear your boots again.

If you get a stone in your boot or you can feel a fold in your sock while walking, stop immediately and remove your boot to take the stone out or straighten your sock before the friction starts to rub up a blister. If your boots continue to hurt as you walk and you think you are getting a blister, stop as soon as you can and treat the blister or the sore area before it gets any worse. If the skin is just beginning to rub, put a small moleskin patch on it. Moleskin patches are made from adhesive felt and are widely available from pharmacies and drugstores. They provide padding to take the pressure off the sore area as you walk.

If a blister has developed but you have to go on walking, you can drain it if you have a scalpel blade in your first-aid kit. Blisters can turn nasty if they become infected, so drain the blister only if you have a clean scalpel. Poke a small hole in the blister to allow the fluid to drain out, then cover with a clean plaster or moleskin patch to prevent dirt from entering the open blister, and refit your boots.

If you do not drain the blister, you should still cover it with a clean dressing. The aim is to protect the fluid-filled blister sac, so build padding with raised sides and a hole in the middle; do not cover the top of the blister as this will put pressure on the fluid-filled sac and may cause it to burst. Use a moleskin patch with a hole in the middle (or cut a small hole in a flat patch) and secure with plasters before refitting your sock and boot.

At camp, wash your feet and change the dressing on the blister. The next morning, make sure that the blister is well padded before you put on your boots and start walking.

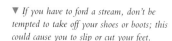

▼ *A specially prepared blister kit is useful on any walking expedition. Take action as soon as you feel a sore spot.*

▲ *You may be more comfortable with a backpack harness that allows some air to circulate between the sack and your back.*

Socks

Whether you wear two pairs of socks or just one thick pair, change them for a clean pair every day, washing the dirty ones as you go if you do not have enough clean pairs for every day. Walking socks should never have mends in them, as these cause friction against the skin and can lead to blisters.

WEIGHT OF YOUR PACK

How much weight adult men and women can carry comfortably will depend on their personal fitness levels, how many hours they will be carrying the load, and what sort of terrain they will be walking on. As a general rule, try to keep down the weight of your pack to under 11kg/25lb, as more than this is likely to turn a pleasant walk into an endurance march. With modern lightweight equipment and food rations, especially if you are sharing the burden of carrying equipment with others, your pack need not weigh more than this. If you are walking in hot weather, the amount of water you take with you will increase the weight of your load, and you may need to look at ways to reduce the overall weight of your camp kit to compensate for this.

▼ *If you have to ford a stream, don't be tempted to take off your shoes or boots; this could cause you to slip or cut your feet.*

Walking Techniques

Everyone knows how to walk: it's not a skill you need to master from scratch before setting off on a trip, but there are some tips and dodges that can ease your way when walking on rough, steep or slippery ground, helping you to avoid accidents and putting less strain on your feet and joints. Developing an easy, elastic stride means that you expend less energy with each step, enabling you to walk longer distances with greater pleasure.

WALKING AS A GROUP

If you are walking as a group, especially if some members are inexperienced or young, aim to have one experienced adult walker at the very front of the party and another at the very rear so that stragglers don't get left behind.

If the group has more than ten people, you may consider splitting it into smaller parties, as it is not much

▼ *In hostile country, keep your party close together and keep checking the route ahead to warn everyone of upcoming hazards.*

fun walking as a long crocodile of people for several hours. It is also easier to keep control of a smaller group, making sure everyone keeps together, takes their rest stops at the same time, and does not wander too far from the footpath or route.

The lead walker, at the front of the group, should set the pace, and this should only ever be the pace of the slowest person in the group, although it should be steady. A particularly slow walker should never be left to walk on their own; other members of the group should take it in turns to walk with them to give encouragement. Some people will naturally walk faster than others, but if those at the front of the group do get some way ahead, they should stop and wait for the others to catch up. The front group should never get so far ahead that they cannot be seen by those at the rear.

This is critically important if not everyone in the group is equipped with a map and compass because those at the back may not be sure of the route to

▲ *If the group gets split up when walking in remote locations, wearing bright clothing makes people easier to spot.*

follow. The leader can also act as scout, watching out for obstacles or potential hazards and finding the best route across or around them.

While the group should be careful that the slowest walkers are not left behind, the latter need to do their best to maintain a steady pace. If they dawdle and linger, or demand too many stops, the whole group can become discouraged and impatient and the walk will not be a success.

WALKING EFFECTIVELY

There is one important way of making your walking more effective, less tiring and safer, and that is to take long strides. If you walk from the hips, rather than from the knees, your strides may be slower but they will be longer, and you will be able to put your feet down carefully and surely.

Each step you take uses up energy, so if you can cover 90cm/3ft with each stride instead of 60cm/2ft, you will be

▲ *When walking up or down steep slopes, particularly on unstable ground, plant each step sideways to the slope.*

▲ *When walking in extreme conditions the party should keep close together, if necessary using a system of ropes.*

covering a lot more ground for the same energy output. It's a good idea to practise lengthening your stride during everyday walking so that it becomes natural to you.

WALKING UP AND DOWNHILL
When going uphill, take shorter steps than usual, and keep your body weight forwards, but try to keep to the same walking rhythm that you had on level ground. When walking downhill, again take short steps, keep your body weight back and bend your knees slightly, so that the shock of your downward motion is absorbed by your thigh muscles rather than your knees. Descending can be hard on the knees, especially if you are carrying a heavy pack, and you may want to take more stops to make it easier on your legs. Steep ascents and descents will be much easier if you walk in a zigzag.

DIFFICULT TERRAIN
If a slope is composed of sand, snow or loose material, such as scree, stand sideways to the slope and step sideways up or down it. Treat descents over wet grass, rocks or loose ground with care, as even walking boots with good grips can slip. Avoid walking over loose, large rocks and boulders, which may

become dislodged and start to fall. Walking poles will help you to keep your balance over uneven ground.

If walking over level snow, you may find the going easier with skis. In an open area, a group should walk in single file and within touching distance of each other, so that if there is a sudden blizzard that cuts visibility, you will know where everyone is. In a very heavy blizzard it is usually safer to stop and take shelter, but if you must keep walking, everyone should walk with one arm on the shoulder of the person in front of them.

THINK AHEAD AND LOOK AHEAD
Even if you are following a footpath, look at the features of the landscape around you, such as lakes, rivers or woodland, and check that it matches the landscape shown on your map to ensure you are following the correct route and are walking in the right direction. If you are at all unsure, take a compass bearing.

Always be on the lookout for the easiest route around possible hazards, such as boggy land, streams or unstable rocks, that some in the group may have difficulty with. If walking uphill, be prepared to descend a little if you have to in order to find a safer route

upwards, and vice versa. If you cannot see the whole course of a stream or river, do not use it as a route down a mountain, as water will take the shortest route, and this may be over a cliff. Likewise, when descending a hill, make sure you can see the whole slope, as some slopes end in cliffs.

COUNTRYSIDE ETIQUETTE

Respect the environment and other users of the countryside when walking, especially in a group.
- Give way to other walkers, cyclists and horse riders.
- Take all litter home with you.
- If you are walking over farmland where crops are growing or livestock are grazing, keep to footpaths, close gates behind you and do not touch or deliberately frighten the animals; if you are walking with a dog, put it on a lead (leash) and do not allow it to approach or worry livestock.
- If you have to walk on roads or tracks that have vehicles on them, walk facing the oncoming traffic, unless you are approaching a sharp bend when it is better to walk on the outside of the corner where you will be seen more easily by the oncoming traffic. Take special care if you come to a blind summit.

Daily Walking Routine

On a long-distance walk it may take you a few days to settle into a daily pattern of walking, striking a happy medium between feeling relaxed and enjoying a sense of achievement.

WALKING PROGRAMME

At what time you start and finish your walk is something for the group to decide between them according to personal preference, but it will also depend on where you are walking and at what time of year.

If you are walking in a temperate or arctic climate in the winter months, there will be fewer hours of daylight than in the late spring, summer or early autumn, and as you will not be able to walk for as long, you will not be able to cover as much distance. You may prefer to walk right through all the few hours of daylight there are before making camp, rather than stopping for lengthy rest stops mid-route.

If you are walking in a hot climate, you may wish to start your walk at dawn and finish in the late morning, around 11am, when the sun will already be very hot. You can either make camp then or rest up in the shade until the mid afternoon, around 3.30pm, when the day will start to cool down and you can move on again.

Try to divide up your day so that your lunch break comes roughly half way through the walk. This is for practical and psychological reasons: it makes sense to restock your energy levels with food and rest halfway through the day, and it makes the day's programme more balanced, so that you are not faced with an unpleasantly long afternoon walk after a short, easy stretch in the morning. You may want to make an exception if you prefer to have lunch at a particular site, such as somewhere with a view or shelter, or where you can replenish your store of water.

▼ *Get into a comfortable rhythm, but try to match your companion's pace to avoid the walk feeling like a forced march.*

REST STOPS

Try to keep these brief: a 5–10 minute stop every hour on the hour should be enough for most walkers, but be flexible if someone is having a bad day and needs to stop more often or for longer. In hot weather or if the walking is very strenuous and you are sweating a lot, take more stops to have a drink to avoid becoming dehydrated. If you are walking with children, you may need to build in more stops than this, depending on the age and strength of the children, but plan the stops before you set off and be firm with the children if they try to manipulate you to make more stops along the way: the more stops you make, the more difficult it is to get into a good walking rhythm. Likewise, it is a good idea to agree within the group that going to the toilet, drinking and checking the map will all take place during these hourly stops. If you need to drink as you walk, use one of the drinking systems in which you carry the water bag in your pack and drink from a tube leading from it.

When you stop for a long period, such as at lunchtime, or while waiting for slower walkers to catch up, put on an extra layer of clothing to make sure

▼ From a high viewpoint on a good day you may be able to see many miles of the route ahead of you.

you do not get too cold. If you take your boots and socks off while you rest, be careful not to get your feet too cold or even sunburned, and do not walk around bare-footed in case of thorns or sharp rocks.

When starting your walk after a stop, check the area in case a camp fire has not been put out properly, or items of kit or litter have been left behind.

TAKE EXTRA CARE WHEN TIRED

Be aware that at the end of the day's walk, when you will be feeling physically tired, your concentration can wander, and it is at this point that accidents are most likely to happen. Don't take short cuts from your route and avoid skipping rest stops in order to get to the campsite quicker: remember that the original schedule was carefully thought through in the first place, and if a rest stop was planned, it is probably needed.

▲ Rocky terrain can be hard on the feet and especially on the knees. Be sure to take plenty of brief rests.

SICK OR INJURED WALKERS

If someone in the group becomes injured or unwell on the walk, give them first aid attention straight away. Dress the injury or make them as comfortable as possible. If the casualty is unable to move, the group needs to work out how to fetch help. If the casualty can walk, they should be escorted by a fit person in the group, with the two walking in the middle of the group so as not to be left behind. You may well need to change your route to find the swiftest or easiest way back to camp or to find medical assistance.

Cycling

Cycle camping trips were traditionally confined to the road system until the arrival of the mountain bike opened up new possibilities of off-road routes not previously available to the cyclist.

CHOOSING A BIKE

A multi-speed touring bike is comfortable and speedy for road riding, but if you are planning to include rough tracks in your route a mountain bike is more rugged and reliable. Its fatter tyres and heavier frame make it harder work on tarmac and when climbing hills. Hybrid bikes, a compromise between the tough mountain bike and the fast, light tourer, are a versatile alternative.

If you are choosing a new bike, make sure its frame is the right size for you and check that the saddle is comfortable, as a bad saddle will ruin your trip. Buy the best tyres you can afford. The rear tyre will wear faster than the front one, so it can be a good idea to switch them around when they are partly worn.

Before any long trip your cycle should have a full service: if you can't do the servicing yourself take the bike to a specialized cycling shop.

SETTING UP YOUR BIKE

It's important to ensure that your bike is set up correctly to suit you. This means adjusting the position of the saddle and the handlebars for comfort and maximum pedalling efficiency. With the ball of your foot on the pedal

▼ *Cycling helmets are made of shock-absorbing foam that does not recover: replace any helmet that has suffered an impact.*

when it is at the bottom of its rotation you should have a slight bend in your leg. When you start pedalling, you should be able to reach the pedals without having to move your hips. If this is not the case you will need to change the height of the saddle.

You'll find that you can adjust your saddle backwards and forwards slightly, as well as tilting it up and down – experiment with this to see what feels most comfortable.

Handlebar height and reach is also a vital consideration. You don't want to be too stretched out as this puts strain on the hands, wrists, arms, shoulders and back, so again experiment with adjusting the bars to find the optimum riding position. If you're not sure how to do this your local bike shop will be able to help. If you are riding a mountain bike you may find that the straight handlebars offer too little variation in hand positions, so that your arms get tired and stiff. Drop handlebars on a touring bike avoid this problem, and you can buy extensions for mountain bike handlebars to give you an alternative grip.

CLOTHING AND EQUIPMENT

If you are planning a touring trip using a bike as transport, consider your clothing and equipment carefully. You need to keep the weight and bulk down, otherwise you may find the bike becomes too difficult to control. How much you can carry comfortably will depend on your bike and your level of physical fitness, but as a rule, aim to keep the combined weight of your gear below 11kg/25lb: about the same as a walker's backpack.

▶ *Padded cycling shorts act as a cushion to make sitting on a saddle all day more comfortable.*

A good cycling helmet is a vital accessory, and modern helmets are so lightweight and aerodynamic you'll scarcely notice you're wearing one. Your helmet should fit snugly on your head when fastened, and not be able to move around or slide forward and obstruct your vision. The chin-strap shouldn't be too tight.

▲ *Padded cycling gloves will protect your hands from blisters caused by gripping the handlebars.*

▲ *A cycling computer can be attached to your handlebars to keep you informed of speed, distance and route gradient.*

▲ *A cyclist's tool kit includes all manner of elements that could come in handy for emergency repairs during your trip.*

▲ *When weight is an issue, a compact multi-tool combining a range of knives, scissors and pliers can be invaluable.*

Clothing

It is possible to buy specialized bike clothing that will keep you warm (or cool) and dry in virtually any weather conditions. Check guidebooks and local information services to find out what conditions to expect.

Your basic kit should include a helmet, a waist-length waterproof cagoule top and waterproof trousers if you are likely to run into heavy rain. Thermal base layers can be worn beneath your waterproofs. Choose clothing that can be layered and is close-fitting, so it won't flap in the wind or get tangled up with the bike.

Padded gloves will protect your hands from blisters and will also soften the effect of vibration when cycling on rough surfaces. Padded shorts or cycling tights are specially designed for comfort and ease of movement; they

▼ *This pannier sits at the front of the bike, just below the handlebars. It should be used for items you need ready access to.*

are not essential, but are worthwhile if you are planning to cycle long distances. Otherwise, cotton trousers or leggings are appropriate as long as they fit neatly at the lower leg and will not catch on the chain. In warm weather shorts are ideal, but remember to protect your legs with sunscreen.

Some cyclists like to wear clip-in shoes, which attach to the pedals and make for more efficient pedalling, or toe clips; neither of these is strictly necessary. However, you should wear footwear with stiff soles, such as walking shoes: trainers are designed to absorb impact, and will compress with each pedal stroke, wasting your energy.

Luggage

For long journeys it is more comfortable to stow all your luggage on the bike rather than carrying a pack on your back. Use rear panniers strapped to a rigid carrier that keeps the weight evenly distributed over the back wheel. If this is not enough, add front panniers, but make sure they don't interfere with the front wheel or restrict your ability to steer the bike. The general rule when loading luggage is that the weight should be kept as low and as close to the middle of the bike as possible to maintain stability.

Bear in mind that the more kit you carry the harder your ride will be, and with heavily laden panniers your bike will become less manoeuvrable. You should keep items you may need during the day near the top of your panniers for easy access.

Spares and repair kit

Modern bikes are easy to maintain and relatively cheap to repair and service. If you are going to be away from cycle stores or suppliers for a week or more during your trip, you will need to carry a spare inner tube, a puncture repair kit, a multi-purpose spanner (US wrench), appropriate Allen keys (wrenches), brake blocks and at least one spare brake cable for the back brakes. (The rear brake cable is longer than the front one, so it can be used for either front or back brakes.) It may be worth carrying a spare tyre as well.

If you are travelling as a group, it will be useful if some of your spare equipment can be interchangeable between your bikes, so that you can spread the load. Make sure you have a serviceable pump for your tyres and a small pressure gauge to check the tyre pressures on everyone's bike each morning before setting off.

▼ *Your puncture repair kit should include patches of various sizes, adhesive, abrasive paper and chalk to mark the puncture site.*

Cycle Training

Racing cyclists are generally considered to be some of the world's fittest athletes, and cycling certainly does get you fit. Yet you don't have to aim so high to plan an enjoyable trip.

BUILDING STAMINA

Whether you are riding on- or off-road you need to build up your training gradually. There is no point in achieving a massive ride on your first day if you are hardly able to get on the bike the next day.

If you are not used to riding a bike, or haven't ridden for some time, you will need time to get your muscles used to propelling a bike and your bottom used to being on a saddle. Regular short rides will build your strength and stamina and you can try a day's ride from home to see how far you can manage comfortably.

As with most sports, the best training for cycling is actually doing it. You can improve your general fitness by doing weights, running or swimming, but by spending more time

▼ *Woodland tracks are bound to be crossed by roots; on descents, slow down before you reach them and rise out of the saddle.*

on your bike you will get fit just as well while at the same time becoming technically more efficient at cycling. Use your gears to get you up the hills – there is no point struggling in one gear if you have an easier one, and remember, you can always get off and walk to rest those leg muscles.

Families can enjoy cycling together both on- and off-road. Because bikes are so simple to use and maintain children find them easy to relate to and enjoy.

RIDING THE BIKE

Your riding technique will depend on where you ride. All cyclists should obviously be alert to their surroundings, but while a road cyclist's main concern is usually other road users, mountain bikers will find they need to keep a close eye on the rough terrain they're riding over. Always look well ahead and prepare for the rocks and roots you're about to reach rather than looking straight down in front of your wheel – by the time you see objects this close it's too late to take action to avoid them.

The main difference in technique between road cycling and off-roading is one of balance. When cycling down steep off-road sections, get out of the

▲ *When going uphill, if the trail is not too steep, riding out of the saddle uses energy less efficiently but produces more power.*

▲ *Mountain bikes can be safely ridden over small obstacles such as fallen tree branches or sizeable rocks that appear on your path.*

▼ *Familiarize yourself with gear-changing before you set off. Gears will only make pedalling easier if they are used correctly.*

saddle and keep your weight over the back wheel of the bike. If cycling in a group make sure you do not bunch up when going downhill – the results can be disastrous.

Riding single-track paths can also be tricky and potentially hazardous so do practise on some narrow paths in your neighbourhood before planning a long trip off-road. Control is paramount so always stay focused and keep your eyes on the route ahead.

WORKING OUT A PROGRAMME

Keep your training sessions varied, alternating hard and easy days. Some trails, especially those at mountain bike centres, are graded for difficulty which means you can ensure you don't take on too much when you go out for a ride. Try to find trails that offer a variety of terrain – flat, undulating and hilly, both on- and off-road – as on a long trip you may encounter any of these conditions. When training on hills, vary the length and gradients of the slopes you attempt. Train in wet and windy weather, not just on fine days, so that you are fully prepared for all conditions.

Practise riding at a steady pace over different surfaces and concentrate on developing endurance rather than speed. When travelling you will want to appreciate your surroundings. You need to find a pace that you can maintain comfortably without feeling breathless and exhausting yourself.

RIDING SAFELY IN A GROUP

The ideal number for your cycling party is four. If anyone has an accident it is safer for two people to go off in search of help, not one, while someone else stays with the casualty. As everyone's abilities and stamina will vary within the group it is important to watch your pace and keep within the capacity of the group as a whole. Do not allow the group to become too strung out and always wait for each other at the bottom of steep hills. Take frequent rests, eat, drink and keep warm to avoid any risk of exposure. Finally, watch out for signs of exhaustion among your fellow riders.

PUNCTURE REPAIR

1 Take off the wheel. Make sure you keep all the nuts and bolts safe.

2 Using tyre levers, ease the tyre off the rim of the wheel.

3 Carefully remove the inner tube from the tyre, taking care not to damage the valve. Locate and mark the hole.

4 Gently brush the area around the puncture with abrasive paper to roughen the surface of the rubber.

5 Apply the glue, making sure you cover a large enough area around the puncture to secure the patch.

6 Put on the repair patch. Hold it down firmly for as long as required by the manufacturer's instructions.

7 Dust the repair with chalk. Refit one edge of the tyre. Inflate the tube slightly and refit on the rim.

8 Use your thumbs to tuck the tyre edge back into the wheel rim and inflate the tyre fully.

Daily Cycling Routine

One of the advantages of travelling by bicycle is its portability. You can easily transport it by plane, boat, train or car, so you can plan your trip anywhere in the world.

PLANNING YOUR ROUTE

If you are a relative novice, it's wise to choose reasonably flat, well-maintained terrain rather than challenging hills. Beware of absolutely flat countryside, however, as you will have no shelter from the wind and pedalling will be hard if it is against you.

On- or off-road cycling allows you to explore and discover countryside you might never otherwise see. Because you travel so much more slowly than in a car, you have time to take in your surroundings, but because cycling is faster than walking, you can cover more ground. As your fitness develops you'll be amazed at the distances and hills you can tackle.

When planning your day's route, it is worth remembering that you will be able to cover a far greater distance than

▼ *In some places drivers may expect cyclists to get out of their way: don't argue with a truck in the middle of the road.*

your walking counterpart. You should reckon on about four times the distance of a walker: about 80–100km/50–62 miles a day. This makes it feasible to plan detours to particular places of interest: an extra 16km/10 miles in a day's cycling may be worthwhile to get the most from the trip, unless the route involves particularly strenuous ascents and descents.

If you are planning to take your bike cross-country, there are now guide books available to show trails and tracks in popular cycling areas. These trails are often graded according to their level of difficulty, and this will be useful if it is an area you are unfamiliar with. Bear in mind that a bike with 9–13kg/20–30lb of extra weight on it will be much less manoeuvrable than an unladen bike.

MAINTENANCE CHECKS

While on your trip, your daily routine should include checking your cycle at the beginning and end of each day. Use a gauge to make sure that the tyres are inflated to the recommended pressure. Inspecting the treads for embedded stones and other sharp objects may save you the trouble of repairing a puncture later on. Check that the chain and

▲ *When the going gets too rough for the most rugged bike its portability means that you can carry it across obstacles.*

gears are all working and well-oiled. Check the brakes: inspect the brake pads and adjust the tension in the brake cables if necessary. If the cables are too tight the brake pads will be touching the wheel rims; if they're too loose you won't be able to stop.

Check the height of the saddle periodically as weight and vibration may lead it to sink slightly over time. If you have marked the correct position on the post it is easy to restore. Check that the lights are working and do not need adjustment.

When you've finished your ride for the day, don't forget to clean and lubricate your bike (this applies especially to mountain bikers). If you leave the mud and grime on it will be harder to shift later, and it can cause damage to mechanisms such as gears and brakes, as well as causing rust to develop. Keeping the chain clean and free of grit will give you a smoother ride and lengthen the life of the chain and cogs. It should be lubricated each time it's cleaned.

DAY RIDES

On shorter day rides you won't need anything as big as panniers to carry your gear, but try to find a cycling-specific backpack. It should be big enough to store your repair kit, spare clothes and food and water for the day. Many backpacks are now fitted with a hydration system; they contain a bladder for carrying water with an attached drinking tube so you can drink while on the move. However, they can be difficult to keep clean if you use them for extended journeys.

LOADING THE CYCLE

Before setting off in the morning you'll need to stow your camping gear and other luggage on the bike, and doing this neatly and methodically every time is important for your comfort and safety. Make sure that most of the weight is over the back wheel, packed in the rear pannier bags. More gear can be placed on the rear carrier in between the panniers. If you are using front panniers, you must make sure they are packed neatly and will not interfere with the steering of the cycle. Check that all pannier bags are securely attached so they cannot interfere with the wheels once they are turning.

If you are carrying a tent, either strap it on the rear carrier or carry it in one of the rear pannier bags. Spare clothes and cooking equipment should also go at the back. In front will be your stove and food. Light, bulky articles such as your sleeping bag can go on top of the rear panniers.

You may have a pouch on your handlebars for those items that you will need during the day's cycling, such as your waterproofs, your map and compass, and a water bottle. A map board attached to the front of the bike saves time when navigating.

Ensure that all your gear is well secured, cannot interfere with your steering and is well away from the wheels. It is worth considering that most braking systems are designed to stop an unladen bike, so another of

▲ *Try out the cycle and your own fitness on a number of shorter day trips before you start on a long expedition.*

your regular safety checks should be to see how they perform when you are fully loaded.

STOPS AND BREAKS

If you're cycling in a group, agree on a schedule for regular rest stops, with time for a snack and a chance to consult the map for the next stage. If the group varies widely in fitness and skill, some members may set a considerably faster pace. Agreeing in

advance on stopping places will give everyone a chance to catch up. At the end of the day, the fastest cyclists can be persuaded to start setting up camp if they arrive at your destination early.

In hot weather, it may be preferable to have a really early start so that you're riding in the coolest part of the day. You can then take an extended break while the sun is at its hottest. Vary the pace of the trip by building in some easy days and rest days.

▼ *When cycling off-road, be considerate to other users of the countryside and try to minimize your impact on the terrain.*

Kayak and Canoe Touring

Kayaking and canoeing are very old methods of transportation and can vary from a pleasant paddle along a flatwater river or sheltered coastline to a fast and exciting paddle down a white-water river. The only interruption to a continuous, comfortable journey will be extreme rapids, weirs or non-navigable locks, when the boat will have to be carried overland.

▼ *A white-water canoe is fitted with airbags to keep it afloat when full of water. These can be removed for paddling flatwater, and the space used to carry your gear.*

CHOOSING A BOAT AND PADDLES

A huge number of kayaks are now available. They are all single-seaters. When choosing a kayak, check that it has sufficient buoyancy to float when full of water; the buoyancy should be distributed so that the kayak floats level when swamped. It must have a seat and a footrest to brace against, otherwise you will not be able to paddle properly.

▼ *A modern white-water kayak suitable for beginners. This boat could also be used for paddling flatwater and sheltered stretches of coastal water.*

Canoes are available as single- and double-seaters. A double canoe will accommodate two people, as well as all the supplies necessary for several days of touring. A double canoe can be paddled by one person, but putting two people in a solo canoe is a recipe for a swim. Canoes for three or more people are also available. Double canoes vary from expensive wooden models to cheaper alternatives made of synthetic materials, such as aluminium and polymers, which are more resistant to serious damage if you scrape them over rocks in low-water conditions.

▼ *The correct length for a recreational kayak paddle is determined by your height and reach: this one is ideal. A canoe paddle is shorter.*

Paddles need to be robust but as light as possible. They also need to be the right length: to check the length of a kayak paddle, stand it up level with your foot, and reach up to grasp the top blade. You should be able to do this comfortably with your arm slightly bent. A canoe paddle is always shorter than a kayak paddle because it has only one blade. Beautifully crafted wooden paddles have the nicest feel, but paddles with alloy shafts and plastic blades are a lot cheaper. If you are buying or hiring a paddle, try out a variety of models before deciding. Always carry a spare set of paddles in case of damage or loss.

SPRAYDECKS

A spraydeck (spray skirt) fits around your waist and over the cockpit and is used with kayaks to prevent water from getting into the boat. It is not generally needed on flatwater, where the water is calm and there is little or no splashing. If you wear a spraydeck it is essential that you know how to remove it easily, in case you need to exit the boat quickly in a capsize.

▲ *A thermal top worn with board shorts, a buoyancy aid and trainers are ideal clothing for fine-weather paddling.*

PERSONAL BUOYANCY

A buoyancy aid (personal flotation device or PFD) is vital to help prevent drowning and should be worn at all times when on the water, no matter how confident a swimmer you are. Choose a style that allows you to move your arms freely, and one that fits snugly and will not pull off when you are in the water. To check the fit, pull firmly upwards from the shoulders: if it can be pulled off, the straps need tightening.

HEAD PROTECTION

There is no legal requirement to wear a helmet, but it is advisable to wear one, especially for paddling on white water. Make sure it fits: a helmet that is too big can slip off and one that is too small can cause discomfort. Look for a helmet that carries a recognized safety mark.

CLOTHING

Your insulation requirements depend on the weather, so check the forecast before choosing your level of clothing. Whatever you wear should not be too heavy when wet for you to swim in. Polyester and polypropylene are better than cotton for warmth when wet.

If the water temperature is cold and the air chilly or wet, wear a thermal base layer made from polyester fleece or polypropylene, or wear a wetsuit. If wind-chill is an issue, add a wind- and sprayproof cagoule for upper body warmth. Good features to look for in a cagoule are a waterproof fabric, neoprene cuffs, a comfortable neck seal and an adjustable waist. In fine weather, a T-shirt and shorts can be worn, with something warmer in case you capsize.

FOOTWEAR

You cannot paddle well in bulky, heavy footwear, but bare feet are not ideal as you will need shoes that have a good grip on wet, muddy banks. Light pumps or technical sandals are light enough to swim in if you capsize. Wetsuit boots and water-sports shoes have good grips and are padded and reinforced in all the right places, but this is specialized footwear and not strictly necessary for one-off paddlers.

▼ *Additional items might include a hand pump, knife, compass, VHF radio, transistor receiver, flares, sunscreen and a mobile phone.*

▼ *Suitable warm-weather footwear includes technical sandals, which are lightweight, comfortable and widely available.*

▲ *A cagoule offers good protection from the rain, but choose a close-fitting, waist-length style that allows full upper-body movement.*

▼ *A correctly fitting helmet sits on the head without sliding forward. A helmet that does not fit will not give adequate protection.*

▼ *Specialist water-sports shoes will keep the feet warm even when wet, and are a good investment if you plan to paddle frequently.*

Kayak and Canoe Training

Canals and lakes are good training areas when you are acquiring paddling skills, and will often be adjacent to suitable camping land. The one essential requirement before you begin is the ability to swim. You should be able to swim at least 50m/170ft in the clothes you will be wearing in the boat.

CROSS-TRAINING

Improving your general level of fitness will dramatically increase the fun you get from paddling, and reduce the likelihood of injury and tiredness. While paddling vigorously or over a long distance is itself an excellent all-body workout, extra non-paddling exercises such as swimming, cycling or running will benefit your cardiovascular system and build body strength before your trip. Whatever cross-training you choose, do it in moderation but aim to exercise regularly – daily if possible.

Target specific muscle groups with toning exercises. The muscles in the thighs, abdomen, shoulders and back do most of the work in the boat, and press-ups, pull-ups and crunches are good preparation for paddling.

WARM-UP ROUTINE

Start with some light exercise, such as brisk walking, swimming or playing with a frisbee, to warm up and raise your heart rate. Gently stretch each muscle group. Once afloat, take a short paddle then do some more stretches in the boat, leaning backwards and forwards and rotating the trunk.

CAPSIZE DRILL

If you are going to paddle a canoe or kayak you must know what to do if it capsizes. All beginners should learn this as soon as they start out on the water, and most instructors make it a priority.

When a capsize happens you have a surprisingly long time to react. Should you get out of the boat before it goes over, or wait until it has capsized? If you try to get out you run the risk of being hit on the head by the gunwale. It is better to wait until the boat has stopped moving.

Keep hold of your paddle and boat if possible; do not climb on top of the boat. In a real capsize situation, once you are out of the boat you should find your partner, if you have one, and

make sure he or she is fine. See if the river is shallow enough for you to be able to stand on the riverbed, but be wary of the current. If possible, get the canoe and yourself to the shore. In the last resort, you may need to undertake a deep-water rescue with the help of the rest of your party.

▼ *For novices in search of trouble-free water in which to practise paddling, inland lakes are the best location of all.*

▼ *You should not attempt to paddle on fast-flowing water until you are confident that you have mastered a range of skills.*

▼ *Weirs can be extremely dangerous for paddlers, and it is always advisable to stay away from them.*

CAPSIZE AND GET OUT

1 To practise the capsize sequence, start from your usual paddling position, sitting or kneeling upright in the canoe.

2 Let go of the paddle with one hand and take hold of the gunwale of the boat.

3 Lean over to one side until the boat overbalances. Keep hold of the paddle as you go over.

4 Allow the boat to capsize. Continue to hold on to the paddle with one hand and the gunwale of the boat with the other.

5 Stay in the boat until you are completely upside down and the boat has stopped moving.

6 Kick away from the boat and come to the surface – ideally you should still be holding both the boat and the paddle.

GO TO THE FRONT AND SWIM

1 Swim to the front of the boat. If at all possible continue to hold on to the boat and the paddle.

2 Take hold of the front of the canoe, leaving it upside down.

3 Using the paddle if you can, and propelling yourself with your arms and legs, swim the canoe to the shore or to other paddlers in your group.

Daily Routine on a Paddling Trip

If you are taking your first canoe or kayak trip on a canal, many waterside campsites provide excellent facilities and local farmers will rarely turn you down if you ask before camping on their land. Beware of animals in rural areas, particularly in spring when they will have their young with them.

The tent you normally use for camping/backpacking will be fine. Always pitch it well above the water level of a river or lake as water can rise quickly. If the weather will be reliably fine, you could use your boat instead, rigging up plastic sheets or a groundsheet to make a shelter.

COOKING AND EATING

Although cooking on open driftwood fires gives a real sense of outdoor living, many places ban it or allow it in only designated areas. It is a good idea, therefore, to take a simple gas stove with a built-in flint, plus a few pans.

Ensure you take high-energy food supplies, as you will need them to power your muscles and generate warmth while paddling. There are plenty of instant savoury meals and desserts now available from outdoor shops in a wide variety of flavours; read the packaging to check on the calorific value.

If your water supply is suspect, boil it on your stove to kill any bacteria.

KEEPING THINGS DRY

Your main concern when preparing to get afloat each day will be packing your belongings into the boat. All your equipment needs to be kept as dry as possible, which is not always easy in the case of rain or an inadvertent capsize.

Plastic waterproof drums, which come in a variety of shapes and sizes, are ideal for canoes. They are not too large to carry when loaded, and have easily re-sealable waterproof lids. Specialized waterproof bags are also convenient, as they pack slightly more easily in the boat. Buy different colours or ones with see-through sides, so that you do not keep getting out your dry underwear when you want your lunch.

▲ *A sea kayak has little storage space but offers the possibility of extended sea journeys into remote areas full of wildlife.*

When packing up your tent, make sure the poles and pegs are attached securely, or stow them separately in a special bag so that you do not lose them if you capsize.

Tying all your bags and equipment into the thwarts is always a very sensible decision, since any capsize could lighten your load instantly, and possibly disastrously.

▼ *The inside of a kayak is an enclosed space, which makes it difficult to pack. Kit needs to be divided between several bags.*

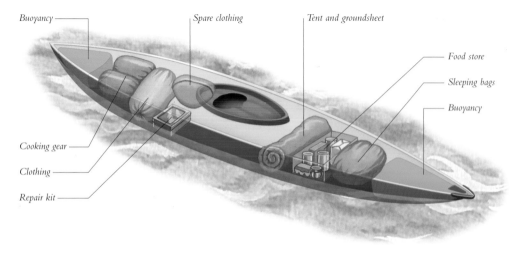

Buoyancy

Spare clothing

Tent and groundsheet

Food store

Sleeping bags

Buoyancy

Cooking gear

Clothing

Repair kit

▲ *Durable plastic containers, known as "BDHs", are ideal for storing small items that must be kept dry.*

▶ *Two paddlers carry their loaded sea kayaks down to the water. Hold the boat end grabs, one in each hand.*

PACKING

A double canoe can easily accommodate all the supplies and equipment necessary for days of cruising, but in a kayak the space is much more confined. Merely getting all your equipment into the boat can be difficult. Rather than keep your kit in one large bag, the secret is to use several small waterproof bags, known as dry bags, which can be packed more easily into the spaces available. Careful packing is essential.

With a canoe, the balance of the boat will determine how easy it is to paddle, so, taking into account the weight of the paddlers (usually, the heavier paddler sits at the back), try either to weigh or estimate the weight of the different bags, then distribute them evenly in the boat to achieve a level trim.

Pack everything into the boat in the reverse order to which you are likely to need it, and keep your map and compass, water bottle and snacks to hand. Most importantly, never have anything positioned in the boat that would impede your exit or that you could get tangled up in if you need to get out in a hurry.

▶ *More than one boat can be transported on a roof rack, and carrying them vertically reduces wind resistance. Both boats must be placed centrally between the roof bars.*

▶ *Use a roll-top dry bag for essentials such as phones, money and keys.*

▶ *Sea kayaks are equipped with watertight hatches, but you should put your belongings in waterproof bags in case of leaks.*

Travelling by Horse

Horseback expeditions are a great way for families and non-walkers to visit remote rural areas. You need to think about how you are going to provide food and water for the horse, as well as for yourself, but, in general, this is an enjoyable way to travel, allowing you to ramble across the countryside, taking photographs and absorbing the wilderness scenery all around you.

CHOOSING YOUR HORSE

For a successful expedition on horseback, it is important to have the right horse. If you are hiring a horse from a trekking centre, find out how much experience he has of carrying riders and gear, and as much as you can about his personality. Some countries have their own training systems for trekking horses, so ask about the training your horse has had.

Get to know not only your own horse but also the other horses in your group trip, finding out which horse prefers to follow the others and which is the slowest traveller. Your pace will be dictated by the slowest horse. Find out if the horses you are going to ride are familiar with people who may have little or no riding experience, and if any packhorses you need are used to being loaded with the equipment you intend to use.

Ask about the stabling arrangements you will be expected to provide, and if the horses will be happy to spend the night outdoors in an unfamiliar area.

CLOTHING

There is little you need in the way of specialized clothing, but when choosing what to wear the keynote is safety.

In many countries, riders wear hard hats, securely fastened with a chin strap, as a matter of course, but this may not be a legal requirement, and you should check if a hat can be borrowed along with the horse, or whether you must take your own. A fall from a horse can be fatal, and a hard hat will always reduce the likelihood of serious injury.

Safe footwear is equally important. Riding boots, jodhpur boots or any leather boot with a smooth sole and a clearly defined heel will prevent the foot from sliding through the stirrup, or becoming caught in the stirrup in

▲ *A wide-brimmed hat will cut out the glare of intense sunlight, but it offers little head protection in the event of a fall.*

the event of a fall, which is a potentially fatal situation. Trainers and boots and shoes with ridged soles and little or no heel should never be worn for riding.

Clothes should be well-fitting and neat without being restrictive. A shirt with a sweater or fleece jacket, and a pair of comfortable trousers, jeans or jodhpurs are ideal. Dark colours will stay smart for longer, and long sleeves are preferable to short sleeves, since they offer some protection from nips from equine teeth. No matter how warm the weather, avoid wearing sleeveless suntops or beachwear.

▼ *The crash hat can be worn with a silk or velvet covering (back left and right); the riding hat (front) is traditional headgear.*

▼ *Short leather jodhpur boots can be worn on their own with riding trousers, or with half-chaps to protect the rider's lower leg.*

▼ *Long riding boots can be made of leather or rubber. The narrow shoe and low heel prevent the foot getting caught in the stirrup.*

◀ *The essential grooming kit: (clockwise from far left) body brush and metal curry comb, dandy brush, water brush, rubber and plastic curry combs, hoof pick with brush, and cactus cloth.*

Wear jackets and shirts buttoned up, as a flapping shirt can frighten a horse, and there is the danger that the shirt could become caught on a tree branch if you are riding through woodland. Some horses may be nervous of noisy waterproof fabrics. Long hair should be tied neatly to avoid scaring the horse or becoming caught. Prominent jewellery, such as earrings and bangles, can cause injury if they become caught up.

EQUIPMENT

Horses are powerful animals and they can carry a considerable weight, but hot weather and long distances are an additional strain, and it is still important to keep your camp kit light, so as not to overload the horse. As well as your own camp kit and clothing, you need to think about the horse's tack, a basic grooming kit, and, depending on how much grass you expect along the route, enough feed for the trip. If you will be in a remote area, carry a spare set of reins and spare stirrup leathers in case your first set become damaged.

PACKING THE HORSE

Panniers designed for horses are available, and these can be fixed over the back of the saddle. Make sure that no item of kit is sticking into the horse's back or side, and avoid having any equipment hanging off the saddle or pannier, as this could spook the horse. All of your gear should be packed into bags or rolls, and the weight of the load should be balanced on the horse.

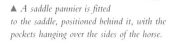

▲ *A saddle pannier is fitted to the saddle, positioned behind it, with the pockets hanging over the sides of the horse.*

▼ *A trail pad is a fleece numnah attached to a canvas cloth. The side pockets provide useful easy-access storage for smaller items.*

PICKING OUT HOOVES

Picking up one foot at a time, use the hoof pick to scrape dirt and stones from the underneath of the hoof, working from the horse's heel towards the toe. After removing large pieces of debris, use the brush on the hoof pick to clean remnants of dirt from the triangular part of the hoof at the heel, known as the frog. The frog is sensitive and easily damaged, so work gently.

FITNESS AND TRAINING

A horseback trek is a far gentler way to visit the open country than walking or cycling, and physical fitness is not a priority. Also, you do not need to be an experienced equestrian as the horses are likely to be mild and steady and you will rarely break out of a trot. However, anyone who has never ridden is advised to spend some time on horseback before they go to make sure they feel comfortable in the saddle.

▼ *If you are an inexperienced rider, taking a course of lessons before the trip will give you the confidence to perform the basic commands.*

Daily Routine on Horseback

Taking care of the horses' needs is one of the main tasks on a mounted trek. The agenda for every day has to be planned with the horses in mind.

ON YOUR ROUTE

Spend some time working out your route before you travel, and ask advice from local people or riding institutions as to which trails will be suitable for horses, including where water will be available for the horses to drink. Try to keep to trails constructed with horses in mind, if possible. If you will be following a popular route, plan to take rest stops or breaks for lunch at areas where you will be able to tether the horses off the trail, so that they are not blocking the route for other users.

The etiquette of wilderness trails is that walkers, vehicles and cyclists all give way to horses. Not everyone you meet will be prepared to do this, however, so be on your guard when riding past other trail users, because sudden movements or noises, such as the revving of a car engine, can spook your horses. If you meet another horse party, then those coming downhill should give way to those going up.

SAFETY CHECKLIST

- Wear your own properly fitted hat, with the chin strap fastened, at all times when mounted.
- After a fall, replace a hat that has been subjected to impact.
- Wear safe footwear at all times when mounted and use the correct stirrup iron size – about 2.5cm/1in wider than your boot.
- Avoid riding on roads if visibility is poor or at night.
- Do not wear jewellery.
- Ride with your coat fastened, and don't take off a coat or sweater while mounted.
- If your eyesight is not perfect, wear soft contact lenses if possible. If not, ask your optician about the safest spectacles.

CAMP ROUTINE

Try to select a well-drained, level stretch of land, and picket the horses at least 60m/200ft away from each other and well away from any water, such as a lake or river, which they could contaminate with urine or droppings. Aim to make camp when there are at least two hours of daylight left, so that the horses have time to graze before it gets completely dark.

However tired you may be, you must deal with your horse before you tend to your own needs. Remove the saddle and bridle, and fit the headcollar, then groom him and provide him with food and water. Visually check the horse's head, body and hooves and run your hand over the back where the saddle has been, and down all four legs. Treat any sore spots immediately, using equipment from your equine first-aid kit. Clean out the hooves with a hoof pick, and brush off any mud from the legs and body, using a body brush.

▲ *Horseback treks are a hugely enjoyable way to travel across open country, but good planning and preparation are essential.*

The next morning, before refitting the saddle and saddle pannier or trail pad when tacking up the horse, check that there are no burrs or small sticks attached to the saddle area of the horse, which could cause sore spots on his back during the course of the day.

FEEDING HORSES

Unless you have had confirmation that grass or feed will be available for the horses at your camping ground, do not assume that it will be. Buy an adequate supply of appropriate horse feed from the organization that supplied the horses, or else provide your own.

If you decide to take horse feed with you abroad, check to see if there are rules and regulations about the kind of feed you can take into the country. You may need a certificate stating that

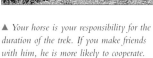
▲ *Your horse is your responsibility for the duration of the trek. If you make friends with him, he is more likely to cooperate.*

the feed is free of weed seed, as proof that there is no danger of contaminating the area with potentially poisonous or non-native weeds.

The horses will need to eat a good meal once a day. It doesn't matter what time they eat, but for convenience, it makes sense to feed them in the early evening, as soon as you have made camp, and before you prepare your own meal. Try to feed the horses at roughly the same time every day and make sure there is enough water for them to drink. Horses do not need to drink purified water, but their water supply should be as clean as possible, free from chemical pollutants, rotting vegetation and litter.

WILD ANIMALS
If wild animals, such as bears, wolves, hyenas or big cats could be a danger to you or your horses, ask for a safety briefing before you set off from the organization you hire the horses from, and carry required safety equipment, such as a rifle, with you. If it is a high-risk area, remember that food smells can attract animals from a great distance. Pack away unused food and burn food waste. Rather than leaving the horses free or hobbled to graze at a distance from camp, it is safer to keep them in camp, tied to a stock line.

▲ *Choose a campsite where there will be space to tether the horses. If it doesn't have grazing land, you will need to carry feed.*

▼ *Discipline is needed for horses and riders when travelling on horseback in large groups.*

Travelling with Pack Animals

If you are venturing into areas inaccessible to vehicles you must either restrict your baggage to the amount you can carry in a backpack or employ one or more pack animals to carry your load for you.

MULES AND DONKEYS

In areas of the world where the terrain is rocky and steep, the animals of choice for transporting people and heavy loads are mules or donkeys. Both have the ability to survive in conditions where horses and camels do not.

Mules have been used as transport animals for many centuries, though they have a tendency to be bad-tempered and stubborn, and may kick or bite if provoked. They therefore need firmer handling than donkeys. They are the stronger animal, and are capable of carrying up to 100kg/220lb if expertly loaded. They can travel at a good speed but have very wide backs, so riding them for long periods can cause discomfort. Donkeys are smaller and slower, carrying up to 50kg/110lb and requiring to be led on foot. They are gentler than mules, and are very sure-footed in mountain areas.

▼ *Donkeys are better suited to carrying gear than people, and travel at a pace slow enough to appreciate the wilderness.*

Animal handlers

It will usually be advisable to employ handlers to take care of any pack animals you are using. Unless you have experience of pack animals, dealing with them on your own can be difficult and time-consuming. The handlers will be familiar with the animals, and will know how much weight they can carry, what they need to eat and drink, and how long they need to rest; the animals are likely to respond better to the handlers than they will to you.

▲ *Mules are proverbially stubborn animals but will usually respond well if they are treated with kindness.*

This frees you up from taking responsibility for the animals and gives you more time to enjoy the trip. You will be grateful for this if the route is demanding and the living conditions

▼ *In this sort of rocky country it is better to hire mules or donkeys for use as pack animals rather than camels.*

difficult, but travelling with animal handlers does need to be thought through. If no one in your group can speak the handlers' language, you will need to employ someone who can speak to them on your behalf.

It will need to be agreed whether your team is responsible for providing food and water for the animals and their handlers while they are with you. If you are providing it, allocate it as needed, so that it doesn't all get consumed at the beginning. This is especially true of drinking water. If you are carrying the water you need for your entire trip, issue just the required amount each day (as you would to other team members) or you may find that water gets wasted and you could run out.

Checking equipment
If you are riding a mule, check the equipment that the animal will have on its back. Is the saddle comfortable to sit in? Are the stirrups in good condition? Are the pack frames suitable for the equipment you wish to carry?

Hiring agreement
Negotiate an agreement for use of the animals before you set off on the route. The agreement should include the costs to hire the animals, the services of their handlers, food costs for the animals and the handlers, plus any additional equipment you may have to provide or

▲ *Dog power enables you to visit the most remote wilderness areas, and sledding is an increasingly popular form of adventure travel.*

---

pay for, such as tents for the handlers and equipment for the animals.

Try to make the hire agreement with a reputable tourist organization, or in the presence of a respected local, such as the local chief, a priest at a mission station or the officer commanding the local police, to give you some back-up if there turns out to be a misunderstanding about what was agreed. It may also be wise to pay the handlers in their company, though pay only half upfront, keeping the second half back until you are safely back at base. If you have doubts about the trustworthiness of the animal handlers or owners, you may find that offering an additional sum if all goes well will help to make your trip go smoothly.

DOGS
Sled dogs have been working for centuries in Arctic and subarctic regions. In Alaska they were much used during the 1896 Gold Rush, proving far more hardy and reliable than ponies.

The dogs are bred to haul loads and work in teams, and are very sociable, strong and hardy. They have the highest metabolic rate of any mammal and require a large amount of fresh meat every day. Alaskan Malamutes are

long-legged and ideal for pulling loads in deep, soft snow; Siberian Huskies are smaller but faster.

A team of seven dogs can travel about 32km/20 miles a day pulling a sled with a load of about 270kg/600lb – known as a "rig". The teams are carefully assembled: three leading dogs, usually female, are chosen for their intelligence; the middle pair are the speed-dogs and regulate the pace of the whole team; the two nearest the sled are known as the wheel-dogs – normally male, they provide the pulling power.

You can hire teams of dogs and sleds together with experienced handlers, or "mushers" (an Inuit term meaning "one who travels through snow on foot"). This gives you the option of travelling on skis alongside the teams, but the mushers can also offer training in sledding and dog handling. The dogs respond to shouted commands, such as "haw" to go left and "gee" to go right. The key to successful sledding is to relax and loosen up so that you take bumps and twists in the trail in your stride, rather than being thrown off.

Vehicle Transport

If you are going to use one or more vehicles on your expedition, you have to decide what type you will need and whether you are going to ship your own out to the expedition area or hire what you need there.

For off-road expeditions in remote areas you should take at least two vehicles, ideally three, so that if one breaks down it can be towed to safety. You will need four-wheel drive if you are intending to drive in boggy or sandy conditions. At the expedition area you will need to pay attention to loading and maintenance. You should be confident that you can service the vehicle yourself, and if necessary attend a vehicle maintenance course before setting off.

TAKING YOUR OWN VEHICLE

The downside of taking your own vehicle out to the expedition area is that you will be faced with all the costs and bureaucracy involved in this process. The upside is that you will have a vehicle that you know will be in good working order, with all the necessary spares and tools, and which you are confident of driving.

HIRING A VEHICLE

If you are hiring a vehicle from a local company, look it over first to check all the tyres, suspension, steering, lights and brakes, and ask to take it on a test drive. Choose your vehicle carefully: a long wheelbase will give you more space but will lack manoeuvrability; the most powerful vehicles will cope with any terrain but will use a lot of fuel. Petrol engines are lighter and more powerful than diesel, but the latter

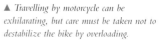
▲ *Travelling by motorcycle can be exhilarating, but care must be taken not to destabilize the bike by overloading.*

cope well in very low gear so are more reliable in rough terrain. They use less fuel, and diesel fuel is often very much cheaper than petrol.

In some countries you must have a driver, whereas in others you will have the choice of driving the vehicle yourself. The advantages of having a local driver are that he will know the country, will be used to driving on its roads and can be your interpreter. The disadvantages are that you lose a seat in the vehicle, you may not get on with the driver, or even understand him, and he may not be prepared to follow your route. Make sure you can work together before you hire him and the vehicle, and promise a good tip if the trip goes well.

SPARES AND MAINTENANCE

Check that you have a spare wheel with a good tyre on it that is inflated, a jack and a tyre spanner (wrench). Also make sure that the hirer has provided any other items that are required, such as a fire extinguisher,

◄ *When hiring vehicles make sure you have thought through the conditions you will be driving in so that your transport is suitable.*

first-aid kit and warning triangle. If you are going to be off-road for any time, you should also have spare oil, inner tubes for the tyres and a puncture repair kit including tyre levers, along with a full set of tools.

Always keep your fuel tank as full as you can, and never pass up the chance of buying fuel. If it is not clean, use a large funnel with a filter in it to filter the fuel before putting it into the tank.

Each night when you have finished your driving for the day, inspect the whole vehicle, especially the tyres, oil level, radiator fluid level and so on.

LOADING
How you load the vehicle is important, and if you are going off sealed roads you should keep your loading down to about three-quarters of the manufacturer's recommended limit.

DRIVING AT NIGHT
Be wary of driving at night in developing countries, as many vehicles have faulty lights and vehicles may be parked or abandoned without any warning lights or signs.

DRIVING IN DIFFICULT TERRAIN
Err on the side of caution: drive slowly and if necessary stop and check the state of the road or track ahead on foot. Stay in the middle of muddy tracks, taking care not to spin the wheels or ground the engine on rocks. Use four-wheel drive except when on firm road surfaces. If you do get bogged down in mud or sand, try reversing out or get your passengers to push. Failing this, dig in front of the wheels to create a gradual slope and try to go gently forwards. Lay down wood, canvas or anything that will help the wheels grip.

MOTORCYCLES
In temperate regions a motorcycle can be an attractive option if you are travelling alone. A heavy-duty bike will be able to cope with almost any terrain but will need constant servicing: wash it daily and check all the connections.

The amount of luggage you can take will be strictly limited, and will need to include spare parts and tools. Keep the

heaviest weight above the rear wheel and don't load too much on the back as it could destabilize the front wheel. Side panniers should be as slim as possible to reduce wind resistance.

If you are travelling in areas where motorcycles are unfamiliar, take extra care around other road users.

▲ *Snow chains should be fitted either on all four wheels or on the rear wheels only. Make sure the tyres are at the right pressure otherwise the chains will damage them.*

▼ *Getting your vehicle out of heavy mud is a skilled job and should be practised before you embark on a trip.*

Public Transport

You will almost certainly use public transport at some stage of your journey, whether just to get to your starting point or to complete most of your travel. Its quality varies greatly from country to country. In some you will find a modern, well-organized, integrated transport system, while in most developing countries the trains, ferries and buses may be crowded and uncomfortable. It is a good idea to take your own food, water and toilet paper.

PLANES

The overbooking of plane seats is a universal curse, but in some developing countries you may arrive at an airport only to find that your flight has been oversold by 50–70 per cent, with no system of seats going to those who booked first. This may leave you with no option but to bribe your way on to the flight. If you are tempted to use a local charter airline or private plane instead, check first to see if your travel insurance policy will cover you for this type of transport.

▼ *If you use small local boats for river trips, make sure they are safe and have a life jacket on board for each passenger.*

TRAINS

In many countries you will be offered up to three classes of travel. If you are making a long journey, and especially if this involves travelling overnight, it is worth paying to travel in either first or at least second class, as third class will probably have uncomfortable seats and will be very crowded.

If you are travelling on your own in developing countries, it is generally better to travel in first class as you will benefit from more space and comfort

▲ *Be on time or early for check-in when flying or you may find that you do not have a seat on the plane.*

and there will be more staff. On long journeys, check in advance to see if sleeping facilities are available. Be warned that sleeping cars may be filled on a first-come first-served basis, and

▼ *If you are travelling by ferry it is a good idea to have a contingency plan in case you arrive late at the port and miss your boat.*

▲ *If you are travelling by train on your own or overnight, it may be worth paying the extra fare to go first class.*

the sexes are not always segregated. Keep your luggage with you at all times. Lock your window closed at night so that nobody can get in at stops.

LOCAL FERRIES
In many countries, ferries have a number of classes. These range from first class, where you will have a cabin, to third class, where you may have to fight for a space on the open deck. In developing countries, ferries may get grossly overcrowded, carrying little or no safety equipment, especially for the deck passengers. Bear in mind that by travelling first class you will attract the attention of fellow passengers, and you should lock your cabin at night.

Some ferries can be seasonal due to the height of the river as a result of the dry or wet season, so check if your travel plans depend on a ferry trip.

BUSES
In developing countries buses are the mainstay of most transport systems. They range from new, air-conditioned vehicles to buses that would have been old when you were born. In hot countries, many buses will leave around dawn to take advantage of the cool part

of the day. Be early for your bus but expect long delays, as it may wait until it has filled all its seats before departing. You will usually be asked to put your luggage on the roof rack, so make sure you carry anything valuable with you.

Long-distance trips by bus can be a good way to meet fascinating local people as well as seeing the landscape at speed. Travelling with an open mind and an open ticket may lead you on some unexpected adventures.

LOCAL TAXIS AND MINIBUSES
If you use a taxi, either find out the rate and then watch the meter, or negotiate a price before the journey. Local minibuses are the cheapest form of transport in some parts of the world, but can become very overcrowded and are often involved in accidents.

▼ *Greyhound buses criss-cross the United States and are much used by backpackers as a cheap way to explore the country.*

CAMPCRAFT

While camping you are at the mercy of natural forces, and your activities
will be dominated by the times of sunrise and sunset, changes in the
weather, the lie of the land, the nearest water and the supply of fuel.
Your comfort will depend on your skills in choosing a suitable site,
erecting a shelter, building a fire and establishing a smooth routine.
When you leave there should be no trace of your stay.

Choosing a Campsite

There are very few perfect campsites, so when choosing a site you will probably have to compromise to some extent. Obviously your priorities will vary depending on how long you are going to stay there, and how large your camp will be, but it is a good idea to have some general principles in mind during the selection process so that you know what to look out for.

RECONNAISSANCE

For a long-term campsite, particularly for a large group, you will need to plan ahead and may have already visited the site before the group arrives. If you choose a site on private land you will need the landowner's permission to camp. However, whether you are looking at an established site or scouting in the wilderness, the points to check are the same.

WHEN TO LOOK

If your campsite is to be an overnight stop on the trail you should start to look for a suitable place at least two to three hours before it gets dark. By that time you will need to have settled in and pitched your tents and your food preparations should be well under way. Be prepared to stop short of your intended destination for that day if you find a spot that looks ideal. You may even want to backtrack a little if you do go on but the terrain ahead fails to offer further viable sites.

WHAT TO LOOK FOR

Try to avoid extreme conditions of any kind. In hot countries you will find it a great advantage to have some natural shade on your campsite. In colder areas your priority is likely to be natural shelter from wind. Always try to find a site that is well drained; this usually means looking for a reasonably high site. Not only will you avoid marshy, damp ground, but you will also not

▶ *Make sure you set up your camp well above the high-tide mark if you are camping near tidal water.*

▲ *In hot countries shade on your campsite will be a great advantage. If you want to use a popular site you will need to book ahead.*

find yourself in a pocket of cold air during the night. If it is windy, you will need space to pitch your tents with the doors facing away from the wind.

It will be an advantage if the site has its own water supply but you should always check to see where the water comes from. Just because local people drink it, it does not mean it is safe for you to drink. Unless you have good evidence to the contrary, you should always regard water as contaminated and treat it accordingly. Don't be tempted to camp too near a water

▼ *Camping by a river can be noisy. Make sure that, if it floods, your camp is high enough above the river not to be affected.*

CAMPSITE CHECKLIST

Check to see if the site is protected from the prevailing wind and that there is a readily available water supply. Once these criteria are satisfied, assess the following points, depending on your area and situation:

• The ground is reasonably level and flat, and is not covered with sharp stones or pieces of wood that could damage your groundsheet or sleeping mat.
• The land is not in a hollow, where a pocket of cold air could collect during the night.
• The land is not in a dried-up watercourse, which could flood without warning.
• The ground is neither boggy nor likely to become boggy.
• You have checked to see if you need permission to camp and have agreed any fees to be paid.

• You are happy that you can drive your tent pegs into the ground or that you can anchor the guy lines in some other way.
• There are no branches or unsafe trees near your tent site or dry-stone walls or other loose stones that are near enough to collapse on your tent or you while you are asleep.
• If the site is near to water, it is well above the flood level of a river or the high-tide mark at the coast, and there is no danger of crocodiles.
• There are no insect nests nearby and no holes or bushes where snakes may live.
• In a hot climate, there is adequate shade from the sun.
• You are not too near a source of water or a patch of wetland that will attract insects and animals during the night.

• There is a plentiful supply of wood for your fire. Unless you have permission, you should use only dead wood or wood lying on the ground.
• The camping area has not previously been used by domestic animals or livestock, which could have left ticks and other insects on the ground.
• There are no domestic animals or livestock in the field and no obvious signs of game trails going through the camp.
• In the mountains, your campsite is protected from a snow avalanche or rock falls from above.
• If the ground is covered in snow, you have stuck a ski pole or stripped tree branch into the snow to see if the ground is firm all over your site, with no hidden crevasses.

source, such as a stream, as it may attract clouds of biting insects in the evening, and may be a place where animals come to drink.

In an area where there is the possibility of attack by bandits or a track record of theft from tourists, it

can be worth calling at a local police post and asking them for advice on where you can camp safely. They will sometimes offer you a site in their own compound. If you are camping in a place – or travelling through the area – for any length of time, try to

build and maintain good relationships with the local people, especially the community leaders. You may find that during your stay you need their help obtaining supplies or settling disputes between yourselves and other local people or traders.

▼ *Trees with seriously undermined roots might be felled by a high wind, so it could be risky to camp near them.*

▼ *If you have to camp among trees check that there are no rotten or broken branches above the area where you pitch your tent.*

▼ *Get some local knowledge about the site: a watercourse may be subject to flooding in the event of heavy rain many miles away.*

Camp Layout

The layout of your camp will be dictated by the site you have chosen, the climatic conditions, the size of the camp and personal preferences. There are, however, some golden rules that should be followed for the sake of the safety and well-being of the campers.

POSITIONING TENTS

Try to pitch the tents with their back into the prevailing wind. If possible, use either a belt of trees or bushes to form a natural windbreak. If hot weather conditions make shade important then choose a place under some trees, but remember that falling twigs and branches will be likely. Make sure your sleeping area is well away from the cooking area and toilet area, and upwind of them if there is a prevailing wind.

TOILETS

If there are no permanent toilets on the site, construct a toilet area downwind of the tents and away from sleeping and cooking areas, with natural screening or a bivvy bag or groundsheet for privacy. You can dig a hole in the ground with a trowel or knife for solid waste, covering it with soil after use and burning toilet paper. Have a separate urination point. Alternatively, you can dig a large ditch to make a latrine, covering it with soil each time it is used. Note that latrines can become a breeding ground for germs unless the soil covering is applied religiously after every use.

USING WATER WISELY

If your camp is near a stream or river use the water systematically:
• Collect water for drinking and cooking upstream of the site. Make sure you are also upstream of animals' drinking spots.
• Wash yourself midstream.
• Wash dishes downstream, scraping food remnants off before rinsing. You can wash clothes downstream but do not use detergent as it will pollute the water.

WASHING AREA

If you are going to have an area dedicated to washing clothes, keep this away from the cooking and sleeping areas. Site any clothes lines well away from where people will be walking, especially at night.

WHERE TO SITE A FIRE

If you are going to have a fire, light it well away from the tents, as sparks can fly out and burn holes in the material. Also make sure it is downwind of the tents, on a flat area well away from trees and bushes.

KITCHEN

Site the food preparation area some distance from where you will be sleeping, so that if an animal is attracted by the smells of food during the night, you will not be disturbed. Also, any flies attracted to your cooking will be well away from your sleeping area. If you can, have an extra tent near the

▲ *A campsite under trees has the advantage of being shady, but you risk twigs and branches falling on your tent.*

cooking area for the storage of food. Do not keep food inside a tent where anyone is sleeping.

SOCIAL CENTRE

Choose an area away from the sleeping and cooking areas where you can set up a working and/or social area in which people can sit and talk or work. This area will become the social centre of the camp. Make sure that everyone accepts responsibility for keeping this shared area clean and tidy.

PARKING AREA

A large campsite will probably be accessible by road or track. If your group is travelling by vehicle, allocate a parking area and make it clear that vehicles cannot drive around within the camp itself, which could be dangerous.

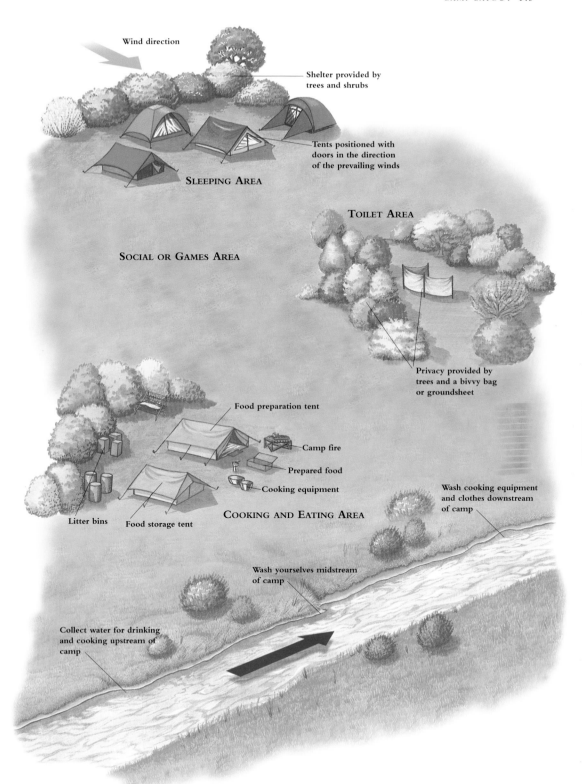

Wind direction

Shelter provided by trees and shrubs

Tents positioned with doors in the direction of the prevailing winds

SLEEPING AREA

TOILET AREA

SOCIAL OR GAMES AREA

Privacy provided by trees and a bivvy bag or groundsheet

Food preparation tent

Camp fire

Prepared food

Cooking equipment

Litter bins

Food storage tent

COOKING AND EATING AREA

Wash cooking equipment and clothes downstream of camp

Wash yourselves midstream of camp

Collect water for drinking and cooking upstream of camp

Erecting Tents

Once you have checked your site for suitability you can get on with erecting your tent. No matter what kind of tent it is, you will need to follow the same system of erection. You should refer to the manufacturer's instructions, especially if this is the first time you have put the tent up, but your memory may also need refreshing if there has been a long gap since you last did it.

It's a wise precaution to practise erecting and striking your tent before you go away (you can do this in the garden or a local open space), so that you iron out any problems and can do the job quickly. On the expedition

▶ *The geodesic dome (shown here without the outer tent) is very strong, but if any of the poles break it will lose its strength.*

ERECTING A DOME TENT

1 Check that you have all of the tent parts. If the inner tent needs to be attached to the outer tent, do it now. Make sure that all zips are closed.

2 Assemble the poles and thread them through the sleeves in the tent. It is easier to push them: pulling them may pull the pole sections apart.

3 Now place the ends of the poles in the fastenings provided in the lower part of the tent so that they put the whole of the tent under tension.

4 Peg out the inner tent. Always push the pegs in at an angle away from the tent. This prevents the pegs from being easily pulled up by the wind.

5 Peg out the outer tent and check to see that the inner tent is attached correctly. If you need to reposition a peg, use another peg to pull it out.

6 Peg out all the remaining guy lines. Gather up any remaining pegs, place them in the tent bag and stow the bag inside the tent.

there may be days when weather conditions are bad and you are forced to pitch your tent in windy or rainy weather, or even in the dark, so the more familiar you can become with the procedure in advance, the better. If you erect the tent using the same procedure each time it will become automatic.

If you are using a tent made of cotton, it is better to pitch it and get it thoroughly wet, then let it dry out naturally before using it.

CHECKING THE SITE
The first thing to do is to check the piece of ground on which you intend putting the tent. Make sure it is flat and does not dip in a way that will mean water collects there if it rains. Is the

▶ *The traditional ridge tent is still widely used on expeditions. It is simple to erect and will withstand a lot of bad weather.*

ground soft enough for you to drive the tent pegs into it? Is it reasonably sheltered from the wind but not too near anything that might crash down on to it, such as a dead tree? When you are happy with the lie of the land, the

next thing is to make sure that there are no sharp objects that could damage the groundsheet, such as stones and twigs. Clear anything of this kind from the site and if necessary remove or flatten any small humps.

ERECTING A RIDGE TENT

1 Take the tent out of the bag and check to make sure all the parts are present, then lay out the inner tent on the ground and peg down the corners.

2 Assemble the frame over the inner tent. Check the poles before fitting them together as incorrect connections can be hard to unfasten.

3 Attach the inner tent to the poles using the fittings provided. Place the flysheet over the poles and where necessary attach to the inner tent.

4 Peg out the guy lines on the flysheet, starting with the four corners. Make sure all the door zips are closed while you do this.

5 Complete the pegging out of all pegging points and guy lines. The flysheet should be tightly stretched and should not be touching the inner tent.

6 Undo the door zip for ventilation and tie at the sides to secure. Adjust the guy lines so that the walls of the flysheet are clear of the inner tent.

ASSEMBLING THE PARTS

If it is a new tent, read the instructions and check that you have all the parts. With most tents, you will put the inner tent up first, but do check the instructions about this. First assemble the poles and get the pegs out of their bag. Then, depending on the type of tent, start your pitching routine. Make sure all the doors are closed when pitching the tent. If you cannot erect your tent on your own, make sure other people are available to help.

Many modern tents, especially geodesic domes, have quite thin poles. To strengthen them, wrap tape around each pole where it fits into the next joint. This will stop the joints splitting in high winds.

▶ *The weather may be calm when you put your tent up, but always use all guy lines provided in case it changes for the worse.*

ERECTING A FAMILY TENT

1 Take the tent out of its bag and check with the instructions that you have all the parts – the pegs, inner and outer tents, poles and guy lines.

2 Lift the poles forming the main assembly to pull the tent up into position.

3 Lock the joints in the poles to create the tent frame.

4 Slide any additional poles into their sleeves. Assemble the porch area, taking care not to damage either the tent fabric or the poles.

5 Peg out the sides of the tent, sticking the tent pegs firmly into the ground and angling them to pull the guy lines away from the tent.

6 If your tent has a separate inner it may be necessary to attach it at this stage, then peg it out. Add the flysheet and peg out all of the guy lines.

ERECTING A PATROL TENT

1 Take the tent out of its bag and check that you have all the parts.

2 Spread the main tent out, upside down, on the ground.

3 Place the ridge pole in the sleeve or loops provided in the main tent.

4 Push the spikes on the two uprights into each end of the ridge pole.

5 Push the spikes through the reinforced holes in the tent canvas.

6 Pull the canvas back over the poles and attach the main guylines.

7 With someone at each end holding one of the poles firmly, lift the tent into an upright position.

8 Peg out the main guy lines so that the frame of the tent will stand up on its own.

9 Now make sure the door flaps are closed, either by lacing them together or by closing the zip.

10 Peg out the walls. Check they will be under the roof so that rain will clear them when it runs off the roof.

11 Peg out the side guy lines of the tent to create the walls.

12 Check the whole tent. If it does not have a sewn-in groundsheet, lay out the groundsheet inside the tent.

Base Camps

For a long or large-scale expedition exploring challenging and inaccessible terrain or requiring a large amount of equipment, it is usually necessary to set up an initial camp to act as a semi-permanent support structure. From this "home base" more lightly equipped expeditions can set off, for instance to trek through wilderness, climb a mountain or conduct an archaeological survey. The base camp acts as a communications hub and supply store. It is likely to be sited in an area that is accessible by motor vehicles and can generally offer a reasonably high degree of comfort.

Setting up this more elaborate kind of camp is naturally a much more complex operation than setting up a small temporary camp. You will probably be using heavier and bigger tents, your cooking area will be of a more permanent nature and you will need to construct a toilet area and make provision for rubbish disposal.

CAMP ROUTINE

You will find it useful to draw up a simple and sensible set of rules that everyone is able to follow. If there are a lot of people in the camp, you may want to post up a programme each day listing meal times and any planned events or meetings. It is also a good idea to have either a lights-out time or

a quiet time, so that those who want to sleep can; you should also try to implement this rule if your camp is set up near other people, who will not want to be kept awake.

CAMP SECURITY

If you are a large party with people coming and going, perhaps sometimes overnight, make sure you have a system of knowing who is where and who will be in camp when. This will not only act as a general safety feature, letting you know where all the members of the group are at any one time, but will also aid with planning the catering.

▲ *A base camp may need to include many different components. Draw up a logical plan for its layout before pitching any tents.*

If there will be times when all or most of the members of the expedition are going to be away from the camp it is a good idea to employ a local person to act as a guard. Even when the camp is not empty, your equipment should not be left lying around in case it is stolen or damaged.

▼ *Long-stay camps need to be supplied with well-maintained and carefully sited toilet and washing facilities.*

BURNING WASTE

Not all waste will be suitable for burning on the camp fire, and a large long-term campsite may require an incinerator, which should be carefully sited well away from the tents. This could be an ordinary galvanized incinerator of the kind intended for garden waste, or you could make one by piercing holes all around an oil drum or metal bin and siting it over an open fire. The ashes should be removed regularly and buried in a pit used for solid waste.

▲ *A daily discussion and briefing involving all the group members will help to keep the base camp running smoothly.*

▲ *A large camp will probably require one or two designated cooks to provide regular meals for the whole party.*

KITCHEN

Hygiene should be a priority in the food preparation area in a large camp. Make sure your kitchen area is kept thoroughly clean and that all waste is properly disposed of each day so it will not attract animals and insects. With a lot of people living together, poor hygiene can quickly result in everyone getting ill, especially in hot countries.

Wash all the cooking pots and equipment in hot water each day. Try to have some hot water on your fire or stove all the time so that people arriving back from activities can always have a hot drink or even some hot water to wash in.

If possible, rig up some sort of structure that enables you to store your eating and cooking equipment, and all your food, off the ground. This is useful and more hygienic than leaving them on the ground. Some kind of table or raised surface also makes the preparation of food much easier if you are cooking for a large group. All fresh food should be stored in sealed containers or cool boxes.

If you are using a fire to cook on, make sure your woodpile is kept tidy

and well stocked. Your reserves of water should always be kept covered and should be well marked to show which water is for drinking and which is for washing.

BURYING WASTE

In a camp that will be occupied for some time it is particularly important not to leave any waste lying around. Waste food will encourage wild animals to scavenge in the camp and will attract flies. If you are allowed to do so on your site, dig two pits at least 60cm/2ft deep: in one you should dispose of any solid waste, such as flattened cans; the other is for the disposal of any cooking or waste water.

Each time you put anything into the first pit, cover it with soil to prevent insects from feeding on the waste. Make sure this pit is well marked so that nobody steps in it. If you are going to bury cans or other packaging, burn and flatten them first.

Place a layer of bracken or grass over the top of the second pit to filter out any scraps of food that may be in the cooking water. This covering should be burnt or buried every day.

CAMP LAYOUT

A large base camp may need to accommodate the following specific areas, whose siting needs to be planned before you start pitching the tents:

- Camp fire: should be central but downwind of the tents.
- Woodpile: near the fire. The wood, especially the kindling, will need a cover to keep it dry.
- Chopping area: next to the woodpile, and clearly marked out to avoid accidents.
- Kitchen area: should be sheltered, fairly near the camp fire and away from the tents, and ideally near the water supply.
- First aid tent: in a large base camp everyone should know where to find the first-aid kit in an emergency situation.
- Storage: should be conveniently sited depending on its use. If you do not have a dedicated first aid tent, keep the first-aid kit near the door of a storage tent.
- Toilets: should be downwind of the site and screened off, but not so far away from the tents that people are tempted to use a nearby bush instead.

Lightweight Camping

This form of camping is so-called because the weight of your camping gear is cut to a minimum, allowing you to transport it under your own steam. All the equipment you use will have been selected because it is made of lightweight material and made to be either carried in a backpack or packed into a canoe or cycle pannier bags.

MINIMIZING YOUR LOAD

Lightweight camping can be an end in itself, although most people use it as a means of carrying out some other kind of activity, such as walking, cycling or paddling in the countryside. The real enthusiasts believe that you should be able to go away for, say, a weekend's expedition on your own taking kit weighing no more than 9kg/20lb. Getting your load down to this level requires practice and experience. However, if you are travelling with another person the target is much

▼ *Lightweight camping gives you the freedom to explore inaccessible areas that few others will be able to reach.*

easier to reach, as much of what you take, including your tent, stove, fuel and cooking equipment, will be shared between you.

CHOOSING EQUIPMENT

If it is to combine the high performance you need when camping with extremely lightweight and compact design, all your equipment needs to be of the best quality. This means it will not come cheap, and you may well find that you have to carry more weight to begin with and acquire better, lighter pieces of kit over time. Very lightweight equipment tends also to be more susceptible to damage; you will need to treat it with care and maintain it well, following the manufacturers' instructions.

Much of the art of travelling light lies in the care with which you choose what to take. Thinking very carefully about where you are going and the kind of terrain you will be travelling over will help you to avoid carrying unnecessary items. The more trips you do, the better you will know how

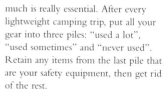

REDUCING YOUR EQUIPMENT

Overloading a cycle, kayak or canoe can make it dangerously unstable, and, if you are walking, carrying too heavy a load will be wearisome and spoil your trip.

Your equipment should weigh no more than 11kg/25lb and, with some care, you should be able to get it down to 9kg/20lb.

When you have all your equipment together, consider how you could reduce its weight.

• Is everything you have essential?
• Do you need to carry the containers some of the equipment may be packed in?
• Do you need all the things in your washing kit? Could you cut the soap in half and take a smaller tube of toothpaste?
• Do you need a knife, fork and spoon, or could you get by with just a spoon?
• Do you really need all the clothes you are thinking of taking?

much is really essential. After every lightweight camping trip, put all your gear into three piles: "used a lot", "used sometimes" and "never used". Retain any items from the last pile that are your safety equipment, then get rid of the rest.

At the same time, make a list of any items you wished you had taken, so that you can add these next time. Soon you should get your kit down to the minimum weight possible.

TENTS

Single-skin tunnel tents made of waterproof, breathable material with a minimal frame of flexible poles are lightweight but pricey. Even lighter are bivvy bags, which dispense with a frame and simply form a waterproof covering for your sleeping bag.

Although lightweight tents can be strong and robust you will need to be careful, especially with the tent's groundsheet, which is likely to be very thin. If you pitch on a sharp piece of wood or rock you may damage it. One way around this is to place your sleeping mat on the ground before you pitch the tent over it, so you can still have the warmth of the mat to lie on but your groundsheet will be protected.

COOKING EQUIPMENT

If you are a really lightweight camper, your cooking equipment will be very basic, which means that you will have to choose your food and utensils carefully, perhaps cutting the latter down to just a knife and a spoon.

If you are cooking on a single stove and using dehydrated foods, make sure you will have enough cooking pots. Choose a pan with a close-fitting lid that will double as a frying pan. Remember to check on the cooking times of packaged food: the longer the cooking time, the more fuel you will need. If you are going to carry food, take it out of its outer packaging but keep the cooking instructions.

Each of these things individually may save only grams/ounces, but added together they represent a significant weight saving.

▲ *Choosing a site with a good view may mean that it is exposed. Be sure that your lightweight tent will withstand the wind.*

▼ *If you have to pitch your tent on very stony ground, protect your groundsheet with your sleeping mat.*

LIGHTWEIGHT EQUIPMENT

For a three-day trek in a temperate climate it should be possible to take the following gear per person without exceeding 9kg/20lb:

- Shirt, trousers, socks, underwear
- Fabric or leather walking boots
- Windproof jacket
- Woollen or fleece sweater
- Waterproof jacket and trousers
- Hat and gloves
- One-person tent, or bivvy bag and groundsheet
- Sleeping bag and insulated mat
- Lightweight backpack
- Canister stove and lighter
- Cooking fuel
- Cooking pot/mug and lid
- Spoon and knife
- Water bottles and purifier
- Food and food storage bag
- Whistle
- Wristwatch
- Map
- Compass
- First-aid kit
- Basic survival kit
- Sunglasses and sunscreen
- Insect repellent
- Wash kit

Alternative Shelters

There may be occasions when you either do not have a tent or you are unable to use the tent you have, but you still need a shelter to protect yourself from the elements. A tent groundsheet can be used to form a makeshift shelter, or you could construct an A-frame shelter from tree branches; in snow conditions you could build a trench; alternatively, you could use natural landforms as shelter.

When choosing the site for a natural shelter, consider whether the ground will be waterlogged if it rains heavily. Cover the floor with a layer of bracken, ferns, heather or any other vegetation available. This will insulate you from the ground and will make you more comfortable; use only dry vegetation and shake it first to get rid of insects.

GROUNDSHEET SHELTER

If you have a groundsheet, or a sheet of ripstop nylon, and a length of cord, tie the cord between two trees about 3m/10ft apart, and place the sheet over the cord. Then take the corners of the sheet and either peg them into the ground or tie a guy line to each corner and guy them out. This will provide you with the simplest of shelters, but it will be considerably better than a night in the open air, especially in windy or rainy conditions. Make sure the sheet comes down to 45–60cm/ 18–24in from the ground, or driving rain will soak you. The bivvy bag included in the survival kit can also be used as an emergency shelter if a groundsheet is not available. On its own, a bivvy bag can be used as a

waterproof cover for a sleeping bag, but if you fix short tent poles or stout tree branches at its entrance, you can form a porch that effectively turns the bivvy bag into a small tent for one person.

A-SHAPED NATURAL SHELTER

If you do not have a groundsheet big enough to make a shelter, find two convenient trees and rest a long branch or piece of wood between them, about 1.2m/4ft from the ground. Make sure you secure it very well, using either cord or natural vines, so that it will take the weight of the frame you are going to build.

Now lean some tree branches on the long branch at 30–45cm/12–18in intervals to form an A-shaped shelter. Fill in the gaps of the structure with

---

BUILDING A GROUNDSHEET SHELTER

1 Look for a fallen branch and place it between two trees about 1.2m/4ft from the ground, wedging it into the trunks or securing it with cord or rope.

2 Unpack the groundsheet of your tent (or use your bivvy bag or space blanket) and throw it over the suspended branch.

3 Arrange the groundsheet so that it hangs over both sides of the branch, coming down at least 45–60cm/ 18–24in off the ground on each side.

4 Take one corner of the groundsheet and peg it out with a tent peg, or guy it with a guy line, or weight it down with a heavy log or rock.

5 Work around the other three corners, securing the groundsheet firmly in place with tent pegs, guy lines, or heavy logs or rocks.

6 With the four corners secured, the completed shelter will provide basic but effective protection from driving wind, rain or snow, or from an intense sun.

bracken, ferns or large leaves, starting at the bottom and working up, in the same way that a roof is tiled. If it rains, the rain will run down and off the sides and will not seep inside.

Alternatively, if there are pieces of plastic, wood or other materials around, you can use these to form the sides of the shelter. Do not use heavy pieces unless you can secure them, or else they may collapse on top of you.

USING NATURAL LANDFORMS

In hot, dry areas, use natural landforms such as caves, overhangs or sand dunes to give you shelter from the sun and wind. Dry-stone walls can also be used as the basis for a shelter. Place tree branches diagonally from the top of the wall to the ground in front about 1m/3ft away, then cover the tree branches with whatever vegetation is available, or with your bivvy bag or a groundsheet. Make sure the wall is stable and is not likely to fall on you while you are inside the shelter.

SNOW SHELTERS

If the snow is deep and you have tools such as a snow saw, machete or long knife with you, and you want the shelter to last for several days, you can build an igloo. For less permanent shelters to give protection from the elements, such as during a snowstorm or while the group takes a rest, you can dig a cave into a bank of snow or a trench in an open space.

LIVING IN SNOW

- Always make sure there is good ventilation inside your snow shelter, especially if the shelter is to be used by several people. Carbon dioxide will build up without adequate ventilation, and this can be fatal.
- Heat from your body will rise to the top of the shelter, while cold air will sink to ground level. Build a snow bench or platform inside the shelter so that you can sit or even sleep in the relatively pleasant warmer air.

▲ *In a desert environment, a shelter constructed from branches and vegetation will provide essential shade.*

Igloo

To make an igloo, cut blocks 1m/3ft long, 40cm/15in high and 20cm/8in deep from one area of hard snow, using a snow saw, machete or long knife. Form a circle with the blocks around the hole from where the snow was cut, then build up the walls, overlapping and shaping the blocks so that they curve inwards. Cut a hole under one of the blocks for the cold air to seep out and for the entrance, then lay blocks along one wall inside the igloo to form a bench. The last block must be larger than the gap in the roof it has to fill. Place it on top of the igloo, then, from the inside, shape it into position so that it fills the gap exactly. Finally, cut ventilation holes through the walls, using an ice axe, machete, ski poles, or a stripped tree branch. In temperatures below freezing, the igloo will last for several days.

Snow cave

If you need shelter but do not have the tools or the energy to build an igloo, hollow out a snow bank, using a shovel, if you have one, or your hands. This is the quickest way to take shelter from high winds and freezing temperatures. Block up the entrance behind you with roughly constructed lumps of snow. Poke a hole in the blocked-up entrance for ventilation, using an ice axe, ski pole or stripped tree branch.

Snow trench

Open, flat spaces offer no natural protection from the elements in the way of trees, walls or hillsides. If you find yourself in need of shelter and you are equipped with a shovel, you can dig into the ground and build a snow trench. The deeper you dig, the more protection the trench will offer. If tree branches are available, make a roof by laying branches over the top; if you have time, you can lash the branches together using rope, cord or vegetation. Pack snow on to the frame, and poke a tree branch, ski pole or the shovel handle through the snow to make air holes. A bivvy bag can be laid over the top if tree branches are not available.

Tree hollow shelter

If you are in a coniferous forest, the natural hollows at the base of the trees will make good temporary shelters. If the tree branches are laden with snow, take care not to dislodge the snow, as it is extremely heavy and will fall on you with an impact. Build a snow bench above the level of the floor to sleep or sit on, as the cold air will sink to the lowest point in the shelter, leaving you in warmer air. Always make sure there is good ventilation.

Camp Safety and Hygiene

When camping, you should be even more aware of safety and hygiene than you are at home, particularly if you are in some remote area where help may be hard to summon. For this reason, all camp members should prioritize their own and each other's health and safety.

TIDINESS

A basic rule to go by is that a tidy camp is a safe camp. On this basis, always try to have as much as possible packed away before you go to sleep each night, leaving out only those things that you may need during the night and first thing the next morning.

Never leave axes, knives or saws lying on the ground at any time, as someone could seriously hurt themselves if they fell on or over one of these. Keep all tools stored away when not in use: apart from the safety issue, this means that everyone will know where to find them. Finally, never tie a rope or washing line between trees in a position where someone is likely to walk into it. At night, mark any such line by putting something light-coloured over it.

FIRE SAFETY

If you are cooking on a wood fire, make sure your woodpile is safe and that your fire cannot spread from the fire area. Use an existing fire pit if there is one on your campsite, and be very careful not to start a forest or brush fire in dry weather. Keep a bucket of sand or soil near the camp fire to use as a fire extinguisher in an emergency.

If you are cooking on a gas stove, do not cook in a sleeping tent and make sure that all gas is stored away from fires and sleeping areas and out of direct sunlight. Never change a gas cylinder in a confined space, and never put an empty cylinder on a fire.

When you eventually strike camp and put the fire out, make sure it is completely extinguished before leaving.

HYGIENE AND SAFETY TIPS

- Whatever task you are doing in camp, tidy up as you go along.
- If you are leaving camp do not leave open fires, stoves or gaslights alight and unattended.
- If cooking in the porch of your tent make sure you have a good level area for your stove.
- Try not to eat food in a sleeping tent as crumbs and scraps will attract animals and insects.
- Keep all drinking water covered and mark it clearly to differentiate it from non-drinking water.
- Store all inflammables well away from fires and out of direct sunlight. Do not store fuel in sleeping tents.

▼ *In a large camp, pitch tents with enough space between them so that walkways are clear of guy lines and tent pegs.*

▲ *The highest standard of hygiene should be maintained when preparing food in camp. Dispose of kitchen waste scrupulously.*

FOOD PREPARATION

Allocate a specific area of the camp site for the preparation of food and keep it scrupulously clean. Always wash your hands in clean, purified water before preparing food and wash dishes and utensils promptly to avoid attracting flies. In hot weather, cook and eat fresh food such as fish as quickly as possible

▼ *If you are sleeping out, do not sleep too near a camp fire in case you roll on to it during the night, or sparks fly on to you.*

after bringing it into camp, and don't keep cooked food standing around cooling, as bacteria will proliferate.

WASTE DISPOSAL

Dispose of all waste food by burning and burying it as soon as possible (see the section Base Camps). If you cannot bury it, pack it into a plastic bag and put it in a bin as soon as possible. Never store waste near the sleeping area, and never leave food uncovered because it will attract wild animals.

TENT HYGIENE

If you are camping in the same area for more than one night, try to keep your tents tidy, clean and aired, if the weather allows. If your tents do not have sewn-in groundsheets, lift the walls each day to air them. If they do have sewn-in groundsheets, open the doors and sweep out the tents each day. Turn your sleeping bag inside out and air it for an hour or so each day, preferably in the sun. Afterwards roll it up until you need it so that nothing can crawl into it before you do.

TOILETS AND WASHING

Dig a hole or latrine for solid waste and cover it with soil each time it is used. Have a separate urination point. To make sure the used water from your washing area cannot run straight into a river or lake, dig a soakaway channel so that the dirty water will be filtered through the ground first.

▲ *When using chopping or cutting tools make sure you have no obstacles or people around you who might get hurt.*

▲ *Keep your wood-chopping axe sharp with a Carborundum stone: a sharp blade is safer than a blunt one.*

▼ *Always cook outside a tent, though you can use the porch to shelter the stove, and never store stove fuel inside a sleeping tent.*

Personal Hygiene

Although personal cleanliness is always important, it becomes even more vital if you are travelling in a foreign country, particularly a developing one, since you may be exposed to many diseases and illnesses to which you have no natural immunity. If you are travelling in a group it is also in everyone's interest that you should all stay as clean and fresh as possible.

BODY

Wash yourself all over at least once a day if you have access to water. The best time to do this will usually be in the early evening when you have returned to camp or pitched your tent and are changing out of your day clothes. Pay special attention to the armpits and groin area, which can suffer painful sweat rashes if not kept clean, and don't forget your ears.

If washing water is in short supply, be careful of the amount of creams and lotions you apply. If they build up on your skin they may begin to block the pores, which could lead to infection.

▼ *When you are active in the wilderness it is even more important to pay attention to personal hygiene than at home.*

FEET

Never walk around bare-footed. You may tread on a thorn or something else that gets stuck in your foot, or on an insect that bites you, which will make subsequent walking difficult. At best, you will make your feet dirty.

At the end of the day, take off your boots as soon as you reach camp and make washing your feet a priority. Be careful if you are drying them near an open fire: it is easy to burn them. Make sure they are clean and dry and check them for blisters. If you are in a wet environment, put anti-fungal foot powder on them. If you are in a hot, dry climate, dress any cuts or abrasions immediately to stop them developing into desert sores. Try to wear clean, or at least different, socks each day.

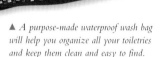

▲ *A purpose-made waterproof wash bag will help you organize all your toiletries and keep them clean and easy to find.*

Hang wet boots on sticks to dry overnight, or stuff them with newspaper if available. Removing the laces and insoles will help them to dry more quickly. Don't try to dry leather boots quickly by the fire or in the sun, as fierce heat will crack the leather.

TOILETRIES

If you will be away in the field for a long time, working from a base camp, take all your personal toilet materials in a purpose-made wash bag. If you leave your base camp for a night and weight is a factor, use a smaller bag, or an ordinary plastic bag, for the small amount you will need while you are away. Keep your toilet bag clean and tidy, with the lids well screwed on tubes and containers to avoid leakage. Avoid glass containers, which may break if your bag is roughly handled; flimsy ones, which may burst if squashed; and pressurized aerosols, which can explode and are not allowed on aircraft.

The number and type of clothes you take is a personal decision and will depend on the nature of your trip and the weather conditions, but you will have to compromise between travelling light and having enough changes of clothes.

- Wash clothes whenever you have the chance, rather than waiting until all your clothes are dirty.
- Take a length of washing line and a few pegs (pins) to help with the drying of clothes.
- Clothes made of natural fibres are usually more comfortable; they retain their insulation properties better when wet and will absorb sweat in hot conditions.

▲ *If water is available, try to wash any dirty clothes whenever you get the chance – at least every other day.*

EYES

If you are travelling in a very dusty environment, take some eyewash solution or contact lens solution with you and give your eyes a good wash out each evening.

If you normally wear contact lenses, consider wearing glasses instead if you are travelling to a hot, dry area. Contact lenses can cause inflammation if dust gets into the eye when you are taking the lens out or putting it in, or when wind blows dust around.

TEETH

When cleaning your teeth, remember to use purified or sterile drinking water. Do not use tap or river water to rinse your mouth unless you are absolutely sure it is clean and free from pollution.

CLOTHING

An adequate supply of clean and dry clothing is important for your health and comfort, but if you are travelling light your wardrobe will be minimal so you will need to wash clothes whenever you have the opportunity. You will find that wearing loose-fitting underwear made of natural materials is comfortable and less likely to rub or cause irritation or sweat rashes.

Keep all your clothes as clean as possible. When washing them is a problem, wear one set during the day, keep another set for the evening and, if you have enough clothes, keep a separate set to sleep in. If water is limited the most important items to wash are your socks: if you keep them in good condition they will help to keep your feet in good condition, but they must be thoroughly dry before you wear them again.

You should try to wash dirty clothes at least every other day, if water is available. Use either some travel wash, which works in both salt and fresh water but can still pollute a water supply, or an environmentally friendly soap, which will wash both you and your clothes but not harm the water supply.

If you are in a wet environment, keep your sleeping and

▶ *In hot weather wear cool, loose-fitting cotton clothing that will wick sweat away from your body and give some protection from the sun.*

camp clothes dry in a waterproof bag and change from your wet day clothes when you return to camp.

In dry, dusty conditions try to keep all clean clothing packed in stuff bags or plastic bags so that they stay free of dust and grit. If you roll your clothing rather than folding it, it will stay less creased. Have a separate bag for dirty clothing so that you do not get clean and dirty items mixed up.

Take a sewing kit so that you can repair any tears in clothes as soon as you notice them to avoid them getting worse, but beware of darning holes in the feet of socks, as walking on the stitching may cause blisters.

Camp Fires

Good preparation is essential for a successful camp fire. To choose the site, look for a place where you are not going to damage any overhanging trees or will risk setting scrubland on fire. Always be aware of these dangers when your fire is burning.

No matter which kind of fire you build, you must have a good supply of fuel. This will usually be wood, but dried animal dung can also be used if wood is not available, though it will not burn as well.

When you have finished with the fire and are leaving the site, leave as little trace as possible. Remove burnt remains of wood from around the fire, bury the ashes and level the ground. If you had to cut out an area of turf to make the fire, replace it before you leave.

TYPES OF COOKING FIRE

Camp fires have different purposes. Some are best used to give warmth, while others are better for cooking, with some of these suited to large-scale cooking and some for smaller pots. A pyramid fire, for example, is easy to build and good for warmth, but if you want to cook on a fire, you need to add some form of structure on which you can safely put cooking pots.

The reflector fire is one of the most complex and time-consuming to build, but it is an effective cooking fire and will cater well for groups using several large pans. It has a wall of wood or clay at one end, which reflects the heat back into the fire. It can be used for any method of cooking and is ideal for roasting food, such as meat or fish.

The hunter or trapper fire has a more basic structure and is most effective for boiling. It is made by placing two logs parallel to each other, about 30cm/12in apart but close enough for your pans to be balanced securely. Lay the fire in between the logs, starting with tinder, then adding kindling and finally the wood fuel. Make sure the logs cannot move either outwards or inwards, wedging them firmly in place with rocks if necessary.

If there is a strong wind, consider building a trench fire as this will shelter the flame below ground level. To build a trench fire, dig a trench 90cm/3ft long and 30cm/1ft wide, and line the base with a layer of rocks. Lay your fire on top, surrounded by a ring of rocks. Pans can be placed on top of the rocks,

---

BUILDING A REFLECTOR FIRE

1 If you are constructing the fire on an area of grass, remove the turf from an area about 1 x 0.75m/3 x 2ft. Store it for later replacement.

2 Lay a raft of dry, thick sticks across the cleared area to protect the fire from the damp soil beneath.

3 Drive two stout sticks into the ground leaning away from the fire and lay a wall of logs or strong sticks against these to form the reflector.

4 When you have completed the fireplace check that it is stable.

5 Place some dry kindling in the middle of the raft of wood. Set light to the kindling and add small twigs to get the fire going.

6 Once you have built up the fire and got it going, the wall at the back will reflect the heat back into the centre to give you more heat for cooking.

▲ *For a rock fire, build a circle of rocks or small boulders, placing the rocks securely so that there is no danger of them collapsing.*

▲ *A star fire is fuelled by pushing four long logs into the heat. Draw the logs back if you want to cook over the hot embers.*

- Never leave a lighted camp fire unattended. If a piece of burning wood were to fall off the fire it could burn your food or your equipment, and you cannot afford to lose either of these.
- Keep something to hand with which to extinguish the fire in an emergency, such as soil or sand.
- If there is a strong wind, use twice as much kindling and place the wood fuel on the downwind side of the fire.

or foods such as meat can be cooked on a spit constructed from whittled tree branches and positioned over the fire in the trench. Ideally, the trench should be angled so that the prevailing wind can blow down it to give a draught.

To create a rock fire, build a rock wall around the fire that is small enough to allow pans to be placed on it. Do not use rocks taken from riverbeds, as these can explode when small pockets of water in the rocks heat up and expand.

The star fire can be used for cooking, but it is better for warmth. Its main advantage is that you can keep moving the logs into the centre as they burn, so that you don't have to collect extra fuel while you rest or cook your food.

BUILDING A HUNTER OR TRAPPER FIRE

1 Choose a piece of bare ground or remove a piece of turf if your site is on grass. Lay two thick logs or tree branches on the ground, parallel to each other.

2 Start to place tinder between the logs. Tinder is the material you will be lighting first, so it must be very dry. You can use dry grass, bark or leaves.

3 Now place thin pieces of wood around the tinder as kindling, standing them upright and supporting each other in a pyramid shape.

4 When you have completed the basic fireplace, check that it is stable and that the surrounding area is clear of any items, such as kit, that may catch fire.

5 Set the tinder alight with a match or other firelighter. As it starts to burn, add more small twigs, balancing them around the pyramid structure.

6 As the twigs burn, add larger pieces of wood, then leave the fire to get established. Let the wood burn down before you start to cook.

TINDER AND KINDLING

To make a camp fire you need tinder and kindling as well as fuel. Tinder and kindling have separate functions. Tinder is used as a firestarter, to kick-start the burning of kindling, which in turn is used to ignite the fuel. Lighted kindling on its own could be used to light fuel, but setting the kindling alight first with tinder means that you need much less of a flame initially to start the camp fire fuel burning. This could be important in wet or humid conditions or where you are finding it difficult to light a flame.

Tinder

Any material can be used as tinder so long as it is highly combustible, and the best tinder will need only a spark to set it alight. Avoid using highly flammable materials such as aerosol spray cans, as these can explode when ignited and the explosion will be difficult to control.

If you know you will be building your own camp fire and you cannot guarantee the weather will be sunny and dry for the duration of your trip, it is a good idea to take your own tinder with you, storing it in a small waterproof container so that it doesn't get wet in a heavy shower. This will ensure that you always have a supply to hand whenever you need it.

SOURCES OF TINDER

- Silver birch bark
- Crushed dry, fallen tree leaves
- Crushed dry, fallen fir cones
- Dry, fallen pine needles
- Dry, fallen seed heads
- Short lengths of dried grass
- Any plant down
- Fine wood or bark shavings
- Bird down
- Dried, powdered fungi
- Short newspaper strips
- Short waxed paper strips
- Short strips of rubber car tyre
- Cotton wool
- Camera film
- Cotton fluff from clothing
- Charred natural fabric, such as cotton or silk

▲ *So long as it is absolutely dry, crisp leaf litter makes excellent kindling for a fire; pine needles and dry grass are alternatives.*

▲ *Twigs and small branches make ideal kindling providing they are dry. Break them into a manageable size before use.*

Manmade tinder materials can be bought from outdoor suppliers, but there are many natural materials that are readily available – free of charge – outdoors. Keep an eye out for new tinder supplies as you follow your route, even if you do not need them that day. If the weather is dry you can store the materials in a waterproof container until needed. In wet weather you can dry damp materials inside your tent or at the side of the camp fire – not so close that they catch fire – until they are dry enough to be stored.

Kindling

Materials used for kindling are types of wood. The best materials are small, dry twigs and sticks. The soft woods flare up quicker than hard woods (those that contain resin burn particularly well), but they can produce sparks and will burn very fast, which means that you may need more of them to light a large camp fire. Kindling should be bigger than tinder in order to encourage a high flame, but it should be smaller than the fuel wood, so that it can be packed between the pieces of fuel.

▲ *Pine cones can be used as fuel if dry, and are worth collecting if they are plentiful, but they do not burn particularly well.*

▲ *Dry bark found on the forest floor can be used as kindling. Do not strip bark from trees because it can cause considerable damage.*

FIRE STICKS

Firesticks are kindling that has been "feathered" to make it catch fire more quickly. To prepare a firestick from a dry twig, make small shallow cuts down the length of the twig with a knife. Then tease out the fronds so that they bend outwards to catch the flame more easily.

Avoid collecting kindling straight from the ground as it will be damp and will take longer to burn. Carry it with you in a waterproof container if possible; if you have to use damp wood as kindling, shave off the outside and use the inner part, which will be dry.

Using tinder and kindling

When your camp fire is ready to light, ignite the tinder using a match, lighter, artificial flint striker or traditional flint and steel. When it is burning, hold the tinder against the kindling. As the flame takes hold and rises, pack the kindling in between pieces of fuel wood on the camp fire, which should start to burn.

CHOOSING WOOD

If you are planning to use a camp fire to cook your meals, you will be relying significantly on wood as your fuel supply, so find out as much as you can about the burning properties of the wood available in the area before you travel. Know how to identify the wood you need, and make sure you are equipped with the right tools to deal with it.

Some woods, such as telegraph poles and treated fencing or building timbers, are dangerous to burn because they contain chemicals that give off a toxic smoke: do not use these even if you see them lying on the ground and are sure they are unwanted debris. Natural woods can also be unsuitable: bamboo can trap water in its stems, and this may explode when heated on the fire.

Different woods burn in different ways. Some burn faster than others and produce varying amounts of heat, making them particularly suited to different methods of cooking – those that burn quickly are better for boiling and those that burn slowly and give out a lot of heat are better for roasting. Knowing the character of your wood fuel will help you to use it in a more efficient way, reducing the quantity of fuel you need and the amount of time spent sourcing it. Be prepared to use different types of wood on your fire if you plan to boil some ingredients and roast others for the same meal.

Hard woods are generally regarded as the best woods for roasting or grilling foods because they burn hot and for a long time (avoid using willow unless it is very dry because it has a high water content and therefore burns poorly). Soft woods burn quickly, and for a shorter amount of time, and are best used for boiling.

Whatever the type of wood, it must be dead and well dried if it is to burn well (one exception is ash, which burns well whether it is dry or green). Wood picked from the ground will be damp, and this will burn with an unpleasant amount of smoke and not enough heat (the fire's energy is used up drying out the wood). Instead, look for dead wood that is caught up in branches: a vertical position means it will be drier.

HARD WOODS

▲ *Apple and cherry burn well and give off a pleasant and sweet smell. They grow in sunny areas of temperate climates.*

▲ *Holly is found in woodland areas in temperate and cold, dry climates. Holly and yew burn equally well whether green or dry.*

▲ *Narrow-leaved ash usually grows in wet temperate conditions so it will need to be well dried before it can be burned.*

▲ *The silver birch grows in mountainous regions of temperate climates. It lights easily and the bark makes good kindling.*

SOFT WOODS

▲ *Cedars and other coniferous trees make excellent kindling and good fire fuel, giving out a lot of heat.*

▲ *Horse chestnut is common to cooler temperate climates. Like all softwoods, it burns quickly and gives out a lot of light.*

▲ *Small-leaved lime is common to warm temperate and hot, dry climates. It is not easy to light but will give off a good heat.*

▲ *Cones from spruce and any other coniferous tree can be used as a fuel but will not burn with much of a flame.*

Useful Knots

The following knots have been found to be useful for life in the wilderness. It is a good idea to practise them so that they can be tied as second nature. They are designed to be tied with natural fibre rope, and may not be as successful with synthetic ropes.

FISHERMAN'S KNOT OR WATER KNOT
This is used to join two ends of a rope together to form a loop, such as a sling, or to tie two ropes of similar thickness together. It is not secure enough to be used for tying climbing ropes together, or any ropes that are to bear a heavy weight.

1 Lay the two lines parallel, tying an overhand knot with one end around the standing part of the other. Turn the half-completed knot end-for-end.

2 Tie an identical overhand knot with the other end. Pull first on both ends to tighten the knots, then on the standing parts to tighten the knot.

BOWLINE
This creates a non-slip knot in a rope. It can be used to make a loop at the end of a rope, or a waist loop for a climbing rope, when you do not have a climbing harness.

To make it more secure, once you have tied the knot, finish it off with two half hitches. It can become less secure if the rope is very stiff, or wet and slippery.

1 Bring the working end across the standing part of the rope to form an overhand loop.

2 Rotate the hand clockwise and so produce a smaller loop in the standing part of the rope.

3 Ensure that the working end points upwards, from back to front, through the smaller loop.

4 Lead the end behind the standing part, then tuck it back down through the small loop from front to back.

5 Arrange the bowline with a long end (longer than shown) and secure further, if necessary, with tape or a half hitch.

CLOVE HITCH

This can be used to suspend a light object at right angles to the suspension point or to tie a boat to a pole. The pull of the clove hitch must be steady, because the knot can work loose if it is not under tension. It can also jam if it becomes wet. If the knot has to last for any length of time, tie the two ends together to secure it more permanently.

1 Hold the rope in a straight line and make an overhand loop of any size at any convenient point in the line.

2 Add an underhand loop further along the line, so that there is now a pair of loops consisting of two opposing halves.

3 Arrange the two loops so that they are the same size and close together in the line of rope.

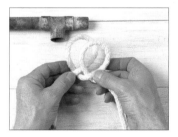

4 Rotate the two loops a little, at the same time, in opposite directions, in order to position them so that they overlap precisely.

5 Insert the rail, spar, rope or other foundation through both of the loops and pull on either one or both ends to tighten the resulting hitch.

ROUND TURN AND TWO HALF HITCHES

This is a strong and secure knot or hitch, which can be used to secure a rope to a pole or ring, tow a broken-down vehicle or secure the guy lines of a tent. It will even make a haulage knot for securing a load or climbing. Before you trust a heavy weight to the knot, check the condition of the rope: if it feels soft and amenable, it is worn out and should not be used.

1 Take a turn around the anchorage of the pole or ring and bring the working end alongside the standing part. Apply a single half hitch by tying an overhand knot with the working end of the rope.

2 Add an identical second half hitch and draw the two snugly together to complete this dependable knot.

REEF KNOT OR SQUARE KNOT

This knot does not jam and can easily be untied. It is used for tying together two ends of rope or, in a first aid situation, two ends of a triangular bandage or sling. It is strictly a binding knot, reliable only when pressed against something else or tied in both ends of the same material. If any strain on the knot comes from an angle, it can turn into a slipknot.

1 Bring two ends of rope together, left over right. Tie a half-knot: the two entwined parts will spiral to the left. Bring the ends together, right over left.

2 Tie a second half-knot. The two entwined parts will now spiral to the right, opposite to the first half-knot.

SHEEPSHANK

The sheepshank's main use is to take the slack out of a fixed rope or line. It can also be used to shorten a length of rope or to bridge a damaged section, but the rope must be kept under tension, otherwise the knot can come undone.

1 Fold the rope and fold it once again, shortening it as required, into a shallow S-shape with two loops.

2 Make an incomplete overhand knot – known as a marlinspike hitch – in one standing part.

3 Pull the adjacent loop through the marlinspike hitch in a locking tuck that goes over-under-over the rope.

4 Turn the half-finished knot end-for-end and make another marlinspike hitch in the other standing part.

5 Insert the remaining loop over-under-over, securing the hitch, then tighten both ends of the knot until they are snug. Ensure that the load falls equally on all three standing parts; if one is damaged, it must lie between the other two and be slightly slacker than them.

DOUBLE SHEET BEND

This knot is used to bind two ropes of different thicknesses, or where one or both ropes are made of wet or slippery material. Check that the ends of both ropes are on the same side of the knot, otherwise it will be unsafe.

1 Create a loop in the end of one of the ropes. Take the second rope and tuck it up through the loop. Bring the end beneath the loop in the first rope.

2 Tuck the working end beneath itself so that both short ends are located on the same side of the knot. Bring the working end around and beneath the loop and its own standing line once again, keeping it to the right of the original pass. Finally, tuck the end through alongside the initial tuck to complete the double knot.

PRUSIK KNOT

This slide-and-grip knot is used to attach a sling, strap or loop to a main rope in order to hoist or lower a weight. The sling is tied with a fisherman's knot to the main rope, which will need to be secured at each end. The main use of the Prusik knot is as a rescue knot for ascending or descending with a rope – for example, out of a crevasse. The knot allows the sling to be slipped up or down the main rope when not under strain, but will jam tightly if suddenly jerked or strained.

1 Make a loop with part of an endless sling and lay over a climbing rope. Bend over and down behind the rope.

2 Pass the standing part of the sling through the working loop.

3 Pull some slack out of the initial loop and take it up and over the climbing rope once more.

4 Take the working loop back down behind the climbing rope again.

5 Tuck the remainder of the standing part through the wrapped loop and tighten the knot.

SIMPLE SIMON OVER

This knot is good for general camping use. It is especially effective in slick synthetic lines and, once mastered, it can be tied easily. It has rarely appeared in print, but it merits being more widely known as it is a secure knot and a very useful one to have at your disposal when faced with tying slippery, synthetic lines in a howling gale out in the field.

 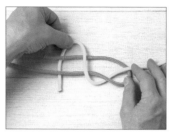 

1 Make a bight in one of the two lines to be joined. Bring the working end of the other line over it. Tuck the working end down through the bight.

2 Bring the working end out to the left (in this instance), then take it over both bight legs and, in a snaking "Z" track, back again beneath them.

3 Lay the end back over its preceeding part (the "over" of the knot name).

4 From the outside of the bight, tuck the working end up and through and finally lay it alongside its own standing part. Tighten, working the slack out.

SIMPLE SIMON UNDER

This is a variation of the Simple Simon Over knot, above. It is more secure than the Over knot and it will cope better with dissimilar cord sizes and textures. To make the Under knot, first complete steps 1 and 2 of the Over knot.

1 After bringing the working end of the line back beneath both bight legs, tuck it beneath its preceding part (the "under" of the knot name).

2 From the outside of the bight, tuck the working end up through and finally lay it alongside its own standing part. Slowly work the slack out of the knot.

VICE VERSA

Some intractable materials – such as wet and slimy leather thongs or bungee (elastic) shock cord – are difficult to keep in place and will slither out of other bends. The Vice Versa is one way to keep these kinds of rope lines securely in place. The various tucks and turns that make up this knot are the secret of its very reliable strength and security.

1 Lay the two lines to be joined parallel and together.

2 Take the working end of the line on the right-hand side and bring it beneath the other standing part.

3 Pass the end over the other line and then tuck it beneath itself.

4 Take the other working end on the left-hand side, passing over the first of the two lines. Now bring the second working end back beneath the other line and up past the front of the knot (with no tuck).

5 Cross the right-hand end over the left-hand end and tuck it through the left-hand loop alongside its own standing part. Similarly, take hold of what has become the right-hand end. Tuck the remaining working end through the right-hand loop alongside its own standing part. Gently pull on all four emerging lines at once to securely tighten this knot.

Using an Axe

Axes are useful for cutting down trees, removing branches and cutting up timber. As long as the axe is sharp and in good working order and you are aware of the dangers, accidents should not happen. Dress appropriately, with jackets and shirts fastened up to avoid them flapping around and getting caught, and wear strong footwear; do not wear open-toed sandals or bare feet.

Trees should never be felled or branches lopped unless you have the express permission of the landowner.

MAINTENANCE

Sharpen a blunt axe on a Carborundum stone, which can be used either wet or dry. Replace a split handle and check the axe head to see that the wedge is tightly fitted in and there are no chips out of the blade. After use, clean the blade and cover it before storing.

▼ *When cutting branches from the trunk of a tree, start from the base and work upwards (left); do not work downwards (right).*

▼ *When chopping a log, weaken the log with a V-shaped cut by first making one cut from the right and one from the left.*

▼ *When splitting a log in half, position the log to be cut on a large log to raise it off the ground, and secure the log to be split with your foot before you start to swing the axe.*

▲ *Carry an axe with the blade in the palm of your hand, facing outwards and away from your body in case you should fall over.*

CLOTHING

Make sure your clothes are neat as loose clothing could get caught as you swing the axe. Protect your feet with leather walking boots or walking shoes; you should not have bare feet or wear flip-flops or open-toed sandals.

PREPARATION

Before starting work, clear the area all around, including smaller overhead branches, or the axe may catch. Check that the ground you are standing on is firm and clear of obstacles. Make sure that nobody is within at least two axe-plus-arm lengths away from you. This is not just to avoid hitting someone but also to avoid wood chips flying up into their eyes as you chop.

CHOPPING DOWN A TREE

Decide where you want the tree to fall, and make a cut facing in that direction. On the other side of the tree, start to cut through the tree above the first cut. Remove any low branches that can be easily reached on the side away from the direction of fall, chopping parallel to the trunk rather than towards it. This should encourage the tree to fall

▲ *You should always wear stout footwear and close-fitting clothes when working with an axe or any other sharp tool.*

in the correct direction. When the tree is about to fall, shout "Timber!" and move to one side, so you will not be caught by the bottom of the tree swinging back or up. You can also use your axe for cutting and splitting the tree trunk into logs.

▼ *Make sure you have a clear area around you before starting to use an axe to chop logs, in case of any flying wood chips.*

Using a Saw

Saws can be used for any wood-cutting job, and they do not leave the same amount of wasteful wood chips and debris as an axe. A high level of safety is required, as with an axe, because a saw has the potential to be a highly dangerous instrument.

MAINTENANCE

Before use, check to see that the blade is tight in the handle and that the teeth are sharp. Check from time to time that the teeth are not becoming clogged with wood shavings or resin from the wood. After use, clean the blade to remove wood shavings, and pack it away clean and dry. Keep the saw well oiled or greased to prevent rust. When not in use, mask the blade, either by using a plastic clip or mask or by tying a length of robust sacking around the saw several times.

CLOTHING

Wear jackets and shirts buttoned up and generally avoid wearing loose items of clothing, as the teeth of a saw could easily catch in them. Sturdy gloves will protect your hands in the case of the saw slipping, and may make it easier to grip the wood; mittens restrict your fingers and will not give you a firm enough grip.

TRIMMING A TREE

A saw can be used for cutting up small timber and is ideal for trimming a tree before or after it has been felled. Trim

▼ *When felling a tree the first, lower cut needs to be made on the side on which you want the tree to fall.*

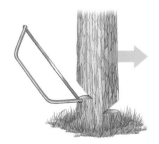

the tree from the bottom and work upwards. Hold the tree with a tight grip, keeping your fingers well away from the moving blade.

FELLING A TREE

Make the first cut in the direction you want the tree to fall, then make the second cut on the opposite side of the tree, above the first cut. Work slowly until the blade has made a good deep cut in the wood. If at any time you feel tired, stop for a break. If you are using a two-handed or two-person saw, put your main effort into the pull stroke.

▲ *Rest the timber you are cutting on a secure base and get someone to hold it if necessary: never try to saw on the ground.*

Once you are about a quarter of the way through, push above the saw cut to take the pressure off the blade. If the saw blade jams, do not force the blade out. If necessary, take the blade out of the saw handle and work it out slowly, using a little oil or grease.

▼ *When two people are using a saw together, each of them should only ever cut on the pull stroke.*

Striking Camp

When it comes to striking camp, it is important to have a proper system for dismantling everything so that everyone knows what they are doing. How complex the job is will depend on whether you are taking down a small overnight camp or a large base camp. The most important thing is to clear the campsite so as to leave no trace of your presence after you have gone.

OVERNIGHT CAMPS
If the weather is fine, dismantle your tent first and hang it up to air while you are dealing with everything else. Pack all the rest of your gear into your backpack, then fold up your tent and add it to your pack.

If it is raining, pack your backpack first, while you are inside your tent, then pack the tent and add it to your pack. Make sure you dry the tent at the earliest opportunity (see below). When

▼ *In a large camp set up a system and have somewhere where you can stow equipment and baggage that has already been packed.*

▲ *Ideally, pack the tent away when it is dry and clean. If you have to put it away wet, unpack it and dry it as soon as you can.*

you have finished packing, spend a little time walking around the site to see if anything has been left lying around before you depart.

BASE CAMPS
The size of this type of camp and the number of people concerned will make dismantling the camp a more complex operation. Make sure that everybody is involved and knows which jobs they

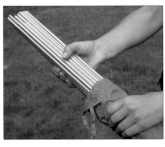

▲ *The tent poles should be counted and checked for any damage, then packed away in their own bag.*

have to do, and when. It is a good idea to keep one tent up until everything else is done, so that as you take the other tents down and pack up your cooking and other equipment, and any constructions such as clotheslines, you can put everything in this tent. If it rains, this will also stop all your kit getting wet. Alternatively, have a large groundsheet ready to spread over the kit that has been packed if the weather becomes stormy.

STRIKING TENTS
As with pitching tents, the way in which you take the tent down will depend on the type of tent, but there are some general rules that should be followed for all of them. If you are taking down a large tent, make sure there are enough people working with you to take it down safely, so that the tent is not damaged.

When you strike your tent you may need to pack it up while it is wet. If you leave it for more than a few days, however, a cotton tent may become mildewed and a synthetic tent can start to smell (its cotton inner will also become mildewed), so get it dried as soon as possible.

If the tent has a sewn-in groundsheet, clean the inner tent thoroughly then turn the inner tent over to make sure the groundsheet is dry and clean. If not, let it dry then clean the groundsheet with a cloth.

▲ *Clean all your pegs so that they are ready for use next time. Make sure none has been left in the ground before you go.*

Make sure all the tent pegs are clean and straight and ready for use next time, and that you have the right number. Also check that all the guy lines and pegging points are in working order and any zips are working.

When you have taken down the tent, make sure that all the different parts, such as poles and pegs, are together in their respective bags before packing them away in the main bag.

COOKING AREA

Make sure you fill in all the pits you have dug. If you have been using a fire, make sure it is out and that the fireplace has been filled in and the ground covering replaced.

TOILETS

If you have set up your own toilets, make sure that all waste products are well buried, holes or trenches are filled in and the ground cover is replaced. All screening materials, unless they are naturally growing in the area, should be removed.

If you have dug a latrine and used it for some time, mark the site before you go so that others following you will not use the same site.

WASTE

Either burn all the waste and bury the residue, or take it away with you. Never leave plastic bin liners full of waste at a site, as animals will quickly

rip them open, allowing the contents to blow away. If the animals try to eat the plastic, it can kill them.

Finally, it is a good idea to walk around the site once everything has been taken down and packed to see if any items of kit, any tent pegs or pieces of litter have been left lying about. There is nearly always something.

▲ *If the weather is dry and sunny, turn your groundsheet over to dry it off and clean it before packing up your tent. Pack your other equipment while it is airing.*

▼ *Make sure all your equipment is clean and dry before you pack it so that it is ready to use when you arrive at your next stopping place.*

NUTRITION
& FOOD

Whatever kind of expedition you are planning, food will play an important part in its success. If you are using up a lot of energy trekking, cycling or climbing, you will need hearty meals at the beginning and end of each day to keep up your strength, and communal cooking and eating in camp can be a great morale booster even in harsh conditions. Without the modern conveniences of refrigeration and hot water on tap, rigorous attention to food hygiene is vital.

Planning your Food

Carefully chosen rations are vital to the success of a trip, and it is important that everyone eats a balanced diet. At the planning stage you can decide what types of rations will be used and how they will be prepared at the camp and in the field, and find out about any special dietary requirements.

TYPES OF RATION

There are four different types of food you can eat when camping. These are fresh food, dry food, ready-to-eat meals in pouches and canned food. Their advantages and uses are described in detail on the following pages.

Unless you are travelling in the most arid and remote terrain, you are likely to use a combination of the various types of food during your trip – for instance, enlivening the dry food you take with you with fresh items bought locally. The different rations available will suit different stages of the trip:

▼ *Lightweight rations may be needed in the field. They should be easy to prepare and require the minimum of equipment.*

EATING HAPPILY

Cooking and eating is a central aspect of camp life, and it is important to make it as enjoyable as possible, even at times when the range of available food is limited.

• As well as asking about special dietary needs, try sending out a food preference form in advance so that people can tell you which foods they particularly like.

• Take some special luxury foods with you, including items that are group members' favourites. These can be brought out on a special occasion, such as reaching the expedition's goal or somebody's birthday, or at a difficult time when the party needs a lift.

• In transit, pre-packed picnic food or eating in cafés may be best.

• At camp, plenty of storage space, good cooking facilities and no need to carry the food mean that fresh and canned food may be eaten.

▲ *Try to include as much fresh food in your diet as possible when it's available and you have the means to prepare it.*

• When you are out in the field or on activities everything has to be carried on your back, and so dry and pouch meals are ideal.

Whatever type of food you use, always bear in mind that you are responsible for disposing of any waste, such as empty wrappers and cans.

PLANNING RATIONS

When planning your food, consider whether there are any constraints on the amount or type of food you are going to use during the trip, such as:
• weight
• bulk
• fuel
• the size of your party
• packaging
• cooking time
• ease of cooking
• cost

Will it be easy to buy local food during your journey? If so, this will help to make the packaged food you take more palatable; if not, you'll have to think harder about the flavourings and seasonings you can carry with you.

When you are planning your menus, don't forget to choose food that you and the other members of the group actually like: don't take anything you wouldn't normally eat just because it is in freeze-dried or pouch form – if you don't eat it at home, it won't seem any more appealing in camp.

SPECIAL REQUIREMENTS

Check in advance with all the members of your party in case anyone has specific dietary needs that will affect your catering plans. If anybody going on the trip has special requirements due to food intolerance or allergies, moral or religious beliefs, it is important that you know this at the planning stage so that you can accommodate their needs.

FOOD BUDGETS

Work out the food budget for your trip by basing it on a figure per person per day and adding an amount for contingency. You will need to arrive at this figure through a combination of educated guesswork and thorough research about your destination; running out of money for food would be disastrous, so the food budget needs to be as accurate as possible.

If you are cooking for a large number of people you will benefit from economies of scale. Bear in mind, too, that food costs will be lower in developing countries than in the developed world. Your food budget will need to be higher if you are a small group, and much higher if you are expecting to eat some of your meals in cafés and restaurants.

FOOD PACKING

If you decide that you are going to use pre-packed rations, make sure they contain everything you will need for the length of time covered by the ration. Apart from the food itself, each package should include toilet paper, a can opener (if cans are included), matches, salt and cooking instructions for everything in the package.

If you are planning a large and complex expedition involving different camps and locations, it is a good idea to mark all the food packages clearly before you leave, to make sure that the right rations go to the right locations. Again, make sure you include any utensils needed to use the food, such as a can opener, in the package destined for each location.

Use a simple marking system that everyone will understand without needing to refer to you – in case you

are not around when they are being loaded on to your transport. Be careful of colour coding as some people are colour blind.

Try to keep packaging materials to a minimum, as you will have to find a way of disposing of them when you have used the contents. Make sure the package is secure, but don't make it too hard to get into as there is nothing worse, after a hard day, than having to fight to get at your food.

If food is going to be carried on the back of a pack animal you may need to pad any sharp corners of boxes or containers. If your rations are to be carried in a vehicle they will need to be packed to withstand jolting in transit, especially on unmade roads.

IMPORTING FOOD

If you are travelling overseas you may be thinking of carrying food from your own country with you, possibly in advance of your arrival. Before doing so, it is worth finding out about any import regulations and restrictions, and the costs this will entail. You may find that carrying food with you rather than sending it to your destination in bulk is a cheaper and easier option.

▼ *Pasta is a good filler: light to carry and quick to cook, it is a nourishing source of carbohydrate.*

▼ *Chocolate is just one of a range of favourite foods that can be carried as a luxury item and given out as a treat.*

▼ *Food supplies for a large expedition need to be clearly labelled before the packing begins to make sure that they are transported to the correct destination.*

Local Foods

One of the most enjoyable aspects of travel is being able to sample the foods of the country you are visiting, but food can carry disease and it is important to make sure that eating local foods, either served in restaurants or prepared at your campsite, does not make you ill and spoil your trip.

AVOIDING FOOD POISONING

Whether you are at home or abroad, it's important to eat fresh food that has been properly cooked, but whatever the quality of the food it can be contaminated from external sources, such as dirty water, dirty hands or flies.

In many countries the mains water is not reliably clean, so it is best to avoid uncooked food such as salads, which may have been washed in it. Avoid ice cubes in drinks and if you have doubts about the cleanliness of plates and glasses, drink from the bottle through a straw and leave the bottom layer of food on the plate.

Make sure you wash your own hands scrupulously before preparing food or eating with your fingers and avoid food handled by others who you feel may not have been so thorough. Flies may

▼ *Eating local food is an exciting part of the whole experience of travel, but make sure you only eat well-cooked dishes.*

settle on food that is left standing on buffets, and chutneys or sauces left open on the table are especially likely to be contaminated.

EATING OUT

Try to find out where the local people eat, as these places will almost certainly offer the best-value food, and they will give you an authentic introduction to local cuisine and culture. In popular, busy restaurants the ingredients are more likely to be completely fresh and cooked dishes won't stand around waiting to be eaten.

In countries with unreliable food hygiene standards the locals' stomachs may be stronger than yours. If they eat from stalls beside the road or in market places, which may not be hygienic, you should be wary of following their example, as the food could give you diarrhoea or dysentery. For the same reason, avoid buying any cold food displayed in shops, and eat only ice creams sold sealed in packaging and made by well-known firms.

When eating in local restaurants, ask to watch the food being cooked and ask for yours to be cooked well. Be careful of shellfish and meat, which may have gone off before being cooked. Shellfish are especially risky as they may contain concentrations of

▲ *Be careful of food that is on open display in restaurants; choose popular places where the dishes are unlikely to hang around long enough to be contaminated.*

toxins. Ideally, eat only those shellfish that you have seen alive before they go into the cooking pot.

AVAILABILITY AND PRICES OF LOCAL FOODS

Unless you are taking all your food with you, you will need some idea of what types of food you can buy in the area you are going to and what are the local delicacies, as well as the prices. This information can be obtained either on a reconnaissance trip from a local contact or from an up-to-date guidebook. The price of seasonal foods may fluctuate, but you will at least have a general idea.

COOKING LOCAL FOODS

Fresh vegetables, salad ingredients and fruit need to be well washed in a weak solution of antiseptic and then rinsed in purified water before they are eaten. If you don't have time for this process – for example, if you want to snack on

▲ *In hot countries all fresh food – such as fish and meat – should be cooked and eaten on the day it is bought.*

a piece of fruit while visiting a local market – choose a piece of fruit that you can peel before you eat it and make sure the peel is intact before you buy. Make sure your hands are clean when you peel it.

Avoid watermelon and watercress in countries where food hygiene is suspect, as both of these foods contain large amounts of water and can make you very ill if they have been grown under conditions of poor hygiene.

OBSERVING LOCAL CUSTOMS
If you are lucky enough to be invited to eat with local people, make sure you understand the customs of the region. In some countries it is important to use only the right hand to handle your food, as the left is considered unclean; in others you may cause offence by showing your hosts, or the people you are eating with, the soles of your feet, so you should keep them flat on the floor or tuck them under you if you are sitting on the floor. You may find that if you eat everything on your plate it will immediately be filled again, or your host may serve you with particular delicacies which it would be impolite to refuse, even if you don't like the

look of them. As a tourist, it is up to you to find out which rules of etiquette apply in the region you are visiting, and to observe them.

DIET RESTRICTIONS
Your research when planning your trip will highlight any dietary restrictions that apply at your destination, but if you have specific dietary needs, especially if these are for health reasons, you should make a point of finding out specific information and asking direct questions. In some parts of the world, eating strictly vegetarian meals may be difficult, especially when eating in cafés and restaurants. Foods produced for vegans can be even more difficult to find in some countries, as will, for example, organic, gluten-free or diabetic foods. In other parts of the world, vegetarian food will be the only option. Other foods, especially different types of meat, will have taboos attached to them in different parts of the world, usually for religious reasons.

DRINKS
Tea and coffee, which require water to be boiled, are safe to drink, but you should stay away from unpasteurized milk, non-bottled water and locally made cold drinks. It is safest to stick to brands that are internationally recognized, and to make sure that the

seal on the bottle or can is unbroken when you buy the drink.

Alcohol will not be openly available in many countries because it is against the prevailing religion or local customs. In some of the more extreme regimes, it can be a criminal offence to drink or be in possession of alcohol. If you arrive at the border of such countries with alcohol in your baggage, it can be confiscated and you can be fined or refused entry into the country.

▲ *Unpasteurized milk may carry harmful bacteria and should be avoided in areas where hygiene standards are unreliable.*

Dry Foods

The main advantage of dry foods is their lack of weight, especially if you have to carry large amounts of food on your back. The taste, however, is not as pleasant as that of fresh or tinned food, or even pouch meals, so they may require some extra ingredients to make them palatable.

Despite being lightweight, these meals do require hot water to rehydrate them. If you plan to cook over a wood fire, with a water source nearby, then you will need only a pan, but if these options are not available, you will need a stove, water and a pan, plus fuel, all of which are heavy items.

There are two types of dry food: air-dried and freeze-dried. As with all food, you get what you pay for. You can cut the cost by buying in bulk and packing individual portions in small, well-sealed plastic bags. If you do this, make sure the contents of the bulk container are well mixed up first.

AIR-DRIED FOOD

The food is placed in a drum and the moisture is removed by passing hot air through it. This system has been used for many years and is very simple, but it does tend to destroy the cell structure of the food, so that when it is reconstituted it tends to be rather mushy. In addition to changing the texture of the food, it can also affect the taste adversely.

FREEZE-DRIED FOOD

This newer, more expensive, process can be used to prepare both fresh and cooked food. The food is flash frozen, which means that it is frozen very rapidly so the water in it forms ice crystals. The food is then put into a vacuum at very low temperatures and the ice crystals are drawn off as water vapour. When reconstituted, the results look and taste far more like the original.

IMPROVING THE TASTE

It is a good idea for people to sample any dried food you intend using on your expedition to find out the best way to cook it and to see if the tastes are acceptable. Adding spices or fresh foods, such as onions or other vegetables, will improve the flavour.

If you have time, allow the dried food to soak for some time before you start to cook it. Also use more water than the manufacturer's instructions suggest, to ensure that the food is properly rehydrated. Make sure you cover the pan while the food is soaking, so that nothing is able to fall or crawl in before you start cooking.

You may be able to vary your diet by eating dried fruit and even dried meat and fish, depending on the country. Wash these thoroughly before you use them, and be wary of any that are not packaged.

▲ *If there is time before the meal, add water to the dried food and leave it to soak for a while before starting the cooking process.*

HEALTH CONCERNS

If you are living almost totally on reconstituted dry food, you may begin to suffer from constipation. Include plenty of dried fruit in your diet to help avoid this, and drink plenty of water. Also, if you are going to use this type of food almost exclusively for a long time, you may need to take some sort of mineral supplement to create a balanced diet.

If you are short of water, never be tempted to eat dried foods that have not been reconstituted, as they will use up body fluids that you cannot afford to lose.

PREPARING DRY FOODS

1 Empty the packet of dried food into a cooking pot and give it a stir to break up any lumps.

2 Add clean water and leave to soak if possible. You will need more water and longer cooking times at high altitudes.

3 Cook over a gentle heat, stirring, to avoid scorching. Cook thoroughly to allow time for complete rehydration.

Canned and Pouch Foods

Cans and foil pouches offer many of the same advantages: the food is of fairly high quality, it can be eaten cold if necessary, and it has a long life. Pouch meals have now taken the place of cans in military rations, where their reduced weight is a great advantage.

CANNED FOOD

The advantage of this form of processing is that it is suitable for almost any food, and, unless the can is punctured, it should be edible. If, however, the can is bulging, it means that bacteria are at work and it should be thrown away. Most canned food now comes with a sell-by date on it. The food is usually already cooked

so it can be eaten cold straight from the can in an emergency, though it usually tastes better heated. Vegetables and fruit usually come in their own syrup or brine and will require less water in the cooking process, but the weight of the liquid adds to your load.

Although many cans have a ring pull, these can snap off, so everyone should have a can opener. Write the contents on the cans with a permanent marker pen, so that if the label comes off, you know whether you have rice pudding or stew for supper.

When you have eaten the food, you should either take the empty cans with you or burn them first and then bury them at least 90cm/3ft underground.

POUCH FOOD

The main advantage of these ready meals is that they can just be dropped into boiling water and left for 10–15 minutes to heat, then taken out, torn open and either eaten straight from the pouch or poured on to a plate. As with cans, pouch food can be eaten cold in an emergency because the food is already cooked.

Further advantages are that more than one kind of meal can be prepared at the same time in the same pan, and

◀ A number of companies offer chemical heating units that can be used to heat both canned and pouch food in an emergency.

portion control is easy because most pouches contain one portion. Finally, when you have finished cooking, there are no dirty pans to wash up.

The main drawbacks are that the pouches are not as strong as cans and usually have to have an outer case or covering to protect them from being punctured. Also, at present, most of the meals packaged in this way are stews and casseroles, which can be rather monotonous, though more varieties are coming on to the market every year. Finally, this kind of food is probably the most expensive to buy.

▼ If you intend to use canned food extensively, make sure everyone on the expedition has a can opener.

PREPARING POUCH FOOD

1 Fill a pan large enough to hold the pouch with water and bring it to the boil on the stove.

2 When the water is boiling, drop in the pouch and boil for 10–15 minutes. Several pouches can be heated at once.

3 Either eat the food from the pouch or pour the contents into a bowl. Be careful, as the pouch will be very hot.

Packing your Food

Well-prepared rations will be carefully packed and clearly labelled, with full instructions for their use included in the package. The contents will vary depending on the climate, the type of activity being undertaken and the method of transport. All packaging should be as lightweight as possible, but the food should be packed securely so that it is not crushed and stays dry and free from contamination.

PREPARING RATIONS

The food you are going to use on the expedition will come in its own packaging, and you will have to decide whether to keep it in this or repack it in special ration packs, perhaps with a set menu for each day. If you decide to dispense with the original packaging, remember to keep the cooking instructions and details of any special storage conditions. If cans are included, include a can opener in the package. You may also need to add such items as toilet paper, salt, pepper and matches.

You may need to pack some rations for specialized uses, such as high-altitude or lightweight rations. Make sure these are clearly marked in a way that will be understood by everybody, or you could end up with the wrong rations going to the wrong place.

RATION PACKS

- The ideal ration pack should be self-contained for the period it is designed to cover.
- The ration pack should include clear instructions on how to cook all the food in the pack.
- It should be packed in suitable packaging to withstand the climatic and travelling conditions it will be exposed to.
- The pack should be easy to get into and use.
- The contents, or the type of ration, should be marked on the outside of the pack in a way that is easily read and understood.

FOOD CONTAINERS

If you are carrying a small amount of food for a weekend backpacking trip, use a series of rigid plastic resealable containers, which will keep the food away from the rest of your kit and protect it from being crushed or soaked, or from coming into contact with stove fuel and so on. Such items as washing-up liquid and cooking oil can be carried in small plastic bottles with screw tops.

Make sure the food containers you choose have tight-fitting, airtight lids to help keep the food fresh. If you buy them in graduated sizes they can be stored neatly inside each other

▶ *Whenever possible, buy fresh fruit and vegetables locally to supplement your pre-packed rations.*

▲ *Double-check your rations, as when you next open the packages you may not be in a position to make any additions.*

when not full of food. Buying them in different colours may be helpful, to give you some idea of what is inside each container, but make sure all food

containers are well labelled with the contents. Keep cooked and raw meats in separate containers, well apart to prevent cross-contamination, and in camp make sure they are covered at all times to prevent flies settling on them. Never leave any food containers open when you are camping or you could attract animals or insects to your food. Keep food containers out of the sun and packed away when not in use.

PACKING RATIONS

Your mode of transport will be a major factor in deciding how much weight and volume you can carry and how you will pack the food.

If you are going to carry all your food in a vehicle, weight will be a relatively unimportant factor and it should not be difficult to keep your food stores dry. However, if you are intending to travel on dirt roads, the way you pack your food will be important: it needs to be kept well away from fuel in a strong box, which is securely wedged in so it will not jump about in the vehicle.

If you are travelling with one or more pack animals, both the weight and the method of packing will be important to ensure that the animal is not overloaded or unevenly loaded. Any packaging with sharp edges will need to be well padded to stop it

FOOD SAFETY

- Check all canned and pouch food before you pack it to make sure that the containers are sound and unpunctured.
- Check the sell-by dates of pre-packaged food.
- Make sure all your food containers have airtight, close-fitting lids with no splits.
- Never pack raw meat or fish in a way that would allow it to cross-contaminate cooked food.
- If you buy fresh food in hot countries, don't store it at all: cook it on the day you buy it.
- Do not store any food in direct sunlight or on the ground.

CARRYING WATER

Water is a heavyweight item, but it is vital to carry enough at all times, and there are many types of water carrier on the market.

- If you use water bags, make sure they are well protected from sharp objects or rubbing, as either may cause the bags to leak.
- Check for leaks in the bags at the end of each day's travel.
- If you need to purify your water, mark each container as it is purified. You can do this using a piece of coloured cord or tape tied to the handle.
- If you are using a lot of jerry cans to carry water, number them so that you can keep track of how many you have used and use the cans in sequence.
- If you use canvas water bags you can keep your water cool by hanging them outside your vehicle or on the side of pack animals. This is due to the evaporation of water from the walls of the bag.

▼ *Collapsible water containers are useful but after a lot of use they may eventually split along the folds. Check older ones for leaks before you use them.*

▼ *Water bags are available in all sizes and when not in use they take up very little space, but they can be punctured when full if not treated with care.*

rubbing the animal's skin and developing sores. If you are carrying food in a canoe or kayak, you will need to make sure it stays dry and the space available will be limited. Pack food inside waterproof containers and wedge or strap them tightly into the boat. When backpacking, weight will be the most important factor, and you need to adopt the principles of lightweight camping.

▶ *Plastic containers will keep food safe from water and insects.*

Planning your Outdoor Kitchen

If you are a lightweight camper, your kitchen will be little more than a fire or stove sited a little way from your tent. If you are establishing a camp on one site for more than a week, however, it will be worth planning the layout of your camp kitchen, and you may even want to build some simple structures to make your life easier.

ESTABLISHING THE COOKING AREA

The first thing to do is to fence the cooking area off in some way so that people cannot just wander through it unawares and get in the way of the cook. If there are children in the camp you may want some way of deterring them from getting too near the stove or helping themselves to the food while you are preparing it. Your store tent and woodpile, and any structures you build for the kitchen area, will all help to establish its boundaries.

Next, choose where you are going to put your cooking site, be this a stove or fire. If there is a suitable natural feature such as a flat rock, use this as your base; otherwise, if you can, build a framework off the ground as the base for the fire, so that when you are cooking you will not have to bend over all the time. Make sure this framework is substantial and will not wobble or

collapse once you have built the fire and loaded it with cooking pots. Allow some space for the cooks to stand. If you are using a fire, keep the woodpile well stocked, but make sure it is kept tidy, as leaving pieces of wood around could cause people to trip over them.

You will need to put your store tent near the cooking area, but don't have it so near that it gets in the way of the people doing the cooking.

PROTECTING THE KITCHEN

You may choose to build one or two structures in the kitchen area to keep eating and cooking equipment off the ground. If you construct a simple table you can use it to prepare all your food and also as a serving area, and some form of dresser will keep the cooking equipment tidy and help to demarcate the kitchen area. If your campsite has trees growing around it, they

◀ *In a long-term base camp the kitchen will be easier to organize if you can set up some kind of dresser to keep all your cooking equipment together and off the ground.*

▲ *A safe cooking fire is spacious and well thought out. Large timbers around the fire provide both a safety barrier and seating.*

can be useful in several ways, though you should not build your fire or site your stove too close to them. Leafy trees will provide shade for keeping food cool, and in a hot climate they will also offer welcome shade for the cook, to offset the heat of the fire. You can also use any branches within reach as racks on which to hang utensils, mugs and food. It makes sense to store as much off the ground as you can, to keep things clean and make them easier to find, and to clear the area where you are preparing food.

THE EATING AREA

In a large camp it's a good idea to establish a designated eating area to help keep the rest of the site tidy and free of food debris. If you are in a place where it rains regularly, you might consider it a good idea to have a shelter over both your fire and the eating area. Discourage people from eating in their tents as crumbs and spilt food may act as a lure for animals later on. You will need to dig two waste pits near the kitchen (see the section Base Camps) or have two bags, one for dry waste and one for wet waste. Insist that everyone disposes of all waste responsibly.

▲ *A mug tree is useful for keeping mugs clean and organized. On a campsite it can be the branch of an actual tree.*

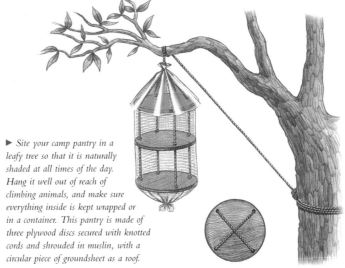

▶ *Site your camp pantry in a leafy tree so that it is naturally shaded at all times of the day. Hang it well out of reach of climbing animals, and make sure everything inside is kept wrapped or in a container. This pantry is made of three plywood discs secured with knotted cords and shrouded in muslin, with a circular piece of groundsheet as a roof.*

THE CAMP PANTRY

If you have a store tent, all dry and packaged food can be kept in it, but fresh food will need to be kept as cool as possible. For this you can use a hanging camp pantry. You can buy these in various styles, but you can also make one with a few pieces of wood, a length of muslin (cheesecloth) or nylon mesh, and some cord. Hang the pantry from a rope slung over the

▼ *By constructing a fire or stove stand you will save yourself a lot of bending down, but you must make sure that it is very stable and will not collapse when loaded with fuel and heavy cooking pots.*

branch of a large tree and make sure it stays in the shade for as much of the day as possible. Any food that you keep inside it should be well wrapped up or packed in an airtight container.

BEAR BAGGING

In case the camp is visited by animals attracted by the smell of your fresh food, the pantry and any other bags containing food should be hung far enough away from the trunk of the tree to prevent them climbing to get to it. This is particularly important if you are camping in bear country. Unless you can hang your food around 4m/13ft high and 3m/10ft away from the trunk you may lose it all to a hungry bear. You should also hang food downwind of your camp so that if any bears do want to investigate it they don't need to pass you to get to it. To rig up your bag or pantry, weight the end of a rope with a small rock tied into a bag and toss it over a high branch, keeping hold of the other end. Lower the rope until you can reach the rock, which you can discard. Tie your food bag

to one end of the rope and use the other end to haul it up to a suitable height. Make the end of the rope fast around the tree trunk.

If you are camping in an area with no trees, this arrangement will not be an option for you. In this case, try to avoid the need to store fresh food at all by taking dehydrated, pouch or canned food supplies instead. If you do have to keep fresh food at ground level, use thick double wrapping to mask the smell of the food, and avoid any particularly smelly foods if you don't want to risk attracting animals to your camp. Pack the food in sealable plastic containers and don't keep it inside or around your sleeping tent.

▼ *Empty food cans should be cleaned out or burned, then squashed and taken away from the site when you leave, or buried at least 90cm/3ft underground.*

Food Hygiene and Storage

You will be faced with many hazards in the wild, so the last thing you should do is add to them by failing to practise sound food hygiene. If you are part of a group, bear in mind that everyone's health depends on the whole group taking equal care in this respect. If any members of an expedition do not follow the basic rules of food safety, they risk causing bouts of diarrhoea or even a serious case of food poisoning.

FOOD PREPARATION
Make sure that anybody preparing or cooking food washes their hands

▼ *You should have separate chopping boards for different types of food to prevent any cross-contamination.*

▲ *Be scrupulous about washing your hands before you start to prepare food, whether it is to be eaten raw or cooked.*

▲ *All the plates, cups and bowls from which you eat should be properly washed in hot water after each use.*

frequently. Keep raw and cooked foods separate during preparation, and, if possible, use different chopping boards and utensils for each type. If you cannot do this, make sure they are thoroughly washed before changing from one type of food to the other. For more advice on the preparation of food, see the section Local Foods.

CLEANLINESS
Cooking pans, plates, cups and cutlery must be washed thoroughly in hot water after each meal, and with antiseptic added to the water every three or four days, if possible. To cut down the possibility of spreading infection, each person should use only their own eating equipment and drink from their own mug or water bottle.

In a base camp or semi-permanent camp kitchen, use an antibacterial fluid to clean all working surfaces and utensils at least every three or four days. In hot climates this

▲ *Make sure all your cooking equipment is thoroughly cleaned and disinfect everything every three or four days.*

should be done every day. Make sure that all dishcloths and drying towels are washed regularly.

Check that wooden cooking utensils are kept clean and in good condition. If they get chipped or badly scored, discard them and buy new ones as they are likely to harbour germs.

SERVING FOOD
Well-cooked, piping hot food will be safe to eat, but if it is left to sit around at a lower temperature, bacteria will start to multiply. For this reason, if you are going to serve a lot of people, call them before you take the food off the fire, so that it is still very hot when it reaches their plates.

Serve each dish using a different spoon, if possible, and clean up any

◀ *Specialized lightweight equipment is excellent for backpacking expeditions but may not be robust enough for use in a larger base camp.*

▲ *Although it is bulky, a large plastic bowl for washing dishes will be useful in camp.*

▲ *Collapsible mesh covers are invaluable for keeping flies off dishes of food.*

▲ *A weighted fabric cover can be used to protect dishes of all sizes from flies.*

spillages as soon as they happen. If you have to touch any prepared foods – including bread – wash your hands first: this applies whether you are serving it or picking it up to eat.

Finally, keep all food covered until you are ready to serve it, and, if the food is cold, get it ready and serve it in the shade.

DRY FOOD STORAGE

All items should be stored in a cool, dry, well-ventilated place, raised off the ground. Try to make sure your storage is bird- and rodent-proof and never leave food containers open. If you do not have a lid for a pot use a piece of muslin (cheesecloth) to cover it.

▼ *Proper serving implements, such as ladles and large spoons, are essential if you are catering for a large camp.*

No food should be kept in a sleeping tent at a base camp. If you are on a lightweight camping trip this is less easy to arrange, but you should pack all your food away in containers or put it in your backpack.

If you buy dried fish or meat from local traders in tropical countries, make sure you wash it well before eating it. It may well have been dried out in the sun, which will have allowed flies and other insects to settle on it.

FRESH AND COOKED FOOD STORAGE

Unless you are cooking in a semi-permanent base camp and have some form of refrigeration or effective cool boxes, do not keep either fresh or cooked foods for long periods, and never for more than 24 hours in a hot country. Keep all food out of the sun

and covered with muslin to keep flies away, and never store cooked and uncooked food together.

If you are camping within reach of local markets or food producers, try and buy all your fresh food daily, then you can cook it straight away and storing it will not be a problem.

As an alternative to going to the market, you may have local traders coming to your camp or base. If you want to use this arrangement, make sure you stipulate a time and place, as you will not want a succession of people turning up throughout the day trying to sell you food.

If you can, try to spread your purchases around a number of different traders when you are visiting a Third World country. Your money will make a big difference to small farmers and traders in the locality.

SERVING MEALS

- As well as the cooks, people serving food must have the highest standards of cleanliness, both personally and with the equipment they are using.
- Serving food should not be a free-for-all. Either ask everyone to sit down and serve them where they are going to eat or get them to queue up so that you can serve the food on to their plates: don't let them use their own spoons.
- Make sure all your serving equipment is clean and you use a separate implement for each pan.

Cooking over a Fire

Most cooking is more successful when it is done on a good bed of hot embers rather than over a fire with lots of flames. So this means preparing the fire by burning a good amount of fuel until it has died down to a bed of embers, then placing your pots safely either directly on the fire or on its surrounds.

HEAVY-DUTY POTS
Use heavy-duty cooking pots when cooking on a fire. If your pots and pans are too thin and flimsy they will not heat evenly and the food inside is likely to burn. The fire may also damage the cooking pots themselves, especially if you are cooking directly on the fire. If you have constructed a structure to support the pots (see the section Camp Fires), they will be exposed to less intense heat.

Have a padded oven glove or something similar to lift pots off the fire, as the handles may become very hot. Be careful when lifting pots on or off the fire that you do not get smoke in your eyes, as this could lead you to drop the pot.

If a pot is extremely heavy, use two people to lift it off the fire and warn others in the cooking area to get out of the way while you are doing so.

PROTECTING COOKWARE

If planning to cook on open fires, coat the outside of cooking pots with a paste made up of washing powder and water, and allow it to dry before putting the pots on the fire. When you come to wash the pots, this coating will wash off with the layer of soot on it.

▲ *Make sure the pot is completely stable when you put it on the fire, and will not fall over during cooking.*

You may lift the pot by pushing a stick through the handle with one person on each side, but if you use this method make sure the stick is strong enough and will not break when the full weight of the pan and contents is brought to bear.

On a windy day, be careful that ash from the fire does not blow into your cooking pots or food.

PLANNING COOKING TIMES
Before you start cooking, think about the way you are going to use the fire: for instance, you may need access to the hottest part of the fire to grill some meat, while pots are simmering gently over a cooler part, so make sure you can reach everything easily. If you are cooking a meal with a number of different elements, consider which foods will take longest to cook, and start with these.

If you want to cook a number of dishes all at the same time, and have enough people, you can make one person responsible for each dish, making sure it is ready on time and does not burn.

KEEPING EMBERS HOT
Once you have constructed your fire (see the section Camp Fires), and it is burning, don't forget it while you are cooking. If the bed of embers starts to cool down, you may have to stop cooking and burn some more wood. Since stopping the cooking process is

▼ *When you put a pan on the fire, try to arrange the handle so that it is shielded from the fiercest heat.*

▶ *Woodland will supply shelter and fuel for your camp fire, but be careful to choose a site for the fire that is not too near the trees.*

rarely ideal, a better solution is to use part of your fire, where you have the bed of embers, for cooking, and keep a wood-burning fire stoked on another part to create a steady supply of hot embers that you can rake across when you need them.

Make sure you have a good supply of wood for the fire, as you will not want to have to hunt for more wood halfway through cooking a meal.

CAMP OVEN
If you have a camp oven, place it at one end of the fire and bank earth or sand around it to make it secure and keep it at a constant temperature. The door should face away from the fire so that food can be put in and taken out easily and safely.

Remember that, as in most ovens, the temperature will be higher in the upper part than in the bottom. You do not want fire directly under the oven, as this can turn the bottom of the oven into a hot plate and cause anything left on this to burn.

▼ *Let the fire die down to a bed of glowing, ash-covered embers before cooking on it, so that food cooks rather than burns.*

COOKING IN THE CAMP FIRE
It can be great fun to cook a meal using the minimum of utensils, though this is not usually practicable if you are catering for a large number of people. With this type of cooking it is particularly important to have a good bed of embers and no flame on your cooking fire. You can use aluminium foil to keep food moist and protect it from burning on the outside, and from getting covered with ash.

You need to make sure that everything is cooked thoroughly when using this method. One secret is to cut everything into fairly small pieces or thin slices. If you are using ingredients such as potatoes or apples, try to cut them into pieces that are all of roughly the same size, so they cook evenly.

Be careful not to burn yourself when putting things on the fire, or taking them off.

FIRE SAFETY
Make sure everyone using the camp fire follows these rules:
• Site the fire well away from trees and other vegetation.
• Never throw wood on a fire, but place it on gently.
• Always have water available in case you need to put it out.
• Never allow people to mess about around a fire, especially when it is being used for cooking.
• Keep the area around the fire clean and tidy.
• Keep the woodpile well clear of the fire.
• If you have pans of water or food on a fire make sure someone is looking after them.
• Use an oven glove or padded glove to take pans off the fire.

Cooking on Stoves

If you are going to use a stove for cooking, you will need to decide how many burners you need, or even how many stoves if the party is a big one. A single-burner stove will be the lightest to carry, but meals will be limited and slow to prepare.

USING STOVES SAFELY
Make sure you always operate a stove of any kind in a well-ventilated area and never store any fuel in or near a sleeping tent. This is especially important if you are using a gas stove. Never change a gas cylinder in a confined space or near a naked flame. If you need to remove it to dismantle the stove, leave it to cool first then take off the cylinder quickly and check that it has sealed itself and is not leaking.

A stove will not burn as hot as a fire, so you can use much lighter pans on it. If the stove is burning on full power,

▲ *Always set up your stove on a flat, stable surface to ensure that it will not tip over while it is in use.*

▲ *In windy conditions use a windshield, either a purpose-made one or something like a log, a rock or another piece of equipment.*

USING A GAS STOVE

1 Outside (not in a confined area) attach the gas cylinder to the burner.

2 Light the stove by turning on the gas and applying a flame.

3 Let the stove cool if dismantling it, and remove the cylinder quickly.

USING A METHYLATED SPIRIT STOVE

1 Assemble the stove and place it on a flat, level surface. Fill the burner.

2 Carefully light the methylated spirit (methyl alcohol).

3 Extinguish the flame by placing the screw top over the burner.

however, the food may still burn if you don't watch it carefully.

If it is very windy, either use your stove's windshield or improvise one using something from your kit or natural materials such as logs. Make sure you don't position anything so close to the stove that it catches light.

When you have finished cooking, turn the stove off. If you need to dismantle it, let it cool down before doing so, and give it a good clean

▼ *A double-burner gas stove is a more efficient way to cater for a large group.*

before packing it away. If it requires special tools to maintain it, make sure they are packed with the stove for easy access when you need them.

COOKING ON A SINGLE-BURNER STOVE

If you are backpacking and have just a single-burner stove, you will have to plan your cooking carefully, as you will not be able to cook anything that requires more than one pan per course.

Before you start cooking, make sure that your stove is in good working order with plenty of fuel. To avoid wasting any fuel, do all the food preparation before lighting the stove. Once the pan is on top, the stove may become top-heavy and unstable, so do not leave it unattended.

COOKING ON A MULTI-BURNER STOVE

If you are cooking on a multi-burner stove, perhaps with a grill as well, you should be able to cook the sort of

meals you do at home. Unless you have an oven in which to keep things hot, remember to plan your cooking so that all the different parts of the meal are ready at the same time.

Only the cooks should be around the stove and cooking area. This is particularly important if you are having to cook in a tent or confined space, where someone could kick or knock over the stove and food, which could be very dangerous.

▼ *The army mess tin is designed to be used with the army solid fuel stove.*

USING A SOLID FUEL STOVE

1 Open the can of fuel, remove the foil covering and assemble the stove.

2 Light the fuel. If it is in gel form, be careful not to get any on your hands.

3 Extinguish the flame using the lid and leave to cool before packing away.

USING A PETROL STOVE

1 Make sure the fuel tank is full and assemble the stove.

2 Give the tank several pumps with the plunger and turn the valve.

3 Light the stove. After cooking, turn off the burner and release the valve.

Lightweight Camp Menus

If you are going to have to carry all your food on your back, in cycle panniers or in a canoe, your main concern is likely to be the lightness of your food rather than its variety. Nevertheless, after a week or so eating the same freeze-dried dishes, you may feel your priority was wrong. Beyond pre-packaged, freeze-dried meals there is plenty of lightweight food on supermarket shelves, and with a little imagination you can devise interesting and appetizing menus for each day.

When choosing your food, consider how many cooking pots and burners you will have to cook on. You should also take the time to read the cooking directions on the food packets. Some soups, for example, take just a few minutes to cook, whereas others can take 20 minutes, meaning that you will need to use (and carry) extra fuel.

BREAKFAST

If you want to be up and on the move quickly, a bread roll with jam may be as much as you have time for. If you have a camp fire, the bread can be toasted over the fire. There are plenty of muesli (granola) and other cereals on the market that are ideal for a speedy breakfast, but for these you will need milk or yogurt. In cold weather you can warm yourself up with instant porridge (oatmeal), which can be mixed

▼ If you use aluminium or enamel eating equipment be aware that they get very hot when filled with hot food.

with either hot water or milk. You can buy it packed in individual portions for camping, and in different flavours such as cinnamon and apple or maple syrup and brown sugar.

If you want a more substantial cooked breakfast to keep you going through the day, you could heat a small can of beans, or beans with sausage, and eat that with bread. A more expensive option might be a suitable recipe in the form of a pouch meal.

Make sure you have plenty to drink at breakfast time. It doesn't matter if your drinks are hot or cold, but you could have hours ahead of you where you will be losing fluid by walking or working.

◄ A mug of soup, hot baked beans and an instant pudding can be prepared using the smallest stove in just a few minutes and they make a warming and sustaining meal.

LUNCH

If you are on the move during the day you will probably want only a brief break at lunchtime and won't want to eat anything that will slow you down. Lunch will usually be in the form of a high-energy snack meal that will need very little preparation and will be easy to eat. Nuts, fruit, chocolate and energy bars are the sorts of foods that will give you this high energy but will not require the body to over-exert itself digesting them.

DINNER

The evening meal will be your main meal of the day, when you have made camp at the end of your journey, or finished work. It should be a substantial three-course affair.

The first course can be a packet of instant soup, which just needs hot water poured on to it. The main course might be either a dehydrated meal or a pouch meal. If you're eating fish or meat, make sure you also have plenty of carbohydrates, in the form of rice, instant mashed potatoes or pasta, with it. All of these are easy to cook and light to carry.

The final course can be something like an instant pudding or fruit cooked with custard, both of which can be bought in dehydrated form. If you buy one of the varieties that just need hot water added to make them, you will save yourself the trouble of having to wash up one of the cooking pans you used for the main course.

COOKING DEHYDRATED FOOD

- Do not eat dehydrated food without adding the correct amount of water: it will dehydrate you.
- Add extra water at high altitudes.
- Soak ingredients such as dried vegetables in the cooking water before you start to cook them, to improve rehydration.

- Cook over a gentle heat, and keep stirring as the food cooks to avoid burning.
- Taste before adding any salt, as some dry foods are very salty.
- Get water boiling before adding rice or pasta.
- Thicken liquids with instant potato mash, raw eggs, grated cheese or powdered milk added at the end of cooking.

◀ *Dried pasta is quick to cook and provides a substantial evening meal. Bring a pan of water to the boil and tip in the pasta. Leave to boil for about 12 minutes, stirring occasionally, then drain and add to your chosen sauce. Heat through and serve.*

TRAIL SNACKS

Because of time constraints, or by preference, you may decide to snack during the day rather than stop for a meal break. The food you choose to take with you will be a matter of personal preference but it will also be dictated by the sort of climate you are travelling in. In hot countries, for instance, chocolate or anything with chocolate in it will melt and be very messy. Nuts, dried fruit, dried meat, biscuits and cheese are all suitable for eating on the move. Avoid salty foods that will simply make you thirsty. Some high-energy bars may not be to everybody's taste, so try them out before you set out on your expedition.

If you do decide to eat trail snacks make sure that any wrappings are not thrown away: put them into your pocket until you find a waste bin to throw them away.

▼ *Cereal bars are sustaining and can be substitutes for breakfast if necessary.*

◀ *Dried fruit and nuts are high-energy snacks and are easy to eat on the trail.*

▲ *Chocolate gives a quick burst of energy but it can make you thirsty.*

PACK SIZE

Although it is a more expensive way to buy food, you may consider buying some things packed in individual portions, including coffee, sugar and creamer. These little packs will help with portion control and, as many are plastic, they will offer some protection against wet, damp, dust, sand and insects. The downside is that you have more packaging to get rid of.

The alternative is to pack up your own individual portions. Apart from specially sealed pouch meals, you can repackage cereals, pasta, soup and pudding mixes in light, small freezer bags, which you can recycle later to carry away litter. Don't forget to add labels to your packages identifying the ingredients and including any necessary cooking instructions.

DRINKS

Tea, coffee and drinking chocolate are all light and easy to carry, and adding sugar to hot drinks will increase your calorie intake.

The most important drink is of course water. If you are living mainly on dehydrated food, it is important to make sure you are drinking enough fluid during the day, especially if it is hot and you are working hard. You can buy supplements from chemists which you can add to your water bottle, to put back into the body many of the trace elements which you will be losing if you are sweating a lot.

ADDITIONS TO YOUR MENU

If you come across berries on bushes or other natural fruit, or carry some dried fruit with you, this can turn a rather bland dehydrated pudding into a great treat. If you pick wild fruit, you must always be confident that you have identified it correctly before you eat it, especially when travelling abroad, and be sure you know that it is edible and not poisonous. If you do find ripe berries to pick, try to avoid bushes growing beside busy roads as they tend to get coated with pollutants from the exhaust of passing vehicles. No matter where you get your wild food from, wash it before you eat it.

Cooking without Utensils

Preparing a meal with the minimum of equipment can be an enjoyable challenge, and it is an integral part of lightweight camping. Learning how to do it does, however, also have a more serious purpose: if you can make a meal in this way, it could save your life in an emergency. For this kind of cooking you will need to be able to light a wood fire and let it burn down to give you a good bed of embers.

BREAD

There are a number of ways of cooking simple loaves. Unleavened bread needs to be shaped into fairly thin loaves as it is heavier than bread made with yeast. It should be eaten soon after cooking, but is delicious when freshly cooked.

Mix about two cupfuls of flour – self-raising (self-rising) gives a lighter result but plain (all-purpose) can be used – with a pinch of salt and water to make a thick dough. Knead the dough and shape it into a number of small loaves, about 2.5cm/1in thick and 7.5–10cm/3–4in wide. Place them on a clean, flat rock that has been heated in

▼ *Simple small loaves of unleavened bread are delicious when baked on a flat stone heated by a wood fire.*

the fire. (Make sure you brush the ash off it first.) Leave it for 20 minutes, turning halfway through. Check to see if the bread is cooked through by breaking one of the loaves open. Alternatively, roll the dough into a sausage shape and wrap it around a stick that has had its bark removed. Hold it over the fire and cook for about 10 minutes, then slide or twist it off the stick and fill the centre with fruit, honey or just butter.

EGGS

Hollow out the centre of a large potato and break an egg into it. To stop ash getting on the egg, place a piece of potato over the top of the hollow. Put the potato in the ashes of the fire and leave for about 20 minutes. If you want to eat the potato as well as the egg, wrap it in foil to protect it from the fire. Alternatively, break the egg into half an orange skin, and leave to cook for about 10 minutes.

MEAT

For a meal in a parcel, slice a couple of large potatoes and place these on some foil. Put some raw meat on the potatoes, and on top of the meat put sliced carrots and then more potatoes.

▲ *If you cut an orange in half and scoop out the flesh, you can use the skin as a container in which to bake an egg.*

Double-wrap the whole parcel in more foil, place it in the embers and rake more embers over the top of the parcel. Leave it to cook for about 30 minutes before opening the parcel. You can use some large, thick cabbage leaves as wrapping for this dish instead of foil.

If you have no foil, cut your meat into cubes, thread them on to a stick from which the bark has been removed, and roast over the fire. Add some vegetables for flavour if you wish.

If you catch a rabbit, kill, clean, gut and skin the animal, wrap it in fresh green grass and then cover the whole parcel with some clay made from mud and water. Bake this in the embers for about one and a half hours, then remove it, break open the clay shell and clean off the grass.

▼ *Meat and vegetables can be threaded on to straight sticks to make simple kebabs for roasting over the fire.*

▲ *Mussels can be cooked in their shells, but take particular care to ensure that they are fresh and from a safe source.*

▲ *Grill fish by laying it out flat on a hot rock, or hang it on a stout log placed next to the camp fire.*

FISH

If you catch fish yourself, you can cook them straight away and be sure that they will be absolutely fresh and delicious. Gut each fish, and open it

▼ *You can make a whole meal by wrapping meat and slices of fresh vegetables up together in a secure foil parcel.*

out flat if you want it to cook more quickly, then place it on a smooth, medium-size stone that has been heated in the fire. Now place this stone on the embers and allow the fish to cook for about 15 minutes or until done. Insert a knife tip in the thickest part of the flesh – as soon as it comes away from the bone it is ready to eat.

▼ *Baked apple is an easy dessert: just remove the core, stuff with dried fruit and sugar, and wrap in foil.*

DESSERT

Take a large apple and cut out the core, then fill the hole with sugar, adding some dried fruit such as raisins or sultanas (golden raisins) if you have them, and wrap in foil. Place the parcel in the embers for 15–20 minutes. Be careful when you open the foil and eat the apple because it will be very hot.

▼ *Baked banana is simple and delicious. Use a spoon to scoop it out of the skin, which will turn black as the fruit cooks.*

Base Camp Cooking

Cooking in a base or standing camp offers many more opportunities than cooking in a lightweight camp. You will probably have more than one stove, a greater variety of cooking utensils and, most importantly, access to a wider range of ingredients. It will be easier to obtain fresh food, and as weight will not be a limiting factor if you have vehicular transport, using convenient but heavy canned food will not be a problem.

The type of dishes you offer will depend largely on where you are and what your programme for the day will be. If most people leave camp for the day, for example, breakfast will need to be more substantial than if you are also providing a cooked lunch.

BREAKFAST

If you are in a hot climate you may not want a cooked breakfast, especially if you are going to have a substantial lunch in camp. If, on the other hand, you are in a temperate or cold country and are going to be in cold weather or doing physical work all day, you may want a cooked breakfast of several courses. This might begin with fruit or cereal, muesli (granola) or porridge (oatmeal), followed by either a cooked meal such as bacon and eggs, or bread/toast with fruit jams or honey.

Try to offer fruit juices as well as tea, coffee or hot chocolate with breakfast (and all other meals), as they are a healthy addition to the diet as well as providing extra fluid.

LUNCH

This will usually be the lightest meal of the day, but people returning to base camp after a morning's exertion may well be quite hungry. Food needs to be quick and simple but sustaining. A good option is soup, sandwiches and either hot or cold drinks. Try to include some fresh fruit with the meal if it is available.

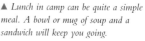
▲ *Lunch in camp can be quite a simple meal. A bowl or mug of soup and a sandwich will keep you going.*

DINNER

This will usually be the main meal of the day, a more elaborate, three-course affair to be lingered over and enjoyed at the end of the day.

Soup will usually be the first course. If you are using soup powder, try to add some fresh vegetables if they are available to make the soup more nourishing and improve the flavour.

The main course will probably be some kind of meat or fish accompanied by rice, potatoes or pasta and some fresh vegetables. Cooking meat or fish in a stew is the easiest way of preparing these foods at camp, particularly if you are catering for a large number of people who may not all be ready to eat at the same time.

Remember to include some spices and other flavourings in your food supplies so that you can give some variety to the camp diet, which might otherwise tend to be bland. With these you can turn a stew into a curry, a chilli or perhaps a sweet and sour dish, depending on taste. But be careful that you do not spice the food to such extent that some people will not eat it. If you find that some people do and others do not like certain spices, you

▲ *A good breakfast is important if you are going to be active during the day.*

▲ *The main meal of the day can be eaten in the evening and should be a fairly substantial and relaxed meal.*

can either cook dishes in two different batches, one spiced and one not, or stick to plain recipes and leave people to add their own flavourings.

Desserts can be as varied as your ingredients and cooking skills allow. If you decide to fall back on such things as instant puddings from packets, you can liven them up by serving them with fresh or canned fruit.

KEEPING FOOD HOT
When you are cooking for a large number of people one of the biggest problems is to serve hot food hot but not burned. One way to achieve this is to have a large pan of simmering water on the fire or stove with a large dish on top. As the food is cooked, it can be placed on the dish and covered with a lid. The heat will be gentle enough to keep everything hot without burning or drying out, and the water can be used later for washing the dishes.

If you have to serve such things as fried eggs and you can only cook say six or seven at a time, then only call for that number of people to receive their food. This way they get all their food hot and you do not have great queues waiting with only half their food served and getting cold.

CLEANING UP
Do not allow your standards to slip just because you are cooking and eating outdoors. In your base camp, there should be no reason why you have to eat all courses of your meal from the same plate or bowl. If you do not have enough plates or bowls, you can quickly wash up between courses.

Make it a strict policy to check that eating and serving surfaces are kept clean and free of food scraps and spills.

SHARING THE COOKING
In a large base camp it is sensible for one or two people to take responsibility for planning and providing meals. This makes it easier to work out how you are going to use your rations and avoids confusion about who is cooking dinner. On the other hand, everyone in camp should be ready to lend a hand preparing ingredients, watching cooking pots, building and fuelling the fire, serving food and cleaning up after meals. You may want to arrange a rota so that you know you always have some help, and don't get too many people hanging around the kitchen area when you are busy cooking.

It is quite possible that various members of the party, apart from the designated cook, will have a particular culinary skill. They may be especially good at cooking fish or making bread, or spicing a curry, so always be open to offers to take over the cooking of a particular course or even a whole meal. But make sure a guest cook doesn't squander your entire stock of, say, lemons or cheese in one fantastic dish: insist that they tell you what they are going to make so that you know it will fit in with your other plans for the meal, or the day's cooking.

COOKING EGGS

Apart from the fact that they are fragile and need to be carefully packed for travelling, eggs are the perfect camp food: popular, adaptable, nourishing, cheap and quick to cook. As well as frying and boiling and scrambling them, try baking them in potato skins in the embers of the fire, or stirring them into hot soup, Asian-style.

▼ *Scrambled eggs need careful cooking. Keep stirring and watch them constantly to avoid overcooking them.*

▼ *Fried eggs take only a couple of minutes, so cook them at the last minute when the rest of the meal is ready.*

Base Camp Sample Recipes

The following recipes will give you an idea of the varied and interesting meals you can achieve when cooking on a simple stove or open fire. Any of these dishes could be cooked at a base camp, where you are likely to have more time and equipment, as well as access to canned and fresh food. Each recipe will serve 6–8 people.

MAIN MEALS
Dishes that can be cooked from start to finish in a single pot make the best sense for camp cooking,

Fish Hotpot
675g/1½lb fish, such as cod or plaice
30ml/2 tbsp vegetable oil
250g/9oz hard cheese, grated
450g/1lb tomatoes, sliced
500g/1¼lb boiled potatoes or 300g/11oz
*   boiled rice, to serve*

Wash and cut the fish into 3cm/1¼in squares, and pour a little oil over them. Grease the pan. Put the fish in the bottom, cover with a layer of cheese and then some sliced tomatoes. Repeat these layers until all the ingredients have been used. Cover tightly and cook slowly for 20–30 minutes.

▼ *A cheesy fish hotpot makes a warming yet light main course.*

▲ *Corned beef is an invaluable standby for camp cooking as it is already cooked and just needs to be heated through.*

Spaghetti and Corned Beef
1 onion, chopped
30ml/2 tbsp vegetable oil
350g/12oz corned beef
400g/14oz chopped tomatoes
400g/14oz spaghetti in tomato sauce
50g/2oz hard cheese, grated
500g/1¼lb boiled potatoes, 350g/12oz
*   cooked and drained pasta or fresh crusty*
*   bread, to serve*

Heat the oil in a frying pan and gently fry the onion until soft. Dice the corned beef and add to the onion with the chopped tomatoes and spaghetti. Simmer gently for 5 minutes. Sprinkle with cheese and serve with potatoes, pasta or bread.

▲ *Chilli con carne is a camp fire classic, warming and easy to eat. Keep the heat gentle so that everyone enjoys it.*

Chilli Con Carne
15ml/1 tbsp vegetable oil
450g/1lb minced (ground) beef
1 large onion, chopped
400g/14oz chopped tomatoes
400g/14oz cooked and drained red kidney
*   beans or baked beans*
1 beef stock (bouillon) cube
375ml/13fl oz water
5ml/1 tsp chilli powder
300g/11oz boiled rice or fresh crusty bread,
*   to serve*

Heat the oil in a large pan and fry the beef until brown. Stir in the onion, tomatoes and kidney beans. Crumble in the stock cube and pour in the water. Bring to the boil and simmer for 5 minutes. Add the chilli powder. Simmer gently for 30 minutes, stirring occasionally. Serve with boiled rice or chunks of bread.

COOK'S TIPS

- Be inventive: by adding some fresh vegetables and imaginative seasoning you can transform the flavour of quickly prepared canned ingredients.
- When making stews, choose fresh ingredients that cook quickly, such as fish and minced (ground) meat, to save time and fuel.
- Cut vegetables into small chunks for speedy cooking.

▲ *Any meat and potatoes left over from dinner can be appetizingly fried up for a quick lunch dish the following day.*

Leftover Hash

50g/4oz/4 tbsp butter
450g/1 lb cooked potatoes, grated
450g/1 lb cooked leftover meat
½ onion, grated
300g/11oz can sweetcorn kernels
salt and pepper to taste

Melt the butter in a heavy frying pan, then add the potatoes, meat, onion and corn and mix well. Season to taste and brown over a medium heat.

DESSERTS

Proper desserts, not just a portion of fresh fruit, will be much appreciated and will satisfy hefty appetites.

Fruit Fritters

150g/5oz self-raising (self-rising) flour
25g/1oz granulated sugar
1 egg, beaten
175ml/6fl oz milk
115g/4oz fruit (cooking apples, bananas, pineapple, pears or oranges)
vegetable oil, for frying
caster (superfine) sugar, for sprinkling

Mix the flour and sugar in a bowl. Add the beaten egg and milk to make a thick batter. Peel, core and grate the apples, or slice or dice other fruit, and add to the batter. Pour some oil into a pan so it is at least 1cm/½in deep. Once the oil is hot, cook spoonfuls of the batter mix until golden. Sprinkle with caster sugar and serve hot.

▲ *Crunchy syrup-coated cornflakes make a satisfying contrast with soft stewed apples in this easy-to-make dessert.*

Ginger and Rhubarb Crumble

8 sticks rhubarb
sugar or honey, to sweeten
water
20 ginger biscuits (cookies)
50g/2oz butter
natural (plain) yogurt or double (heavy) cream, to serve

Cut the rhubarb into chunks and put them in a pan with the sugar or honey and a little water. Stew gently until soft. Crush the biscuits in a plastic bag. Melt the butter in a pan and stir in the crushed biscuits. Divide the rhubarb between serving bowls and sprinkle the crumble over the fruit. Serve with natural (plain) yogurt or cream.

▼ *Fruit fritters can be made using any fresh fruit you have available. Serve them freshly made and piping hot, sprinkled with sugar.*

Swiss Apples

800g/1¾lb cooking apples (or you could use pears, or canned fruit such as peaches or apricots)
50g/2oz sugar
40g/1½oz butter
15ml/1 tbsp golden (light corn) syrup
cornflakes
double (heavy) cream, natural (plain) yogurt or custard, to serve

Peel, core and slice the apples, then cook them in a little water with the sugar before placing them in serving bowls. If using canned fruit, drain off a little of the juice or syrup and divide between the serving bowls. Melt the butter and golden syrup together in a large pan, then stir in enough cornflakes to use up all the syrup mixture. Serve this on top of the fruit with cream, yogurt or custard.

▼ *This quick alternative to a baked crumble topping is made with crushed ginger biscuits and butter, and goes well with rhubarb.*

Clean Water

When living outdoors, clean water will be the most important single item that will determine where you can go and for how long. You may have to plan your route and campsites to take into account the availability of water.

FINDING WATER
The first thing to do is to look at the countryside around you for signs of streams, rivers, lakes or the sea. If you are in the desert, look for vegetation, which requires some water to survive. Also look in dried-up watercourses or at the base of cliffs, as water has previously flowed here, and even if you cannot see it you may find it by digging down 60–90cm/2–3ft.

If you are near the coast, by digging above the high water line you will soon

▼ It is a good idea to equip yourself with more than one method of treating your drinking water.

▲ For your own safety you should always treat all water as potentially contaminated, even when travelling in wild areas.

find a little pool of slightly salty but still drinkable water. Fresh water is lighter than salt water, so drink from the top of the pool. (Always remember that you should never be tempted to drink seawater itself under any circumstances, as its saltiness will quickly lead you to become dehydrated.) In rivers where

there is a lot of silt, the deeper down you get your water, the cleaner it will be, as most of the silt and debris travels in the top layer of fast-moving water. Remove any remaining silt and debris before purifying the water by pouring it through either a finely woven, sock-shaped filter bag or an ordinary sock filled with a layer of sand and then a layer of small pebbles.

▼ A Millbank filter bag will remove some impurities from water, but not all.

CONTAMINATING ORGANISMS			
Methods of purification	Protozoans (5–15 microns)	Bacteria (0.2–10 microns)	Viruses (0.004–0.1 microns)
Boiling	Kills	Kills	Kills
Iodine	Does not kill all	Kills	Kills
Chlorine	Not effective on larger micro-organisms	Kills	Kills
Silver	Does not kill all	Kills	Does not kill all
Filters	Eliminates	Eliminates if pores are small enough	Does not eliminate
Purifier	Kills	Kills	Kills

▲ *Boiling water kills all impurities and is the best way to make sure that it is safe for all purposes, including drinking.*

PURIFYING WATER
The chart on the opposite page shows the benefits and disadvantages of all the methods of cleaning water. Once it has been purified, drinking water should always be kept in clean, sealed containers, labelled to avoid confusion.

BOILING
The safest way to purify water is to boil it vigorously for at least 5 minutes and allow it to cool before drinking. If, however, you want water quickly or in large quantities, you might choose another method.

CHEMICAL TREATMENTS
There are three different chemical agents currently used to treat water: iodine, chlorine and silver. When using any of these, always read the directions on the packet or bottle as in some cases an overdose can be harmful.

Iodine
This is available in liquid form or as tablets. After treatment with iodine, the water should be left to stand for 20–30 minutes. Neutralizing tablets can take away most of the smell and taste.

Iodine should be used on a short-term basis only, and should be avoided by pregnant women, children or anyone with a thyroid condition.

Chlorine
This is easy to use and takes only about 10 minutes to sterilize reasonably clean water and 30 minutes for more suspect water. Neutralizing tablets are available to take away most of the swimming-pool taste of chlorinated water.

Silver
This may be less effective than the other chemicals, but is longer-lasting and leaves no taste. The sterilization process may take at least two hours.

▼ *A water purifier is simple and quick to use. Fill with water and leave to stand before pouring out drinking water.*

FILTERS AND PURIFIERS
A purifier both filters and sterilizes the water, giving safe drinkable water, whereas a filter only sieves the water, which then needs to be chemically treated or boiled.

When choosing a filter, you need to know if it will filter enough water for the trip (you will need 2–3 litres/ 3½–5¼ pints per person per day in temperate climates, and up to 6 litres/ 10½ pints in extreme hot climates, more if you are working hard). You should also check to see how fast it works. For a purifier, you need to know how fast it works and whether the cartridge can be cleaned, or a new cartridge fitted. Disposable cartridges tend to be compact but involve more expense.

▼ *Water filters need thorough cleaning and servicing after use or they can become ineffective.*

YOU & THE ENVIRONMENT

When you venture into the wilderness you immediately begin to form
a very intimate relationship with it; even though the forces of nature are
infinitely more powerful than you, you have a responsibility to protect the
natural world and not to disrupt the fragile ecosystems you are visiting.
By respecting the wild environment, you can help to preserve its integrity
while travelling safely through it.

Personal Safety

When going into the wilderness, your personal safety will be in the hands of yourself and the people around you. It is important that you plan carefully, refer to your risk assessment, prioritize good hygiene and emphasize to the team the importance of safe behaviour at all times, whatever the activity.

RISK ASSESSMENT
Keep the results of your risk assessment in mind throughout the trip and add to it or rewrite it as necessary. If your assessment concluded that equipment such as helmets and buoyancy aids (personal flotation devices) should be worn, then wear them, even if they are uncomfortable or get in the way. Contact specialized organizations for up-to-date advice on health and safety concerns in the area.

▼ *Establishing a set of clear safety rules that everyone follows will mean that you can all safely enjoy wild places.*

HEALTH
Steps to make sure you and your team are physically fit and mentally prepared for the trip should be taken before you set off; this is especially important if you are planning challenging activities. One or two people, if not everyone, in the team should have an appropriate level of experience for the activities. Going ahead with activities without the right amount of skill and experience in the team is foolish and will almost certainly result in an accident.

Check that your personal and team first-aid kits are well-stocked and that you know what's in them and how to use it. Any appointed first aider or medic should be up to date with their training. Encourage everyone in the team to pay close attention to their personal hygiene, and at camp in the wilderness, make sure you have improvised facilities that enable them to do so. This should avoid unnecessary bouts of diarrhoea, or worse.

▲ *When chopping wood make sure there is a clear area around you so that no one will be hit when you swing the axe.*

PROTECTING YOUR HEAD
You are at risk from falling rocks wherever there are cliffs or steep slopes. If you are climbing, wearing a helmet can increase your safety, not only from falling rocks but from falling equipment dropped by other climbers!

Any falling object can cause serious injury, especially if you are not wearing a helmet. For instance, in tropical countries many people are killed and injured by falling coconuts. The answer, of course, is not to walk under coconut trees unnecessarily, and the same could be said of cliffs and steep slopes. However, if you are taking part in a climbing expedition, the important thing is to be sensitive to the potential dangers and ready to protect yourself from falling rocks at all times. When climbing, be careful to keep your equipment secure for the safety of those below.

▲ *Every party should include at least one person with a medical qualification or comprehensive training in first aid.*

▲ *When you are cooking, make sure all cooking pots are supported in a stable, level position and cannot be knocked over.*

▲ *If you are going on a canoeing or kayaking trip, every member of the party should know how to cope with capsizing.*

▼ *Before you set out through unfamiliar terrain, find out about potential risks such as poisonous snakes and insects.*

SAFETY AND EQUIPMENT SUPPLIES

Always make sure your basic survival kit is with you at all times. Check that your personal equipment and clothing are suitable for the worst possible conditions you could encounter, and during the trip check it regularly to make sure that everything is in good working order. Carry out repairs as soon as damage occurs.

SAFETY RULES

Work out a simple but comprehensive set of safety rules, which everybody in the party agrees to sign up to, and then stick to them. While you are travelling you may see other people, including local inhabitants, who are not following the rules you have drawn up regarding drinking water, for instance, but these people will be immune to many bacteria that could cause you illness. Or they may not be, and may end up suffering from diseases and illnesses that you would not want to contract, so don't be swayed by their example.

STAYING SAFE

Many mountaineering accidents happen on the descent, on relatively easy ground, when climbers, who are relieved to be away from the dangerous terrain they have coped with, forget to concentrate fully on the last stage of their climb. On any kind of expedition, silly accidents may happen at base camp or in safe areas, because people have started to relax. It is vital that every team member is aware that they need

to concentrate on safety all the time, not just at the testing times when they might be in personal danger.

Looking after the Environment

Part of the reason so many of us want to visit and enjoy the wilder parts of the world, or just our own local countryside, is for peace, beauty and quiet. So, when planning your trip, be it a weekend's hike or an expedition of many weeks, make sure you don't spoil the very aspects of the countryside that you have gone to enjoy.

CONSIDERATION FOR OTHERS

Remember that many people live and work in the area that you are visiting, so respect their homes and land and don't do anything to disrupt their lives. Never park your vehicle in a place that will obstruct gateways or access roads, and always ask permission before setting up camp.

If you are canoeing down a river and people are fishing, do your best to avoid them and not to disturb the river any more than you have to.

RESPECT FOR COUNTRY LIFE

If you are walking or riding in a national park, or another area where there is an established path system, stay on the paths to avoid causing soil erosion. Similarly, keep to footpaths when crossing farmland, though in this

▼ *Be extremely careful whenever you light a camp fire or use matches, as bushfires can destroy a wilderness area extremely quickly.*

▲ *Avoid disturbing livestock when walking through pasture land; stick to recognized footpaths and close gates behind you.*

case you should do this to avoid damaging crops or frightening livestock. Make sure you refasten any gates you have to open to go through, avoid damaging fences, hedges and walls by climbing them, and keep any dogs under proper control.

Be very careful if you light fires, as these can easily get out of control, especially in hot, dry, windy weather.

Dispose of every scrap of litter by putting it in bins, burning or burying it, or taking it home with you.

LEAVING NO TRACE

The responsible traveller, according to the saying, should take only memories and leave only footprints. This applies equally whether you are going for a walk in the countryside, setting up a camp in the wilderness, or visiting a distant country with a culture and economy that is vulnerable to the effects of foreign tourism.

▼ *Dispose of your litter responsibly: the debris left by a large base camp can have a devastating effect on the natural environment.*

▲ Be considerate of the resident wildlife: don't set up camp near a nest or obvious feeding site, disrupting their lives.

PROTECTING WILDLIFE

Never be tempted to feed wild animals, however much they may invite it. The practice can make them dependent on humans for food, with the result that when you move on they will lose their food source. It can also lead them to lose their natural fear of humans. With large animals this might mean that their behaviour around other people eventually becomes dangerous and they will have to be destroyed.

It is illegal to bring wild animal products into many countries. If you are tempted to buy animal skins, ivory, eggs or any other animal products, make sure that what you buy has a certificate saying it has been farmed at a recognized centre, otherwise it will almost certainly have been poached from the wild. Note that it is illegal to buy rhinoceros horn products anywhere in the world.

If you are near or on a beach, try to avoid doing any damage to coral and underwater life in general, and do not buy shells, shell jewellery, and coral or turtle products. Buying such goods will encourage the local people to continue destroying their local environment and wildlife for economic reasons.

RESPECTING INDIGENOUS CULTURES AND CUSTOMS

Before travelling to a new region or country, read a good guidebook to find out as much as you can about the local culture and customs. As well as enriching your experience of your trip, this could avoid the embarrassment of doing the wrong thing or inadvertently insulting people you meet.

If you are travelling abroad, be aware of the national religion and of the attitude towards religion in the country. If the national language differs from your own, try to find the time to learn something of it. Even if you have only mastered the basics by the time you go, your efforts to speak to the local people in their own language will always be

▼ Don't be tempted to buy seashells offered by local traders, as continued collection can damage the natural marine environment.

▲ If you are lucky enough to see wild animals, don't feed them or encourage them away from their normal habitation.

appreciated. Wearing the correct clothing is also important to avoid giving offence, especially in Muslim countries but also in the religious buildings of many faiths, so find out about this and other customs before you go, and be sure to follow them.

If you wish to take photographs of local people, their homes and belongings, always ask permission and be prepared to pay for the privilege. You should be especially careful when taking pictures of women. In general, treat people with the respect you would expect to receive yourself.

▼ If foreign travel introduces you to new cultures, consider yourself a guest in someone else's home and respect what you see.

Natural Hazards: Wildlife

Depending on where you will be travelling, you may come across any number of wild animals, reptiles, insects and sealife, all of which could harm or even kill you. Taking sensible precautions, including vaccinations, being aware of the creatures' habits, and staying alert to the dangers will help to protect you against attacks.

MAMMALS

All wild mammals will avoid human contact and will attack only if they feel they are in danger, if you startle or frighten them and do not allow them a means of escape. Most attacks happen when humans encounter animals accidentally, so it makes sense to create plenty of noise and let them know you are in the vicinity.

Females can be just as aggressive as males, and are far more so when they are protecting their young. The sensible course is to avoid getting too close to any wild mammal and never to try to touch them – this applies to livestock, such as sheep and cattle, as much as it does to foxes, deer, bears and large cats.

Bears will not seek you out, but may be attracted to your camp if they smell

▲ *All female animals will defend their young, and in the case of lionesses this can make them very dangerous indeed.*

▲ *The hippopotamus inhabits African waters and will attack humans if it cannot see another way of escaping from them.*

your food. Keep everything edible well sealed to avoid tempting them, and never keep any food inside your tent.

If a large predator does start to approach you, you should retreat slowly to safety. Do not turn and run away, as this may trigger its instinct to chase after its prey.

SNAKES

A snake will attack a person only if stood on or threatened, and then only if it cannot get away. Many snakes hunt at night, so always carry a flashlight if you are walking around in the dark.

RABIES

In countries where rabies is still prevalent, domestic animals as well as wild animals can be infected. The main symptoms of rabies are excessive salivation and irritable and aggressive behaviour. Have the vaccination before you travel and avoid touching any animal.

▼ *Deer are usually retiring, but mature stags become aggressive during the mating season and should not be approached.*

▼ *Brown bears are more likely to avoid you than to attack, but a female may become aggressive if she is defending her cub.*

▲ *As snakes feed on rodents they are a useful means of pest control. They pose a threat to humans only if disturbed.*

There are far more non-venomous snakes than venomous ones. Constricting snakes are not venomous but can give a nasty bite, which will often become infected. Only the largest constrictors, including boas and anacondas, would attack humans.

LIZARDS, CROCODILES AND ALLIGATORS
Only the largest lizards, such as the Nile monitor lizard and the Komodo dragon of Indonesia, are a threat to humans. Crocodiles, found in the tropical fresh waters of Africa, Asia and Australia, are extremely dangerous and should always be avoided if seen. The American alligator lies motionless in wait for its prey, but is capable of moving at high speed.

▼ *The estuarine crocodile of South-east Asia and northern Australia is the largest and most dangerous member of the family.*

▲ *Learn about the snake species that are native to the area you are travelling in, and be aware of where you may find them.*

INSECTS
The mosquito carries a number of diseases, including malaria and yellow fever. In addition to the protection offered by vaccination, you should dress appropriately, sleep under nets and use a good mosquito repellent when travelling in tropical regions.

Bees, wasps and hornets can be life-threatening if you develop an allergic reaction when stung, or disturb a nest and are stung many times. Make sure you do not camp near their nests.

Ticks, mites, lice, flies, tapeworms and roundworms can cause discomfort at best and illness at worst. Avoid walking barefoot and don't sit or camp where livestock have been.

Scorpions and poisonous spiders are indigenous to South America, Africa,

▼ *In tropical areas, check before you sit down or put your foot into a shoe: scorpions like dry, dark places and may surprise you.*

▲ *Even if you are confident that a snake species is not venomous, you should always leave the handling of snakes to an expert.*

Asia and Australia. Be on your guard, look at what you are picking up and where you are sitting. Always shake out your bedding, clothes and boots before use and pack them away as soon as you have finished with them.

WATER CREATURES
Stonefish fire venom from their dorsal fins if you stand on them, and their sting can be lethal. Box jellyfish are equally dangerous: they are hard to see in the water, and usually sting swimmers who brush up against their tentacles unknowingly.

Sharks are native to temperate and tropical waters. Great White sharks can be aggressive, though this is usually because they have mistaken a human for a seal, their main prey.

▼ *Jellyfish are found worldwide: beaches littered with dead jellyfish bodies will indicate a swarm in that stretch of coast.*

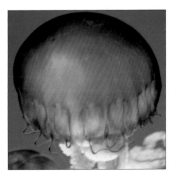

Natural Hazards: Vegetation

You can be at risk of serious injury from some of the plants and trees you may find in the wild. Your skin may be stung or pierced by thorns, or you could become ill after eating a poisonous plant or mushroom.

THORNS AND SEEDS
Many plants have thorns that can be painful if you walk into or on top of them. They can also snag your clothes or go through the soles of your boots. Never walk around barefoot, and when you make camp check the ground where you are planning to pitch your tent, and the surrounding area, for thorns on the bushes growing nearby or on the ground.

Many seeds in the tropics are equipped with sharp barbs intended to get caught in animals' fur. If you tread on these and they get into your boots, they can work up into the skin of your feet and may set up an infection.

INSECT DEFENCE SYSTEM
Some acacia trees in Africa have a mutually supportive relationship with insects such as ants. The tree provides nourishment for the insects and the ants provide defence against browsing animals. So, if you brush against or

touch the tree, a large number of ants will appear from galls on the branches and attack you.

FUNGI
There are far more safe and edible fungi than there are poisonous ones, but some of the species that are toxic are extremely dangerous. The deadly Amanita species, such as the Death Cap and the Destroying Angel, are white, mushroom-shaped fungi that could be mistaken for edible mushrooms unless you know the distinctive signs to look for. These include a cup, or volva, at the base of the stem, a ring around the

▼ *African acacia bushes are protected not only by their savage thorns but by colonies of ants that live on their branches.*

◀ *Brown Roll-rim is a very common mushroom but is severely toxic, with effects similar to leukaemia.*

stem, and white gills. The poisonous Fly Agaric, with its distinctive red and white cap, is easier to identify.

With fungi (as with all wild food), it is sound advice to eat only those species that you are absolutely sure you can identify correctly. It is preferable to go out in the field with an expert, or with a reliable book, to learn how to recognize the most worthwhile edible species. Anything that you cannot positively identify should be left alone.

POISONOUS PLANTS
A good rule of thumb is never to eat or put near your eyes any plant that has a milky sap, such as spurge or members of the buttercup family. There are also a number of plants, such as poison ivy and poison oak, that can cause a burning rash on your skin if you touch the leaves. These and many other irritant plants can be particularly dangerous if you touch them with your

▼ *The Fly Agaric (*Amanita muscaria muscaria*) is easy to recognize – and avoid – because of its distinctive colouring.*

▲ *The Yellow Stainer accounts for half of the cases of mushroom poisoning among those who pick field or horse mushrooms.*

▲ *The Fly Agaric (above left) has distinctive red colouring which may fade to orange after heavy rain.*

▲ *The dangerous Death Cap mushroom. Only one cap is needed to cause serious, possible fatal poisoning.*

hands then rub your eye, when the blistering may cause permanent damage to your sight.

Some common trees of temperate regions, such as the yew and the laburnum, have berries or seed pods that are deadly poisonous. The sap of some members of the mangrove family, known as Blinding Mangroves, can cause blindness if it gets near the eyes.

Any plant that smells of bitter almonds or peaches should be avoided, and mature bracken becomes poisonous as it gets older. As with fungi, it is imperative that you should not eat any part of any plant you cannot identify.

MANGROVES

These trees grow on the edge of tidal creeks in tropical regions, and their knotted roots create a rich habitat for many plants and animals.

Although the trees themselves are unlikely to cause you harm, they attract colonies of shell-dwelling mussels, which can be razor sharp and will cut your feet and legs badly if you try to walk through them. It will always be easier to find another way to or from the water than trying to get through an area of mangrove forest. These forest belts can also be home to salt-water crocodiles and snakes, so you should take great care when visiting them.

NUTS AND FRUITS

The fruits of many plants and trees are good to eat, but you should be aware that some nuts and berries that are good to eat may closely resemble others that are poisonous. A good example is the sweet chestnut, which is delicious roasted, and the horse chestnut, which is inedible. Sweet chestnuts are easily recognizable by their spiny, hedgehog-like husks.

Many tropical fruits look inviting when ripe, and you may even see animals eating them, but you should not regard anything as safe unless you know exactly what it is.

If you have children with you, don't let them pick fruits on their own. If they do make a mistake, they will be more severely affected by any toxin.

▲ *The Destroying Angel is aptly named, being white and fatal. It often grows in places where many edible mushrooms grow.*

▲ *Horse chestnuts, or conkers, are poisonous and should never be confused with the sweet chestnut. If in any doubt at all, do not eat.*

COOKING SWEET CHESTNUTS

1 Slit the skins of the chestnuts to stop them bursting as they heat up, then tip them into a pan of boiling water and cook for about 20 minutes.

2 Drain the chestnuts and peel off the outer skins as soon as they are cool enough to handle. You may need a knife to peel off the inner skin.

Dangers in the Outdoors

The best way to protect yourself from any danger is to be aware of how and when it might happen, and to know how to cope if it occurs. Crossing rivers or open water, walking on ice and snow, and exploring caves and forests are all potentially dangerous activities, but a cautious, sensible and informed approach should keep you out of harm's way.

AVALANCHES

If your party absolutely must travel over snow that you suspect is an avalanche hazard, let only one person go at a time. You can increase your chances of being found if the slope breaks away by tying a long, brightly coloured cord to your waist. The cord may remain visible on the surface even if you are not. A cell or satellite telephone might save your life if you can move your arms enough to use it. You could also carry a passive reflector avalanche beacon, which rescue services can detect from the air or on the ground when they arrive after the alarm is raised. These are now built into many good jackets and ski boots. You can also buy them separately from ski

▼ *Make sure ice is solid before walking on it and avoid it in windy weather, as you could be stranded on a moving ice floe.*

shops. People found within fifteen minutes of being buried by an avalanche have an extremely high survival rate, but after forty-five minutes it is very low indeed.

When caught in an avalanche, try to avoid it by escaping to one side. You can't outrun the falling snow, even on skis or on a skidoo. If you are overcome by the avalanche, try to stay near the surface of the snow using a swimming motion.

QUICKSAND

What appears at first to be solid ground can trap the unwary. Whether it is boggy ground or a special combination of sand and fine dust in dry areas, it is generically known as quicksand.

Avoid any kind of boggy ground, or if you must cross it, try to step only on substantial plants or rocks. If you do find you are sinking too fast to escape, stop struggling immediately and lie back with your arms spread out. You will almost certainly be able to "float" in this position until help arrives; if it feels all right to do so you may be able to swim slowly to more solid ground.

If you need to cross bogs or quicksand and there is nothing to step on, improvise by using ladders or planks, backpacks, or anything that will spread your weight.

▲ *Tempting as it often is to climb in and around natural cave formations, unstable rocks can make them extremely dangerous.*

RIVER CROSSINGS

Many people have drowned attempting to cross what appeared to be quite innocuous rivers, and they are far more dangerous than they appear. Check up and down the river for the best place to cross. Remember that if the water is fast-flowing you will not be able to cross water more than knee-deep

▼ *In mountainous terrain, take care to select a site for your camp that is safe from potential rockfalls or avalanches.*

▲ *An active volcano can be a spectacular sight but you should not venture near the crater without consulting local experts.*

▲ *No matter how scenic, the beach can be a dangerous place. Deep water, offshore winds, sea currents and riptides all present real risks.*

without roped assistance, unless it is deep enough to swim and not turbulent. To fall down in fast-flowing water when wading is very dangerous. Face downstream on your back and keep your feet up. Do not try to stand up again until the water is so shallow you come to a halt.

If you are trying to walk across a river, check the depth with a stick if necessary, and be extra careful with your footing. Untie the waist belt on your backpack so that you can ditch it, or better still rope the backpacks across the river once someone is safely on each side. Roping people across is good, but you must *never* tie anyone on to the rope – rely on holding/belaying the rope only.

SEA CURRENTS

The currents in the sea are not normally as strong as they can be in rivers, but be aware that they may be too strong to swim against. Currents can be caused by the tide, longshore drift, or other local effects, but make sure you know about them. Ask local people if you don't understand what conditions might prevail. Remember that tidal currents may reverse twice a day, or four times a day in some

island environments, and that the combinations of wind with current or wind against current can represent entirely different sea states.

CREVASSES AND GLACIERS

You should never be on a glacier unless you are an experienced mountaineer. You must always be roped up in groups of three, and be fully equipped with mountain rescue gear, which you must be practised in deploying in case anyone falls into a crevasse.

▼ *Don't pitch tents too close to a river: it may look tranquil in dry weather but rivers can rise very quickly when the rain falls.*

CAVES

If you are entering a cave, you should bear in mind that animals often live in them, and you may be cornering a creature that could become aggressive. Even if you do not meet the owners, a number of diseases can be caught from bird, bat and other animals' droppings, so be careful what you touch.

If the cave is a deep or complex system, use a foolproof system to ensure that you can find your way back out again. And if the cave opens on to the sea be aware of tidal variation. Many people have been trapped when their only escape route has been filled with water by the rising tide.

Understanding the Weather

When planning a trip, the weather can be of vital importance, so it is sensible to learn what all the terms and symbols shown on a weather map and referred to on a radio forecast mean. Knowing the highest and lowest temperatures for the area you are travelling to, and the expected rainfall for each month, is also very useful.

ISOBARS

Meteorologists measure the atmospheric pressure at internationally agreed times, every three hours. After plotting these readings on maps, they draw lines known as isobars, which link places of equal pressure.

The closer these lines are to each other, the higher the wind speed will be, because they show that the pressure values are changing quickly over a relatively small area. The isobars on a chart form the shapes of concentric rings which indicate areas of low pressure (depressions or cyclones) and high pressure (anticyclones).

▼ *Low-pressure areas, indicated by closely spaced concentric circles of isobars, are often associated with warm or cold fronts.*

FRONTS

A weather front is marked as a heavy line on the chart, with either small triangles (a cold front) or semicircles (a warm front) on it. A front marks the edges of air masses of different origins and at different temperatures.

A warm front indicates that warm air is advancing and rising over cold air. This usually leads to a bout of heavy rain, followed by a rise in temperature. A cold front shows that cold air is replacing warm air at ground level. This leads to a short spell of heavy rain followed by much brighter weather with showers and gusty winds.

DEPRESSIONS

These may be described as low-pressure areas or cyclones in the northern hemisphere. When pressure falls, the winds blow in an anticlockwise direction (clockwise in the southern hemisphere), often bringing rain.

ANTICYCLONES, OR HIGHS

In anticyclones, winds blow clockwise in the northern and anticlockwise in the southern hemispheres. They are indicated on a weather chart by areas

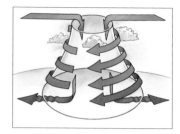

▲ *In an anticyclone, air is descending, compressing and warming. Clouds tend to evaporate and winds are generally light.*

▼ *In a depression, air is rising, expanding and cooling. Water vapour condenses, forming clouds and leading to rain or snow.*

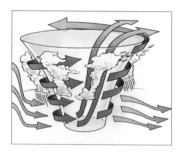

of widely spaced isobars. The pressure is high and the winds are light. Highs bring sunny weather in summer, cold and foggy conditions in winter.

WIND

The speed of winds is measured in knots, but a system called the Beaufort scale is also used to describe the kind of wind indicated by the wind speed.

Regarding wind temperature, as a general rule, summer winds that have come over a landmass will be warmer and drier than those that have come over the sea. In winter, winds that have travelled over a large landmass will be colder than those that have travelled over the sea. In the northern hemisphere, winds from the north will be colder than those from the south, and in the southern hemisphere the reverse is true.

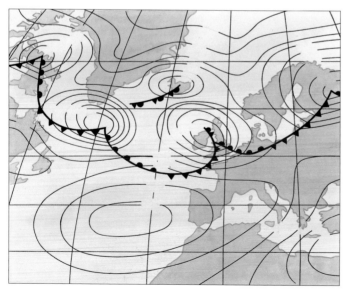

▲ *Cirrocumulus clouds signify a blue sky and fair weather. They often follow a storm.*

▲ *Altocumulus clouds predict fair weather. They will often follow a storm shower.*

▲ *Cumulus clouds indicate fair weather if widely separated; they may produce showers.*

▲ *Stratocumulus clouds covering the sky mean light showers which dissipate quickly.*

▲ *Heavy rain or snow is signified by the dark low cloud cover known as nimbostratus.*

▲ *Stratus clouds look like hill fog. Although not a rain cloud they can produce drizzle.*

BEAUFORT SCALE OF WIND FORCE

Beaufort number	General description	Sea criterion	Landsman's criterion	Velocity in knots
0	Calm	Sea like a mirror	Calm; smoke rises vertically	Less than 1
1	Light air	Ripples with appearance of scales form but without foam crests	Direction of wind shown by smoke drift but not wind vanes	1–3
2	Light breeze	Small wavelets, short but pronounced; crests look glassy and do not break	Wind felt on face; leaves rustle; ordinary vanes moved by wind	4–6
3	Gentle breeze	Large wavelets; crests begin to break; foam of glassy appearance; scattered white horses	Leaves and small twigs in constant motion; wind extends light flags	7–10
4	Moderate breeze	Small waves become longer; fairly frequent white horses	Raises dust and loose paper; small branches are moved	11–16
5	Fresh breeze	Moderate waves take pronounced form; many white horses; chance of spray	Small trees in leaf begin to sway; crested wavelets form on inland waters	17–21
6	Strong breeze	Large waves form; white foam crests more extensive; probably spray	Large branches in motion; whistling in telegraph wires; umbrellas used with difficulty	22–27
7	Near gale	Sea heaps up and white foam from breaking waves is blown in streaks in direction of wind	Whole trees in motion; inconvenience felt when walking against wind	28–33
8	Gale	Moderately high waves of greater length; edges of crests break into spindrift; foam is blown in well-marked streaks	Breaks twigs off trees; impedes progress when walking	34–40
9	Strong gale	High waves; dense streaks of foam along direction of wind; wave crests topple; spray may affect visibility	Slight structural damage (chimney pots and slates removed)	41–47
10	Storm	Very high waves with long overhanging crests; foam in great patches is blown in dense streaks along wind direction; surface takes on white appearance; visibility affected	Trees uprooted; considerable structural damage occurs	48–55

Hot Weather

A basic understanding of the weather is invaluable when you are pursuing any kind of outdoor activity, but you also need to know what to do in extreme environmental conditions. It is not always obvious how to respond to extreme heat and humidity, or to lightning, and many people end up endangering themselves by doing the wrong thing.

In many hot countries, all the weather is extreme. When it rains, very large amounts of water can be deposited in a short space of time. When the wind blows, it is with destructive force. Of course the sun can burn your skin in a short time, even (in fact sometimes especially) on overcast days.

You must always remember that in some places there are large temperature variations. Maritime climates (that is, in places near the sea) can have a fairly constant temperature day and night. In contrast, in the central areas of large continents the temperature may be 40°C/104°F or higher in the daytime but drop below 0°C/32°F at night.

SUN

Prolonged exposure to the sun in any climate will lead you to suffer from sunburn, especially at high altitude or in the tropics or in ozone depleted regions like the Antarctic on the tip of South America. Wear appropriate clothing, sunscreen and/or sunblock to protect your skin. The short-term effects of sunburn can be painful, and the long-term ones fatal, so you must simply not allow it to happen.

HYDRATION

In a hot and humid environment, such as a rainforest or during a monsoon season, your biggest danger is heatstroke and/or dehydration, although you may be surrounded by water. You will be perspiring at the maximum rate possible for your body, but the perspiration will not evaporate from your skin in the 100 per cent humidity. This means that your body does not cool down, so it

continues to sweat as much as it can to try to achieve this. But it makes no difference to your temperature and you lose water at an incredible rate. All you can do in this situation is keep drinking the coldest water you can safely use, to keep hydrated and try to reduce your core temperature.

STORMS

You should find out about and understand any predictable local weather conditions. In hot climates, storms often occur nearly every day as the land heats up, and you should take care not to be caught out. Especially avoid being on the water in a boat, whether travelling by canoe on a lake,

▲ *A cyclone is a funnel of whirling wind that produces extremely low pressure at its base, which acts like a giant vacuum cleaner.*

or at sea. If you are caught by a storm while afloat, tie everything down and try to keep the centre of gravity of the boat as low as possible. In the event of a wreck or capsize, try to stay with your craft if you can.

You can often predict the onset of electrical storms by the presence of cumulonimbus and anvil clouds, often massing together. Beware if you find yourself downwind of these cloud formations – this means the storm is coming your way. Storms triggered by heat tend to hit in the afternoon or early evening, but they can happen at any time. Such storms often bring with them heavy rain or hailstones.

Even if lightning is not hitting the ground and endangering personnel, you should be aware that electrical activity in a storm can damage navigation gear such as GPS, and knock out communications equipment, so this could endanger your party.

Lightning

If you are out in the open space of a desert or savanna, a lightning storm can be very impressive but it is also very dangerous. If the lightning is very close and you feel you are in danger of being struck, crouch down, with your head as low as possible, and put your hands over your head.

You are in more danger from lightning if you are near trees or any upward pointing object. You are also in great danger if you are on water. Surprisingly, however, on land you are safer in the open, as long as you curl up as described. One of the safest places to be is in a car.

Bushfires

Lightning is frequently the cause of bushfires. If one starts near you, or is coming towards you, and you cannot get out of the way, find an open space and consider burning your own firebreak, but remember that fire can jump quite large distances. If you have to escape a fire, remember that it travels upwards: rather than going up to a ridge, stay down in a valley.

Be warned that the fire will flush out all sorts of animal life, so be careful of snakes and larger animals being forced out to share your space. If the fire is near your camp, make sure you get well away from all gas canisters and similar inflammable materials.

Hurricanes, tornadoes and typhoons

There is little you can do in the face of storms of this magnitude, except to hide from them. Don't stay inside a building that could be destroyed by the storm. The best protection is a safe basement of a very solid construction.

Dust and sandstorms

Desert areas are normally windy places, but if the wind becomes strong enough, it starts picking up first the surface dust and then, as it gets stronger, particles of sand. These storms can last from a few hours to a number of days, and if you are caught in one you can become disoriented. In any area where you are going to encounter blowing sand and dust, make sure your eyes and ears are protected with goggles and maybe a headscarf or headdress.

Driving can become very dangerous, as you will be disoriented and unable to see where you are driving. You should stop and park the vehicle with the engine facing away from the prevailing wind. Close all heating/air-conditioning vents to stop the sand being drawn inside the vehicle.

If you are with animals, turn their backs to the wind while you sit out the storm. Camels should sit down, but horses, mules and donkeys will stand.

▼ *If lightning is striking the ground near you during a storm, don't be tempted to shelter under trees as they may be struck.*

SEASONAL EFFECTS

Many tropical countries have very distinct wet and dry seasons, and transport and logistics may be affected in the wet season due to roads and bridges being washed away, and routes blocked by landslides.

Rain

A violent downpour on dry, baked land may have effects some 36–54km/20–30 miles away. The rain will run off into a dried-up river system that may have been dry for many months, and can turn it into a raging torrent in just a few hours.

This can be very dangerous if you are camped or are walking in a dried-up watercourse. It may be that no rain has fallen where you are and you will therefore not expect a flood.

Mud and landslides

Landslides may be the result of heavy rain and they can be even more destructive than a flood. If it is still raining, never try to walk or drive through one, since where one slide has happened, another can follow.

Cold Weather

If you are travelling in or to countries where the temperature rarely rises above freezing, such as those in polar regions at any time, at high altitude, or inshore in very large continents during the winter, you must know how to survive in blizzards, avoid avalanches, and move safely across snow and ice.

Intense cold can damage the lining of the lungs, so always cover your nose and mouth and breathe through a scarf or something similar so that the air is slightly warmed before you inhale it. You are also in danger from hypothermia and frostbite, so make sure all your clothing and equipment is up to scratch.

BLIZZARDS
In a blizzard, heavy snow is accompanied by strong winds. In extreme cases, the driven snow fills the air and can reduce visibility to less than a metre/yard. It can also cause drifting and very quickly build up large drifts, which can close roads and even cover tents or buildings.

If you are caught in a blizzard, always seek shelter and be prepared to sit it out, even though this may take several days. If you are inside a tent when the blizzard strikes, you may have

▲ *Fast-falling snow quickly transforms the landscape, and if it is combined with a high wind, deep drifts can soon build up.*

to dig your tent out occasionally to stop the weight of snow from collapsing it. Also, make sure the snow is not blocking up your ventilation, as people have suffocated in tents or snow holes when the snow has blocked the door or ventilation holes.

AVALANCHES
There are two main types of avalanche: powder snow and slab. Powder snow avalanches usually consist of newly fallen snow and can be very destructive, mowing down whole forests and villages. Slab avalanches are particularly liable to fall in the spring melt. They move more slowly at the edges and the base than in the centre. They also can be very destructive and their weight can crush anything in their path.

Before you visit a cold country, you should find out if the area is prone to avalanches and know what signs to look for that will tell you when there is a high risk of one occurring. These include rapid snowfall, leading to a buildup of more than 30cm/12in new snow, and sudden rises in temperature.

ICE
Be cautious when approaching any expanse of frozen water, as the ice can be anything from 1m/1yd to only a few centimetres/inches thick. If anyone does fall through the ice, they must be got out as soon as possible and treated for hypothermia (see the section Cold-weather Effects). Anybody going to the person's rescue should beware of becoming another casualty.

Remember that thin ice could be covered by snow. When this is possible you will have to make slow careful progress, checking as you go. Walking on skis or snowshoes can reduce your likelihood of breaking the ice.

If you are on steep ground and start to encounter ice, and cannot avoid it, put on a pair of crampons if you have them. If not, pull a spare pair of socks over your boots, which will give more grip than ordinary soles.

Ice can be a hazard for travellers in vehicles as well as on foot. The ice you can see on a road or track is not your greatest problem, however: it is the ice that may be hidden under a light covering of snow or slush that will cause the accident.

▼ *Navigation can be much more difficult when you are travelling through a snowy landscape where visible landmarks are few.*

ALTITUDE

As you gain altitude the air becomes colder. This is because the air pressure is less, and so the air is less compressed. On a clear day the temperature might typically decrease by 1°C/2°F per 100m/330ft of altitude. If you are under or in cloud, this fall might be reduced to about 0.5°C/1°F as a result of the heat that is released by the condensation process.

TEMPERATURE INVERSION

This usually occurs after a clear night in the mountains. The mountain tops become very cold, and this cools the air in contact with them. The air is now heavy, and rolls down the mountain to make the valleys very cold, forcing the warm air of the valley back up the mountains.

SUNBURN

Even in a cold climate prolonged exposure can result in sunburn, especially in ozone-depleted regions such as the Antarctic on the tip of South America, and you should take all usual precautions to protect your skin.

▶ *It is dangerous to approach an iceberg: a boat may be capsized by turbulence if the berg moves, or underwater ice may ram it.*

▼ *Thick snow may mask watercourses, but you should take extreme care when crossing ice in case you fall through and get wet.*

WIND CHILL

Inanimate objects, including thermometers, are not affected by wind chill, so although a thermometer may accurately measure the air temperature, the combined effect of the temperature and the prevailing wind may have a serious effect on the human body, leading to conditions such as hypothermia and frostbite.

Wearing layers of clothing helps to insulate the body, trapping layers of warm air, while cutting down the penetration of the wind and preventing it carrying away heat.

Signalling

Before you embark on any expedition you must consider how you will get help should an emergency arise. You should make sure that others know your plans and route, so that they can take action if you do not return, but if you are ill, injured, lost or stranded in some way you may need to be able to signal to your potential rescuers.

There are two types of distress signal: those that use specialized equipment and those that rely on natural materials. If you are spending time in wild areas, you will find it useful to understand and be able to use both types in case you need them.

If you are going to a national park or wilderness area, you should find out in advance if there is any special system of distress signals that you need to use there, and make sure you and the rest of your party learn it. Alternatively, you may be required to carry a certain amount of specialized survival equipment while you are in the area, and this is likely to include any relevant signalling equipment.

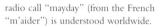

▲ *A rescue helicopter may need to make a difficult or dangerous landing to reach you, so your signals to the crew must be clear.*

BASIC DISTRESS SIGNALS

If you need help you must be able to convey a message that anyone who sees it will understand. "SOS" (short for "Save Our Souls") is an internationally recognized distress signal. It may be transmitted using Morse code (three dots, three dashes and three dots) by the flashes of a mirror or flashlight, or by smoke signals, or it could be written on the ground as a visual message. The

radio call "mayday" (from the French "m'aider") is understood worldwide.

You can also learn the international mountain distress signal, which consists of six flashes of a flashlight, six blasts on a whistle, or waving something for one minute, followed by a minute's silence. The signal is then repeated. The reply from anyone who sees it is three flashes, blasts or waves.

All these signals are taken seriously and you should use them only when you are in trouble.

VISUAL AND AUDIO SIGNALS

If rescue is likely to be coming in the form of a helicopter or plane, you will need to rig up a visual signal that is large enough to attract the attention of the crew. If your rescuers are likely to arrive by land, an audio signal, such as a whistle, will be more effective.

Obviously, any visual ground signals you decide to use must be arranged on sites in open ground, where they can be clearly seen from any direction. You will also need to set up different signals by day and by night, whereas audio signals are equally effective in daylight and darkness.

If you are in a vehicle of some kind, you should always stay with it, as it will offer you some shelter from the elements and you may need to protect yourself from wild animals, particularly at night. A vehicle is also a visual signal in its own right, as it is reasonably large and can be seen from the air, especially if you put bright objects on its roof and beside it. Finally, if you have told people which route you were planning to take, a rescue party will follow it when looking for you.

WHISTLES

Everybody in the party should carry a whistle at all times and should know the international mountain distress signal or any special signals you may

◄ *If you need to make a visual signal, choose an open area where you have a good chance of being seen from land and air.*

have been achieved when climbers in difficulty have phoned home to get relatives to contact the rescue services on their behalf.

PERSONAL EQUIPMENT

If you are in dense scrub or forest, lay your equipment out in a long line on either side of your position, so people looking for you on the ground will have more chance of finding you. Items of equipment can also be laid out on the ground in an open situation to form a visual signal to show an air crew your position.

SPECIAL SIGNALLING EQUIPMENT

A range of emergency equipment is available to help with signalling. You will probably not want to, or be able to, carry all these methods with you, so you need to decide which would be best for your situation.

Transmitters and rescue beacons

This traditional marine method of signalling is becoming far more common for use on land, but the transmitters can have a limited range and are reliant on batteries. Before you

▼ *Strobe lights can be seen over long distances if they are placed in positions of good visibility.*

go into the wilds, arrange two times in the day when you will transmit if you are in trouble – say midday and midnight – then simply transmit for around 15 minutes at both of these times to give the recipients time to pinpoint your position.

Flashlight and strobe lights

A flashlight will allow you to flash a signal or to guide your rescuers to you. Once you switch on a strobe light, it will give a bright flash several times a minute and can be seen at night over great distances.

▲ *A stand allows a flashlight or strobe light to be set up for signalling.*

▶ *Carrying a flashlight will allow you to send the international mountain distress signal.*

◀ *A strobe light fitted with an adjustable strap can be fixed to a cycle frame or hoisted on a pole.*

▲ *A bright orange bivvy bag can be spread out to make a ground marker*

▲ *A folded space blanket can be used to catch the sun's rays and flash an SOS signal.*

▶ *If you take a mobile phone, make sure you load it with all the relevant numbers, but you should use them only in a real emergency and not abuse the goodwill of the rescue services.*

have decided on. They are not only useful for attracting the attention of a rescue party, but can be used by any member of the expedition who strays off the path and gets lost.

MOBILE PHONES

In some countries you may be able to use a mobile (cellular) phone to make contact with the rescue services if an emergency situation arises. This can be a vital timesaver in cases of injury or sudden illness, though its availability should never lead you to lower your usual standards of safety precautions and the correct equipment.

You will need to know in advance the right numbers to call for help or rescue, though some spectacular rescues

◀ *The use of some types of flares requires the possession of a firearms licence, and they can be dangerous.*

▼ *Flares provide both a visual and an audio signal but should not be used without proper training.*

Flares and smoke

These can be bought from specialized stores and ships' chandlers. Some may require a firearms certificate. Flares give both a visual and an audio signal, but they can be dangerous and need to be handled with great care, following the instructions that come with them. You should not let anyone handle them who has not been trained in their use.

Flare and smoke containers will become very hot during use, so wear gloves if possible when you are holding them.

Smoke is useful as a visual signal to attract help from the air or on the ground, though for ground rescue it will need to be on an exposed site that can be seen from a distance. If you do not have smoke containers with you, you can of course light a fire to create a plume of smoke.

Heliographs

A heliograph is a flat, shiny plate, usually silver-coloured, that uses light reflected from the sun to send a flashing light signal. A hole in the middle will help you to direct the sun's rays to the place you are trying to signal to. Heliograph signals can be seen from a great distance. They are quick and require little energy. However, they do need bright, sunny conditions.

By holding the heliograph in the direction of the sun and tilting it

▲ *Tilt the reflector so that the sunlight shines on the plane, and keep it moving to attract the attention of the pilot.*

▼ *A heliograph is a good way of attracting the attention of a pilot too far away to see you, as it is visible over a long distance.*

GROUND-TO-AIR CODE

This international code is designed to be laid out on the ground, using special panels or any natural materials you can find, such as branches, rocks or pebbles. You could also draw the symbols in sand or mud. Make them as large as you can so they can be seen clearly and interpreted correctly.

Some of the messages are particularly useful if you need supplies to be dropped but do not need rescuing, because they allow a plane or helicopter crew to decipher your needs without having to make a risky landing.

Serious injury – immediate evacuation

Need medical supplies

Need food and water

Negative (No)

Affirmative (Yes)

All is well

Unable to move

Am moving this way

Show direction to proceed

Do not understand

Need compass and map

◄ A whistle should be part of the basic survival kit of every member of the expedition.

downwards until the beam of sunlight hits the ground you can make sure you have it in the correct position. Move the panel to flash the light upwards to a passing aircraft or a distant position where a rescuer might spot it.

Water dye

If you are in a boat and need to send a distress signal, a water dye pack can be seen as soon as it is released into the water. The intense colour of the dye patch makes it highly visible, and it can be seen by air rescue more easily than a small boat.

Dye is a very effective way to mark your position on still water, such as on a lake. It is less effective on the sea, where the movement of the waves quickly causes the dye to dissipate and disperse.

Ground-to-air signal panels

Usually made of material in fluorescent colours, these panels can be laid out on the ground as a ground-to-air signal or on a hillside as a ground-to-ground signal. They should measure at least 180 x 75cm/6ft x 2½ft. They can be used to lay out the international ground-to-air code, which it is useful to know (see box).

NATURAL SIGNALS

If you are ill-prepared, or just unlucky, you may not have any specialized method of signalling to hand. You can, however, indicate your position by forming an "SOS" on the ground, or by marking out the relevant ground-to-air signal using part of your kit or any natural materials you can find, such as branches or stones.

You can dig or scrape "SOS" in the earth or snow, or in the sand on a beach. Make the letters as large as you can and build up the sides so that during the day the shadows cast will help the letters to stand out. On snow, you may be able to fill the base of the letters with wood, rocks or earth so that they will be clearer. If you have

fuel from a vehicle, sprinkle some of it along the letters and then light it at night if you hear a plane overhead.

If you use this kind of signal, make sure it is destroyed when you are rescued or if you move away, otherwise other rescuers may see it and endanger their own lives trying to find a non-existent survivor.

FIRES

A fire makes a good signal at night, and if you place boughs of fresh green foliage over the flames during the day it will produce dense smoke, which will make an effective signal both to the air and on the ground. Even if you are not using a fire to keep warm, you should have it prepared in advance, with plenty of fuel ready, so that you can light it quickly if you hear or see possible rescue coming.

▲ Have a fire ready to light if you hear rescuers coming, with some green foliage ready to put on it to create smoke.

▼ In misty conditions a smoke signal may not be seen, and you will not be able to reflect the sun, but a flashlight may work.

EMERGENCY FIRST AID

However carefully you plan a trip, accidents and emergencies can occasionally crop up, and illness may strike even the fittest member of the group. Some expeditions are riskier than others, but if you travel prepared, with a properly equipped first-aid kit and and an up-to-date understanding of emergency life-saving procedures, you can feel confident that you will be able to cope with the unforeseen. Most importantly, you should know your limitations – check out what it is safe for you to deal with yourself and what you should leave for the emergency medical services.

First-aid Kit

If the activities you are planning are relatively low-risk, and you are going to be camping in a place with good road access, so that an ambulance could reach you without too much delay, then a well-stocked standard first-aid kit and the knowledge to use what is inside it will be as much as you need. On the other hand, if you are going to be several hours – or even days – away from road access, both your personal safety and the safety of your group may depend on your emergency skills and

▼ *Do a detailed check through your first-aid kit after each trip and replace anything that has been used or has deteriorated.*

knowledge. Both your first-aid kit and your training will need to be more comprehensive.

BASIC KIT

Make sure that all the items in the kit are well marked and that the kit is kept dry and clean. If necessary, this may mean stowing the container in a waterproof case or bag.

For cuts and grazes, include a good selection of adhesive dressings, both waterproof and fabric-backed. Non-adhesive dressings should be sealed in protective wrappings. Take plenty of sterile gauze pads, the best dressing to stop bleeding from a small wound and

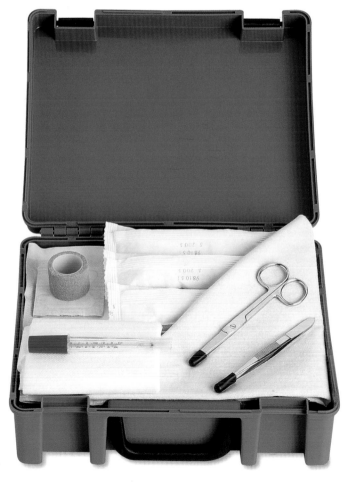

STANDARD KIT

- Surgical gloves
- Wound dressings (2.5–15cm/1–6in)
- Antiseptic wipes
- Assorted adhesive plasters
- Scissors
- Triangular bandages
- Tweezers
- Crêpe bandages
- Sterile scalpel blades
- Moleskin
- Sterile needles
- Sterile gauze pads
- Thermometer
- Cotton wool (balls)
- Safety pins
- Lint
- Roll of adhesive tape
- Sterilized strips (used to close wounds)
- Water purification tablets
- Portable splint
- Face mask for mouth-to-mouth resuscitation

to dress most small to medium-sized wounds, secured with roller bandages. Adhesive tape is an alternative, but some people are allergic to this: try to check before using it. Cotton wool (balls) can be carried to clean the skin around a wound but not to dress an open wound, as the fluff will stick to it.

Scissors in the kit should be sharp, but should have one rounded side to allow the safe cutting of dressings and clothing (for example when treating burns or scalds) without the risk of cutting the skin.

Always carry a notebook and pen in your first-aid kit. In case of serious illness or injury this will allow you to record regular observations of the victim until they can be attended to by a medical practitioner.

As well as your first-aid kit, make sure you have your basic survival kit with you at all times, so that a casualty can be protected from the elements and made comfortable until help arrives.

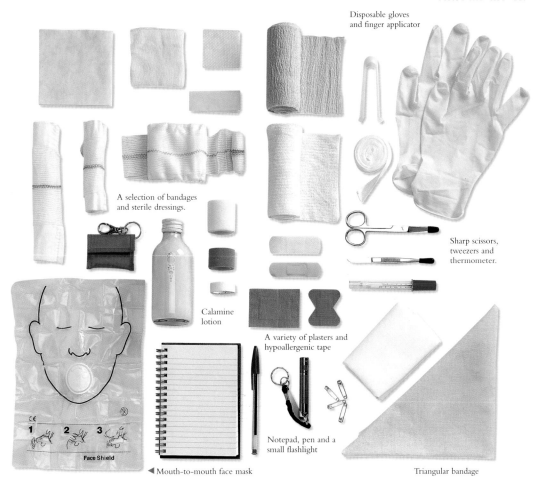

Disposable gloves
and finger applicator

A selection of bandages
and sterile dressings.

Sharp scissors,
tweezers and
thermometer.

Calamine
lotion

A variety of plasters and
hypoallergenic tape

CE
1 2 3
Face Shield

Notepad, pen and a
small flashlight

◀ Mouth-to-mouth face mask

Triangular bandage

▲ *A standard first-aid kit is equipped to support essential life-saving procedures and deal with a range of common injuries; it does not include any drugs or medicines.*

ADDITIONAL ITEMS

The trip you are planning may incur specific risks, either of illness or accident, which you should make yourself aware of and prepare for. The standard first-aid kit is designed to facilitate basic life-saving procedures and deal with common injuries, and you may need to augment its contents. Consider what risks you could encounter and make sure your kit will cover these. If you need to carry more items than those included in the standard kit, add only those that your doctor has recommended and that you

have been trained how to use, to avoid adding unnecessary weight.

If you are going on a long trip in the developing world, you may wish to add a sterile needle kit and an emergency dental kit, in case you have to seek the help of qualified practitioners who are coping with a shortage of medical equipment.

In hot countries, there may be more illnesses and infections than accidents to be dealt with, and this should be reflected in the contents of the kit and any training undertaken.

PERSONAL KITS

The qualified first aider in the group should be in charge of the camp first-aid kit. In addition, all members of the party should carry their own small kits.

DRUGS AND MEDICINES

Any drugs or medicines you add to your kit will be a matter of discussion between you and your doctor, but you will need at least the following:
• Painkillers, both medium and strong
• Treatment for constipation
• Antiseptic cream and powder
• Calamine lotion to soothe sunburn and rashes
• Motion sickness remedies
• Insect repellent
• Eye wash or eye drops or ointment
• Antihistamines
• Rehydration solutions

Assessing an Injured Person

If an accident happens, and one of your party is badly wounded or unconscious, they will not be able to describe their injuries to you, and you will have to ascertain what help is needed by assessing what you see and hear. The ABCDE system will lead you through a step-by-step assessment of the patient.

If the accident occurred in an area that is still dangerous, you will have to decide whether trying to treat the patient in situ would be exposing you and the injured person to a high level of danger. If it would, then you may decide to move the person, even though this is breaking one of the first rules of first aid. If the area is remote, you may have to give more care than is usually recommended in first aid training, because it may be a long time before help arrives. If possible, get two people to write down the grid reference of the location of the accident and set off for help.

▲ *To check a pulse, place two fingertips at the wrist, below the thumb, on the palm side of the hand, and count the pulsations.*

◀ *Always make your initial assessment of a casualty in the position in which you found them, so that your assessment is accurate.*

CHECKING RESPONSES

1 An alert person is awake and will talk spontaneously. Reassure them, and make them as comfortable as possible.

2 The person may seem unconscious but will respond to a verbal prompt. Shout at them and wait for a response.

3 If the person does not respond to shouting or gentle tapping, try a short painful stimulus, such as a rub or pinch.

4 If the three previous steps have produced no response from the person, they are considered unresponsive.

▲ *You may be able to make an improvised stretcher out of two paddles and a buoyancy aid or even a large framed rucksack.*

MOVING AN INJURED PERSON
Never move someone if there is a chance they may have a spinal injury, especially in the neck area, because you risk causing further injury. If you have to move them in order to get them out of danger, you will need to weigh up the risks involved.

If the person is mobile and can walk, however unsteadily, place your arm around their waist, hold their hand and encourage them to lean on you as they walk, taking small steps. If they are unconscious, it is best to drag them. With the person on their back, bend your knees and lift them into a sitting position. Lock your arms around their chest and move backwards, making sure their head cannot fall forwards and block their airway as you move. If the person is conscious but cannot move, they may have a spinal injury and should not be moved – contact the emergency services immediately.

ABCDE SYSTEM

The following system provides a clear and easy-to-remember procedure to follow with an injured person, when you yourself may also be upset.

Assess Safety
- Is the surrounding area safe?
- Look for dangers to yourself and others with you.
- If safe, then approach the person.
- Are they alert?
- Introduce yourself if not known to them.
- Say or shout "Can you hear me?"
- Pinch their ear and ask "Can you feel that?"
- Summon help if possible.

Breathing
- Tilt the person's head back.
- Look in the mouth for any obstruction, and clear as necessary.
- Lift the person's chin.
- Look, listen and feel for up to 10 seconds to determine whether breathing is present or absent.
- If breathing is not present, start mouth-to-mouth resuscitation.

Circulation
- If breathing is present, the person's pulse will be present.
- Look and feel for major bleeding.
- If there is bleeding, apply direct pressure to the wound.

Deformity
- Look for any damage, using a full-body examination.
- Look for bleeding, bruising, pain, loss of function, deformity, swelling.
- Compare one side of the person's body with the other.
- Check the person for a medi-alert, which may be worn around the neck or wrist or kept on a keyring. If you find one, treat the injured person as appropriate.
- Place the person in the recovery position if their injuries allow. Otherwise, make sure their airway is clear and that there is no obstruction to their breathing.

Emotion
- Boost the injured person's confidence by speaking to them and maintaining body contact, even if they are unresponsive.

Follow-up
- Ensure that no symptoms have been missed, and continue to monitor the person's vital signs.
- Ensure they are protected from the elements and from further dangers, such as animals, fire or water.
- Seek medical help as quickly as possible by contacting passers-by, if any, or by phoning or signalling for help from the emergency services.

BASIC LIFE SUPPORT FOR A PERSON WHO IS UNRESPONSIVE

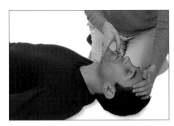

1 Make sure the airway is clear: check for obstructions and remove. Tilt back the head and listen for breathing for up to 10 seconds. If there is no breathing, summon help and give 2 rescue breaths.

2 Watch for signs of a working circulation, such as the rise and fall of the chest, for up to 10 seconds. If there is none at all, begin chest compressions. Do 15 of these.

3 Now give 2 more rescue breaths and continue a cycle of 2 rescue breaths and 15 chest compressions until the emergency services arrive or the person begins to breathe naturally.

Basic First Aid

Wear disposable surgical gloves to treat any wound to prevent cross-infection. You should know how to give mouth-to-mouth resuscitation and how to put someone in the recovery position.

WOUNDS

Even a small wound can cause persistent bleeding and should be cleaned and dressed to avoid infection. Severe bleeding may lead to shock.

Controlling bleeding

If the bleeding is not severe, clean the wound then cover it with a dry wound dressing and bandage. If it is severe,

apply direct pressure with a clean dressing or pad. Lay the victim down and elevate the damaged limb above heart level, then bandage the dressing firmly in place. If blood seeps out of the dressing, bandage another dressing firmly on top of it immediately: do not try to remove the original dressing.

Cleaning wounds

Always clean a wound from the middle outwards, so that any grit or dirt will be moved to the edge of the wound. Cover the area with a clean, dry dressing and secure firmly with either adhesive tape or a bandage.

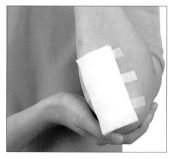

▲ *Clean a minor wound with antiseptic or under gently running clean water before covering with a clean dressing.*

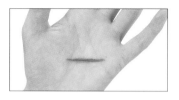

▲ *A laceration caused by a knife or broken glass may damage underlying tendons and nerves, and bleeding can take time to stop.*

▲ *Wounds to fingernails and toenails can easily become infected and very often require professional treatment.*

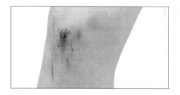

▲ *A fall may cause an abrasion on a knee or elbow. Make sure the wound is clean before covering it with a dressing.*

DEALING WITH A FOREIGN BODY IN A WOUND

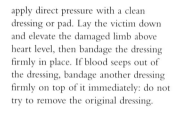

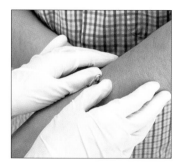

1 If an object is embedded in a limb do not remove it as you may cause further damage. Your aim is to protect the area from infection and get medical help.

2 If the wound is bleeding, apply pressure to the surrounding area, never directly over the embedded object. Elevating the limb may also help.

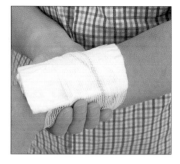

3 Place padding around the object. If possible, as here, build this padding up until it is as high as the embedded object, ready to bandage over smoothly.

4 Bandage over the padding (or on either side of the object if it is long and still protrudes). Keep the wound elevated and get the person to hospital.

REMOVING A FOREIGN BODY FROM THE EYE

1 Examine the person's eye in good light and ask them to look from side to side and up and down. If an object is embedded in the eyeball, or resting on the iris or pupil, do not try to remove it yourself but seek medical help.

2 Ask the person to look down and then gently pull out the upper lid by the lashes. Look on the underside of the upper lid – specks of grit often become lodged here.

3 To remove an object you can see on the white of the eye, flush the eye with clean, tepid water or try (once only) to brush it off with a moistened cotton bud. If this fails, cover the eye with an eyepad (swab) and seek medical help.

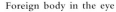

REMOVING FOREIGN BODIES

If you find small objects, such as thorns, protruding from a wound, you may be able to remove them by gently squeezing the skin on either side of the wound, using your fingers. If a small object is embedded in the flesh, or if the wound is more than superficial, you will need to use a small pair of tweezers. Always sterilize tweezers before bringing them into contact with the wound to prevent infection; boil them in hot water or hold over a flame, then allow them to cool down before you start work.

If the object is large or seems to be embedded deeply, do not attempt to remove it as it may be stopping both internal and external bleeding. Seek professional medical help for the injured person as soon as possible.

▼ *A bite from a dog infected with rabies can be fatal, so you should always seek medical help even if the bite is superficial.*

Foreign body in the eye

Hold the patient's eye open and ask them to look in every direction. It is easier to see into the eye if they sit down and you stand behind them and look over their head. If you can see the foreign body resting on the white of the eye, you can try to remove it but do not attempt to deal with it if it is embedded or if it is over the coloured part of the eye. Cover the eye with an eyepad and get medical help.

STINGS AND BITES

In a susceptible person, wasp and bee stings can cause an allergic reaction. Suspect an allergy if there is swelling, dizziness, difficulty breathing, nausea, hives, or a tight throat or chest: take the sufferer to a doctor. If there are signs of anaphylactic shock, call the

▼ *Puncture wounds are caused by long, needle-like objects, including the spines of marine creatures. They can be hard to assess.*

emergency service. A bee may leave a sting attached to a poison sac. Do not squeeze the sac, but scrape it off with a fingernail or blunt knife, and wash the area with soap and water.

Animal bites

If someone is bitten by an animal, first get them to safety to prevent further attacks. If the bite is superficial, wash it with clean water and soap, if available, and cover it with a sterile dressing. If you suspect that the animal might have rabies, or if you are in a developing country, get professional help.

If the bite is deep, press a clean pad over the wound to control the bleeding, and raise the injured part. Bandage the pad in place or replace it with a sterile dressing, then take the person to hospital.

▼ *Cover a wound from an animal bite or sting with a clean, dry dressing and get the person to a doctor.*

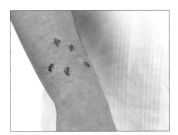

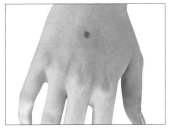

Snake bites

For snake and other potentially venomous bites, prop the person up to keep the heart above the level of the wound. Apply a bandage, or clothing torn into strips, over the whole limb. For example, if you were bitten on the hand then apply the bandage from the shoulder, wrapped around the arm, towards the hand. Make sure that you are able to force a finger under the bandage to ensure it is not too tight. If the arm swells, then undo and re-wrap the bandage so that you are again able to force a finger under it. Seek medical help immediately.

Marine injuries

For stings by jellyfish, Portuguese men-of-war and sea anemones, help the patient out of the water and to a safe place, and pour seawater over the sting area to prevent any stinging cells that have not yet released their venom from doing so. If you have any talcum powder, dust this over the area to bind the stinging cells together, then brush both the powder and cells off with some clean, non-fluffy material.

For puncture wounds from spiny sea creatures, such as sea urchins, hold the stung area in very hot, but not scalding, water for 30 minutes. The spines need to be removed by a medical professional.

TREATING A BLISTER

Cover a blister with a dry dressing or plaster. If a blister bursts, cover it with a non-stick dressing, and change this every day to avoid infection. For more advice on how to treat a blister, see the section Walking.

▼ *Cover the site of a venomous bite with a dry dressing. You should never try to cut into the site of a bite or sting.*

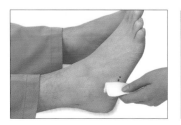

▼ *To stem the blood flow from a puncture wound, elevate the wound above the heart and apply direct pressure over the site with a clean dressing.*

SPRAINS

A sprain is an injury to a ligament, as a result of the ligament being twisted or overextended beyond its normal range of movement. The ligament may have been stretched or completely torn, and it can be very painful. To treat a sprain, follow the RICE guidelines, and seek medical advice as soon as possible for a proper evaluation of the injury.

- Rest the injured limb for at least 24 hours and, if possible, for 48 hours.
- Ice – Apply an ice pack or cold compress intermittently (30 minutes on, 30 minutes off) for the first 12–24 hours. Never put ice directly against the skin, and never use heat or hot water soaks during the first 24 hours after the injury (after 24 hours, apply a warm compress to the area).
- Compress – Apply pressure with an elasticated or crêpe bandage, but loosen this if swelling increases.
- Elevate and rest the injured limb, if possible above heart level.

If you are uncertain about whether an injury is a broken bone, treat it as a broken bone (see the section Bone Fractures). A wrist, elbow or shoulder sprain can be supported in a sling.

▼ *If a burn is on a hand or arm, remove any watches, rings or bracelets while cooling the skin, as the burn may cause swelling.*

▲ *Elevate a sprained ankle comfortably and apply a cold compress. In cold conditions, take care that the foot is not frostbitten.*

BURNS AND SCALDS

Cool the area as quickly as possible with water for 10 minutes (milk or canned soft drinks can be used). Loosen any constriction from the area before it starts to swell. Cover the burn with a non-stick dressing or a clean non-fluffy material, and bandage in place (a plastic bag or food wrap can be used).

Never touch the burned area and do not break blisters or remove loose skin. Do not apply any lotions, ointments or grease, such as butter, to the burn site. If you need to re-dress the burn, do not touch the burn site or remove anything that is stuck to it.

▼ *After cooling the burn area, help to prevent infection by covering it lightly with a sterile non-stick bandage*

SHOCK

This is a serious condition that can be life threatening. It is caused by a sudden and dramatic drop in blood pressure. It can be brought on by any trauma or illness that reduces blood circulation, such as a heart attack, extensive burns, or loss of body fluids due to excessive blood loss or prolonged vomiting or diarrhoea. Severe head or spinal injuries can affect the blood circulation, as can severe allergic reactions.

Initial symptoms of shock include pale, cold, clammy skin, a rapid pulse and sweating. Nausea, dizziness, blurred vision and confusion can follow. If the blood circulation is not restored rapidly, the person will start to gasp for breath and can soon lose consciousness.

To treat shock, lay the victim down and support their legs above heart level. Loosen any constriction at the neck, chest and waist, and keep them warm. Contact the emergency services because medical help is always necessary; monitor their vital signs as you wait. If the person slips into unconsciousness, put them in the recovery position.

RECOVERY POSITION

This is used for people who are unconscious but breathing. A person who is unconscious is not in control of their airway, which can become blocked. To ensure that this does not happen, roll them on to their side, with one arm beneath their head for support, and one hand tilting the head to keep the airway open and the tongue falling forwards, so that fluids, such as blood or vomit, can drain out of the mouth. Bend one leg to keep the position stable. If the limbs are injured and cannot be bent, use rolled-up clothes or sleeping bags as alternative props.

▲ *If a person rescued from drowning is still breathing, put them in the recovery position and keep them warm. Check their vital signs.*

DROWNING

If you rescue someone from drowning, your first step is to get them out of the water safely. A drowning person can easily drag a rescuer under the water: try to reach out to them from the bank or boat with your hand or foot, or hold out a branch or paddle and pull them to safety; get into deep water with them only as a last resort.

Lay the casualty on their back and check for breathing. If they are not breathing, perform mouth-to-mouth resuscitation until their body has become warm and they are breathing on their own. If they are breathing, remove their wet clothing and keep them as warm and dry as you can, using clothing, a sleeping bag or a bivvy bag, then place them in the recovery position and monitor their vital signs. Do not give food or water. Medical help will always be necessary, even if the patient seems fine, because they may fall into a state of shock as they realize what has happened.

▼ *The recovery position is a secure pose that ensures an open airway for easier breathing and allows fluids to drain out of the mouth.*

RESUSCITATION

If a person is not breathing you will need to resuscitate them using mouth-to-mouth resuscitation. Before starting the procedure, you must summon the emergency services, or send someone in your group to make the call.

To begin, lay the person on their back and kneel sideways, facing their head. Check that their mouth is free of any obstructions and tilt back their head. Look, listen and feel for any sign of breathing for up to 10 seconds.

If you are sure that they are not breathing, pinch their nostrils closed. Open your mouth wide and take a deep breath. Put your mouth against the victim's mouth and make a tight seal with your lips around their mouth, to prevent air escaping. Breathe out into their mouth for 2 seconds.

If you are in the correct position, you should see their chest rising as you breathe out. If you do not see the chest rising, reposition their head, keeping the head tilted back and the airway open, and try again. Continue until breathing starts or medical help arrives.

▼ *The head of the unconscious person must be tilted back to ensure that their airway is open. Loosen any tight clothing.*

▼ *You should see the person's chest rising. If not, reposition the head and lift the chin to open the airway before trying again.*

Bone Fractures

In the short term, the various methods used to deal with fractures focus on preventing the fracture from becoming worse. This is all you can hope to achieve in a wilderness situation, without proper medical expertise or equipment. The general idea is to immobilize the fracture and the joints above and below it, and this can be done either by cradling the affected limb or by surrounding it with padding.

Moving a fracture can cause severe pain, as well as damage to surrounding tissue and structures, and possibly further complications, such as shock, from bleeding or from bone penetrating through skin, nerves or blood vessels. Before dealing with a fracture, check that there are no other injuries that require more immediate treatment.

HAND OR ARM IMMOBILIZATION
This can be used on a fracture to the normally rigid bone of the hand or arm. Use your own hands and arms to cradle the injured limb in order to stop all movement. This method is most appropriate when medical help is expected to arrive fairly quickly, or when no other equipment or first aid materials of any kind are available.

If you are dealing with a simple fracture to an arm, and you are confident that bending the limb will not cause further damage, it will be more secure and convenient to put the arm in a broad arm sling in order to prevent movement, rather than to hold it. Have a sling in your first aid kit.

USING PADDING AND BOXES
These props are used mostly for leg fractures, though they are also suitable for arm fractures when bending the elbow to put the arm in a sling would cause further damage.

For this method, hold the fractured limb still, then roll large, loose sausage shapes from sweaters, towels or sleeping bags, and place gently against the limb. Fill any gaps beneath the limb, such as from a bent knee, with just enough padding material to provide support without moving the limb at all. Finally, place backpacks, boxes or other heavy items on either side of the limb to hold the padding in place.

This method is ideal if you can leave the injured person where they are until medical help arrives because it frees you as the first aider to concentrate on taking care of them.

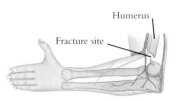

▲ *Fractures of the humerus above the elbow are common in children, whereas adults are more likely to fracture the shoulder end of this bone.*

SYMPTOMS OF A FRACTURE

- The injured person may have a visible history of impact or trauma at the fracture site.
- Bone may be penetrating the skin.
- Swelling, bruising or deformity may be visible at the fracture site. These may worsen over time.
- The person may feel pain on moving the limb.
- The person may feel numbness or tingling in the injured area.
- There may be additional wounds at or near the fracture site.
- The person may have heard the bones crack or grate against one another at the time of impact.

APPLYING A SLING FOR A SIMPLE ARM FRACTURE

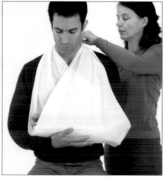

1 Ask the person to keep the arm still. Support the fracture and apply light padding, such as folded bubble wrap or a small towel (nothing too bulky).

2 The fracture should be immobilized completely. Apply a broad arm sling as shown, keeping the light padding in place within the sling.

3 Tie a second bandage across the chest to stabilize the sling and prevent movement when the person is in transit to hospital. Seek medical help.

COMMON FRACTURE TYPES

Simple or closed fracture
There is a clean break in the bone, with no displacement of the bone and no penetration of the skin.

Compound or open fractures
The broken ends of the bone stick out through the skin. The chance of infection is much higher.

Greenstick fracture
The fracture is on only one side of the bone, and the unbroken side bends over like a pliable young tree branch. This type of fracture is common in children.

Comminuted fracture
The bone is splintered at the fracture site, and smaller fragments of bone are found between two main fragments.

Fracture dislocation
The bone breaks or cracks near an already dislocated joint.

Avulsion fracture
A ligament or muscle attached to a bone has ripped off, taking a piece of the bone with it.

SPLINTS
Rigid supports for fractures are rarely used by medical professionals today, but they are useful if you are in a remote location when the accident occurs, and may have a long wait for professional help, or are forced to move the patient to reach a safe area. Improvised examples of splints include ice axes and shovel handles, or even sturdy, stripped tree branches. Add extra padding around the limb, using sweaters or towels, and fix the padding in place with tied bandages, scarves, rope or whatever equivalent you have available. As always with a fracture, your aim is to keep movement to an absolute minimum.

COMPOUND FRACTURES
When you are dealing with a compound or open fracture, it is important to prevent blood loss and reduce the chance of infection at the fracture site, as well as immobilizing the

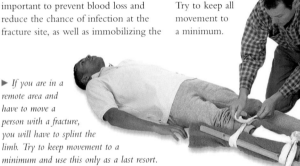

▶ *If you are in a remote area and have to move a person with a fracture, you will have to splint the limb. Try to keep movement to a minimum and use this only as a last resort.*

area. Seek medical help or contact the emergency services urgently, if you can. While you wait, place a clean dressing or sterile pad over the wound site and apply hard pressure, using your hands, to either side of the protruding bone to control the bleeding. Do not press on the protruding bone.

Build up padding alongside the bone sticking out of the skin, and secure the dressing and padding with a bandage, but do not do so if it causes any movement of the limb and never bandage tightly. Monitor the person's condition as there is a risk of shock.

If you are forced to move the injured person to get medical help, you may have to splint the fracture. Add extra padding around the limb and fix in place with tied bandages. Try to keep all movement to a minimum.

USING PADDING TO SUPPORT A LOWER LEG FRACTURE

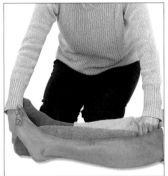

1 Help the person to lie down, then contact the emergency services. Feel the foot and lower leg for warmth and to check the person senses your touch.

2 Place soft padding in the middle of both legs, extending it well above the knee. The foot should be supported in the position in which it was found.

3 If you are forced to move the person yourself, secure the padding in place with bandages, placed well above and below the site of the fracture.

Hot-weather Effects

The effects of the heat on those not used to it can be dangerous, ranging from a bad case of sunburn to life-threatening heatstroke. Staying out of the sun, wearing cool cotton clothing and drinking plenty of fluids are good preventive measures. Other threats to the health in tropical countries arise from water-borne diseases, such as bilharzia, which can be contracted from just a splash of water: avoid swimming in rivers and lakes where there may be any danger of infection. You should have all the necessary vaccinations before you travel, but the commonest infections encountered in hot climates are those contracted from contaminated food and drink or mosquito-borne diseases such as malaria.

SUNBURN

If you are overexposed to the sun without adequate protection you risk getting sunburnt, and it can happen

▼ *Treat heat exhaustion before it turns into heatstroke by getting the person to rest in a shady place and cooling them down.*

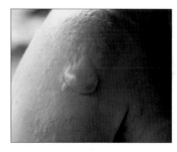

▲ *An extreme case of sunburn can cause blistering of the skin. Treat as you would a burn and seek medical help immediately.*

anywhere: you should always make sure you are well protected. You will be particularly susceptible to sunburn if you are fair-skinned and from a temperate latitude. Those with fair or red hair are most at risk and some parts of the body are particularly vulnerable, such as the nose, the back of the neck and shoulders, a bald scalp and the tops of the feet.

Sunburn can make you extremely uncomfortable and can do lasting damage to your skin, increasing the risk of skin cancer. In more extreme cases, it may mean you are unable to continue your trip, so take it seriously and be prepared.

Treatment If the skin is bright red and sore and feels hot to the touch, get the person out of the sun, either indoors or in the shade. Cool the affected area of skin using cold compresses or by immersing it in cold

water for at least 10 minutes. Apply calamine lotion or any product that has been designed to soothe and moisturize sunburnt skin (many are now available from pharmacies and drugstores). Give the patient plenty of water to drink and encourage them to lie still, keeping the affected area uncovered, if possible, although a loose cotton covering could be used if preferred. If the skin has blistered, treat in the same way as for a burn and seek medical help.

HEAT EXHAUSTION

This is a particular health risk in hot, humid areas, and people are especially subject to it if they are taking part in strenuous exercise in the sun. It is caused by the loss of salt and water through excessive sweating.

The symptoms of heat exhaustion are headache, dizziness, confusion, nausea and sweating, with clammy skin and rapid breathing.

Treatment Move the person out of the sun to somewhere cool, then lay them down with their feet raised. Raise their head while they drink water, followed by a saline solution (1 tsp salt per litre/1¾ pints water). Always seek medical help.

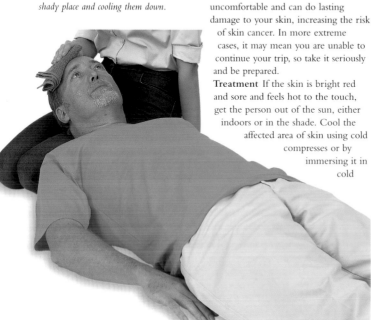

PROTECTING SKIN FROM BURNS AND BITES

All exposed skin needs to be covered with sunscreen to protect against the burning effects of the sun's UVB rays. But you should also apply it to skin that will be under thin clothing, as it may not be an effective screen against UVA rays, which can cause long-term damage.

The brand of sunscreen you choose needs to give protection against both UVA and UVB rays. Apply it 30 minutes before going outside and re-apply it regularly, even in cloudy weather. Look for a protection factor of at least SPF 25, and at least SPF 40 if you are at altitude, on snow or in water, when you should use a water-resistant brand. The protection factor applies only to the burning UVB rays; UVA protection may be indicated by a star system.

Insect repellent also needs to be applied regularly. The standard chemical repellent is DEET, which is available as a liquid, spray, gel or stick. This guards against all biting insects, including mosquitoes. Take care not to get it near the eyes or mouth – spray it on your hands then apply it to your face with care – and don't get it near cuts or grazes, or apply it to skin that will be covered by your clothing. Insect repellent can also be sprayed on to clothing. If you can't bear the smell of DEET, try using natural plant oils such as citronella, eucalyptus or lavender.

Sleeping under specially designed insect netting at night and wearing clothing made from closely woven fabrics, fitted at the wrists and ankles, can help to minimize the use of chemical repellents.

HEATSTROKE

Formerly called sunstroke, heatstroke can follow heat exhaustion, but it can also come on very quickly, leading to unconsciousness within minutes. It is a serious condition that involves the failure of the body's heat control mechanism and can lead to death if the temperature is not lowered.

The symptoms are similar to those of heat exhaustion, but the body temperature will go over 40°C/104°F and there will be little or no sweating.

The person will therefore have dry, rather than clammy, skin. They will be very restless, behave irrationally and have a lack of coordination. They may experience headache and delirium, and can become unconscious.

Treatment The priority is to cool the person down quickly. Move them somewhere cool, lay them down and remove their clothing. Cover them with a wet sheet if available, or sponge them with cold water, until their temperature falls to 38°C/100.4°F. Contact the emergency services for help or get the victim to hospital as quickly as possible.

SKIN CANCER

It is now established that the risk of skin cancer and skin damage is increased by both exposure to the sun over a long period and episodes of acute sunburn. Moles and pigmented areas of the skin should be examined regularly and you should consult a doctor if you notice changes such as a patch increasing in size, developing an irregular outline, showing variations in colour from brown to black within the area, itching, becoming inflamed or bleeding.

HEAT OR SWEAT RASHES AND PRICKLY HEAT

These complaints of the skin in hot countries are often brought on by tight clothing or where the clothing rubs the skin. They can be avoided by wearing loose-fitting clothes of pure cotton, taking frequent cool showers without using soap and drying the body carefully. If rashes do flare up, soothe them with calamine lotion.

TRAVELLER'S DIARRHOEA

This is usually caused by food poisoning, eating unusual foods or drinking contaminated water, and may be accompanied by vomiting. Symptoms will usually pass within a few hours, but if they continue, or the person starts to pass blood and has a fever, seek medical help.

Treatment Encourage the person to drink plenty of fluids, including rehydrating solutions, to ward off dehydration caused by fluid loss.

▲ *Heat exhaustion is caused by the loss of salt and dehydration that results from excessive sweating, so the victim should be given water and a weak saline solution to drink.*

Cold-weather Effects

The risk of frostbite and hypothermia is always present in cold conditions, and the risk increases if there is a wind blowing, since the wind-chill factor can bring the temperature down still further. The onset of hypothermia is the commonest cause of calls to the emergency rescue services, but snow blindness, sunburn, frostbite and trench foot may also develop in cold conditions.

SNOW BLINDNESS

This is a temporary form of blindness caused by the intensity of the sun's rays on snow or ice. A mild case can cause the eye to become red and inflamed; an extreme case can cause permanent damage to the sight. To avoid snow blindness, wear sunglasses or goggles.

SUNBURN

If you are on snow or ice or at altitude, you are in increased danger of sunburn. The snow and ice can reflect the sun's rays and cause burning of the skin on the nose and chin. You must cover all exposed skin or use a high-factor sunscreen (at least SPF 40) or sun block.
Treatment See the section Hot-weather Effects.

▼ Offer a hypothermia victim a warm drink such as sweetened tea to raise their body temperature. Do not give alcohol.

FROSTBITE

In icy conditions frostbite can affect any bare skin. All the extremities of the body, such as the face, nose, ears, hands and feet, are most commonly affected. To avoid frostbite, wear loose clothing, mittens rather than gloves, and a woollen balaclava type of headgear. Try to keep your clothing dry and keep moving your fingers and toes to keep the circulation going.

The signs of frostbite are prickling pain and numbness. If you are in a group, work in pairs to check each other's extremities, looking for pale, hard and stiffened skin, changing to white, then blue and finally black.
Treatment Remove gloves or boots, then warm the affected area slowly, either by placing it somewhere warm, such as in the patient's armpit, or putting it in warm water, before bandaging it. Support the limb in a raised position and seek medical help if necessary.

▲ Someone suffering from hypothermia will become confused. Get them to shelter, wrap them in extra layers and stay with them.

TRENCH FOOT

This is caused when the feet are wet for long periods in very cold conditions, from 0–10°C/32–50°F. It can become a serious complaint if the conditions continue for a long time, as the blood vessels can become constricted, cutting off circulation, which could lead to losing a foot or limb through gangrene.

The feet become uncomfortably numb, cold and heavy and the affected area may swell up and feel prickly or tingling. The toes and ankles are stiff and walking is difficult. Trench foot can be prevented by moving around, keeping the feet dry and loosening footwear to allow good circulation. Changing out of wet footwear should be a priority on arrival in camp.
Treatment As for frostbite.

EFFECTS OF ALTITUDE

The various stages of altitude sickness generally affect climbers at different heights:
- Acute mountain sickness (rare below 2,450m/8,000ft): comes on quickly; headache, nausea, dizziness, shortness of breath.
- High-altitude pulmonary oedema (rare below 3,000m/10,000ft): fatigue, dry cough, headache, fever, rapid heartbeat, blue lips.
- High-altitude cerebral oedema (rare below 3,350m/11,000ft): severe headache, noise in chest, lack of coordination, loss of vision, hallucination.

HYPOTHERMIA

Prolonged exposure to the cold, especially in windy and wet conditions, can cause hypothermia, which occurs when the body cools down to a temperature below 35°C/95°F.

As the body temperature falls, the person will start to shiver, then become confused and lethargic and act in strange ways. They will complain of fatigue and may suffer from visual disturbance, slurred speech and cramp. Their skin will be pale and clammy. The final stage of the condition, when the body temperature drops below 26°C/79°F, is unconsciousness followed by death from cardiac arrest. All members of a party must keep checking each other for the symptoms.

To avoid hypothermia, make sure you are well insulated with a protective windproof layer over your warm clothing. You should eat well, drink plenty of water and stay active.
Treatment Wrap the person in a blanket and cover their head. Move them to a sheltered place and put them in a sleeping bag, bivvy bag, space blanket, or anything similar. Call for medical aid or send someone to fetch help, but do not leave the victim alone. Warm them with a hot drink if possible and some easily digested, high-energy food. Keep talking to them to cheer them up. Give mouth-to-mouth resuscitation if they stop breathing.

ALTITUDE SICKNESS

Mountain or altitude sickness can range from a bad headache and sickness to life-threatening pulmonary or cerebral oedema (fluid in the lungs or brain). It is caused by climbing mountains over 3,000m/10,000ft too quickly.

At high altitudes the atmospheric pressure is lower and the air thinner than at ground level, so that less oxygen gets into the bloodstream. The body is able to adjust to this, up to a height of about 5,500m/18,000ft, but it needs time to do so. The first noticeable symptoms are usually breathlessness and a need to slow down, but a more severe attack of altitude sickness may result in severe headache, chest discomfort, loss of appetite, nausea, vomiting, disorientation, confusion, difficulty with balance and a dry cough. Altitude does not have the same effect on people each time they climb: escaping altitude sickness on one expedition does not mean you will avoid it at a later date.

To avoid the condition, you should climb large peaks slowly (no more than 300m/1,000ft a day) even if you are fit enough to ascend more rapidly. If possible spend a few days at a moderate height (around 2,500m/8,200ft) to acclimatize to that level before beginning a further climb. Dehydration aggravates the condition, so it is important to drink plenty of fluids while climbing.

▲ *The extremities are most prone to frostbite in cold conditions. Warm cold, numb hands by placing them in the armpits.*

Treatment If someone starts to show any of the symptoms of altitude sickness, they should be taken down to a lower altitude as fast as possible, especially if the condition comes on very quickly. The symptoms should disappear after a few days, but if they continue to worsen after this partial descent, the victim needs to get medical help urgently as this indicates pulmonary or cerebral oedema.

▼ *A bivvy bag should be carried as part of the basic survival kit. It will help to retain body heat in an emergency situation.*

Dehydration

This occurs when there is insufficient water in the body, or when the body loses large quantities of water quickly and the fluid cannot be replenished. Dehydration is a medical emergency. It can be fatal, and should be treated as soon as the symptoms are noticed.

Severe dehydration can occur with excessive heat and sweating, through a lack of food and fluid intake, or because of prolonged vomiting or diarrhoea. It is very likely to occur through sweating if you are doing strenuous exercise in a hot climate, if climbing at high altitudes, or trekking cross-country. It is particularly common in the elderly, and in infants and young children, often as a result of diarrhoea, when it will occur rapidly.

PREVENTION

To prevent dehydration, you need to drink enough fluids to replace those lost. If the human body loses as little as 10 per cent of its natural fluid level, it can start to shut down and will need hospital treatment to restore its natural balance, with the victim being put on a drip in order to be rehydrated.

If you are sweating a lot, you will be losing not only water but also salt and, in small quantities, a number of the body's trace elements. The salt and

◀ Hydration backpacks, ideal for cycling and other endurance sports, contain a water reservoir with a drinking tube attached.

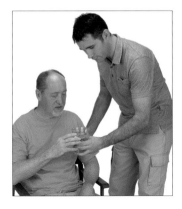

▲ Encourage the casualty to take small sips of drinking water as soon as they start to notice the effects of dehydration.

trace elements need to be replenished as well as the fluids if you are going to continue to function normally.

On average, an adult who is walking or exercising for several hours each day needs to drink at least 3 litres/5¼ pints of fluid in a mild climate, rising to over 6 litres/10½ pints in hot temperatures or if at a high altitude or doing any strenuous physical activity that causes severe sweating. If you drink less than this, you are at risk of dehydration.

SYMPTOMS

An early sign of dehydration is thirst, and in an extreme case you may be unable to quench your thirst no matter how much you drink. Another early symptom is a headache, as the blood vessels in the head constrict due to lack of fluids. Lightheadedness may follow.

You may notice that your urine becomes darker in colour and there is less of it. In the later stages of dehydration, there may be feelings of drowsiness, restlessness and confusion about where you are and what you are doing. Abdominal or muscle cramping are also common.

▲ If you feel dehydrated but drinking water is unavailable, loosen or remove clothing and stop your activities to seek shade.

Treatment

As soon as you notice the symptoms of dehydration in yourself, move indoors or into the shade, and drink as much fluid as you have available or until you no longer feel thirsty. If you suspect a member of your group is dehydrated, encourage them to move to a cooler area and give them something to drink.

What to drink will depend on where you are and what is available. Water alone is not ideal, because it can pass straight through the body. Adding 20–25ml/4–5 tsp of salt and 5ml/1 tsp of sugar per litre/1¾ pints of water is better because it will help to replenish the body's water and salt level. Good alternatives to a sugar and salt solution

---

SEVERE DEHYDRATION

Seek immediate help for anyone who displays any of the following symptoms due to dehydration:
• Vomiting and/or diarrhoea
• Seizures
• Fast, weak pulse
• Fast breathing
• Sunken eyes
• Lack of tears
• Wrinkled fingers and toes
• Dry mouth

DEALING WITH THIRST

DEALING WITH THIRST

If drinking fluid supplies are limited and you need to stave off thirst, there are steps you can take that will help you handle the psychological effects of thirst. This will allow you to focus more efficiently on sourcing water or fluid supplies.

- Suck on something small and smooth, such as gum, a nut or pebble, or a chunk of raw onion.
- Conserve body fluid and reduce sweating by making only calculated moves. In a hot climate, move in slow motion.
- Regulate your clothing. In a hot climate, reduce sweat evaporation by keeping all skin covered; in a cold climate, reduce sweating by loosing/removing clothing.
- Rest or sleep as often as possible, in the shade in a hot climate.
- Do not eat anything if you have nothing to drink; avoid eating proteins if fluids are limited; eat fruit, sweets, crackers and plants.
- Rub the hands, face and neck with a pad soaked in sea water, urine or alcohol, if available.

DEHYDRATION IN CHILDREN

Children suffering from diarrhoea can become dehydrated very quickly. A young child showing symptoms of dehydration, should be given fluids to drink but be careful how much salt you give them: give no salt at all unless they are severely dehydrated, in which case emergency medical help should be sought urgently. For an infant, give as much fluid as they can drink and seek medical help straight away.

VOMITING

If someone is vomiting as a result of dehydration, their condition is serious and you should get medical help. If the vomiting is due to another known cause, such as a digestive upset, but is a potential cause of dehydration, a rehydration solution may help if they can keep it down. Get them to sip the fluid very slowly rather than attempt to drink down a whole water bottle or cup at once, which they may not be able to manage.

A child who is vomiting should be given a small sip (about a teaspoonful) of fluid every 10–20 minutes. You can increase this amount gradually if the fluid stays down.

DIARRHOEA

Mild diarrhoea is characterized by frequent loose, watery bowel movements, and in more severe cases there may also be stomach cramping, tiredness, thirst and/or streaks of blood in or on the stools. Common causes of diarrhoea include food poisoning, certain medications, emotional stress, excessive alcohol consumption, and viral and bacterial infections.

In its mildest form, diarrhoea brings inconvenience and discomfort but it is not dangerous so long as the fluids lost can be replaced. Encourage the individual to drink two glasses of drinking water each time they open their bowels to maintain their level of body fluid.

If the person cannot or will not drink liquids, the replacement of fluids will not be possible and dehydration will result. Hospitalization will then be necessary to restore the body fluids. If the diarrhoea persists for longer than a day or two medical attention should be sought.

▼ *Climbing at high altitudes increases the risk of dehydration. Planning proper water supplies is vital from the outset.*

include a rehydration solution (available from pharmacies and drugstores) that has to be made up with water, an isotonic glucose drink, flavoured gelatin in liquid form, a carbonated drink that has been allowed to go flat, clear broth or diluted fruit juice. All of these will do the job equally well, but caffeinated drinks should be avoided as they are diuretic and can thus aggravate the problem. Drink at least 200ml/8fl oz of fluid every hour and avoid eating solid foods for 24 hours. Make sure that any water used to make up a water-based drink has been purified and is free from contamination. Otherwise, the bacteria in contaminated water may cause vomiting, and this will further increase the fluid loss.

If a severely dehydrated person cannot or will not take a drink, if the thirst cannot be quenched and the symptoms persist, or if there are any complications, seek medical help.

APPENDIX

The following pages feature a glossary, further reading, useful contacts,
a compilation of websites plus an index. If you wish to take your
survival skills any further then the information in this section will
point you in the right direction.

Glossary

Acclimatization: The process of physiological adaptation over time to new or demanding environmental conditions, such as high altitude or extreme temperatures.

Adventure holiday: Organized vacation, usually in small groups, featuring active outdoor pursuits and skills that involve an element of risk and unpredictability.

AIDS (acquired immune deficiency syndrome): Failure of the body's ability to fight disease as a result of infection by the human immunodeficiency virus (HIV).

Altitude sickness: Potentially serious condition caused by climbing mountains too quickly to allow acclimatization to lower oxygen levels at heights of over 2,450m/8,000ft.

Anvil cloud: The very large, flat, spreading top of a thundercloud.

Base camp: Well-established long-term camp, usually set up in a situation with vehicular access, where supplies for a large expedition can be stored and to which more lightly equipped expeditions return.

Bear bagging: Hanging food bags from a tree branch inaccessible by bears and other wild animals.

Belaying: Wrapping a line around a stable object such as a rock or tree to slow or stop it slipping, for instance to protect a climber from falling.

Bivvy bag: Waterproof sack large enough to sleep in, for use as an emergency shelter.

Canoe: Small open boat propelled with a paddle from a sitting position by one or more people.

Carborundum stone: Block of very hard crystalline substance (silicon carbide), used to sharpen blades.

Cardiovascular endurance: Ability to exercise the whole body without becoming breathless or tired.

Contour lines: Lines on a map joining points of equal height, plotted at regular intervals, to indicate hills and valleys.

Crampons: Spiked metal attachments worn under the soles of boots to give grip on snow or ice.

Cumulonimbus clouds: Heavy, dark clouds, of immense vertical height, associated with thunderstorms.

Customs carnet: Document allowing for temporary duty-free importation of goods (such as a vehicle).

DEET: Active ingredient in most insect repellents applied to skin.

Dome tent: Tent supported by lightweight flexible poles threaded through sleeves in the fabric.

Dry bag: Waterproof bag with watertight closure system used for storage in canoes and kayaks.

Fibre pile: Knitted fabric designed for use as thermal component in layered clothing system, which acts as insulation while allowing heat and moisture from the body to escape.

Fieldcraft: Skills needed to survive in wilderness areas, such as the ability to navigate, construct shelter and find food.

Fly sheet: Additional sheet erected over a tent to provide insulation from heat, cold and wet.

Frostbite: Damage to skin and underlying tissue following exposure to temperatures below freezing, which may lead to loss of circulation and gangrene.

Geodesic dome tent: Dome tent with one or more extra poles crossing the sides of the tent at angles to create additional surfaces and reduce wind pressure on any one wall.

Green card: International motor insurance certificate, guaranteeing that a driver's normal motor

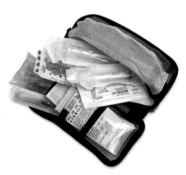

insurance policy covers them for liability in the countries for which the card is valid.

Grid reference: Set of numbers identifying a location with reference to the system of numbered grid lines drawn on a series of topographical maps.

Hazardous pursuit: Any leisure activity that carries a high risk of accident, and may therefore not be covered by a normal travel insurance policy.

Heat exhaustion: Condition leading to symptoms such as headache, dizziness and nausea caused by loss of salt and water from excessive sweating.

Heatstroke: Serious condition arising from the failure of the body's heat control mechanism, leading to rapid rise in temperature, delirium, loss of consciousness and possibly death.

Heliograph: Signalling device that uses a mirror to reflect the sun's rays in flashes, for example to transmit messages in Morse code.

Hepatitis: Inflammation of the liver, most commonly by viral infection; of five named viruses (A, B, C, D and E), A and E are mainly picked up from contaminated drinking water and faeces while B and C are transmitted sexually or through blood and blood products.

HIV (human immunodeficiency virus): The cause of AIDS, transmitted via contaminated blood, injection with non-sterile needles, or sexual intercourse.

Hydration system: Means of carrying and drinking water while on the move; a reservoir, usually in a backpack, is accessed by a drinking tube with a mouthpiece fitted with a valve.

Hypothermia: Fall in core body temperature to below 35°C/95°F.

International Camping Carnet (CCI): Identity card, issued by camping organizations, that guarantees payment of campsite fees.

International Certificate for Motor Vehicles: Vehicle passport, valid for one year, that provides the vehicle's registration documentation in an internationally recognized form.

International Driving Permit (IDP): Document providing proof that the holder possesses a valid driving licence in their home country.

Kayak: Small decked boat propelled with a paddle from a sitting position.

Kindling: Small dry twigs that burn easily, used when lighting a fire to ignite the fuel.

Knot: Unit of speed equal to 1 nautical mile (1.85km/1.15 miles) per hour.

Lightweight camping: Camping using only the equipment that can be carried in a backpack, generally weighing 11kg/25lb or less per person.

Magnetic variation: The difference in direction between true north (the North Pole) and magnetic north, which slowly but constantly changes its position.

Morse code: Signalling system in which letters of the alphabet are coded into combinations of dots and dashes.

Muscular endurance: Ability to exercise specific muscles without becoming tired.

Numnah: Pad placed under a horse's saddle to protect its back and keep the saddle clean.

Pannier: Bag designed to hang beside a horse's saddle or alongside the wheel of a bicycle or motorbike, usually as one of a pair.

Passive reflector: Printed circuit card requiring no batteries that can be built into ski boots and clothing and detected by equipment used by organized rescue groups in case of avalanche.

Pouch food: Ready meals sealed in waterproof foil pouches that are heated in boiling water before opening.

Prismatic compass: Compass with a prismatic eyepiece and hairline sight that allows distant objects and the compass face to be viewed simultaneously for accurate readings.

Protractor compass: Compass mounted on a clear plastic protractor or baseplate that can be held directly over a map when setting a bearing.

Quartermaster: Person in charge of procuring and issuing food stores and equipment.

Rehydration powder: Commercial preparation containing sodium chloride, glucose and other substances, to be added to water for the treatment of dehydration.

Ridge tent: Triangular-section tent supported by a horizontal pole fixed between two vertical poles and held in place by guy lines.

Risk assessment: Process of identifying the risks associated with an activity, how likely it is that something will go wrong and what the consequences will be (to expedition members and the environment).

Salopettes: Trousers, sometimes with reinforced seat and knees, with high bib front and back held up with braces; worn for activities such as skiing.

Scree: Slope of unstable rocky fragments that have broken off a cliff face, usually as the result of weathering, and have accumulated at its base.

Space blanket: Lightweight reflective sheet used to insulate the body in an emergency to prevent hypothermia.

Spraydeck (sprayskirt): Flexible watertight cover for a boat, particularly a kayak; it has a hole for the occupant, the edges of which can be tightened around the body to prevent water getting into the boat in rough conditions.

Sun protection factor (SPF): Number indicating the relative time for which a sunscreen will protect skin against the sun's UVB (burning) rays; the actual time depends on skin type and location.

Third-party insurance: Liability insurance, indemnifying the insured against liability for damage or destruction of other people or their property.

Tinder: Highly combustible material, such as wood shavings or dry pine needles, that will catch alight from a single spark, used to start a fire.

Topographical map: Map showing natural features of a region by means of contour lines and symbols as well as man-made features such as roads.

Visa: Stamp in a passport issued by a country's immigration authority allowing the bearer to enter the country for a specific purpose and length of time.

Wicking: Movement of moisture by capillary action; often used to describe clothing that draws sweat away from the body to the fabric's outer surface, where it evaporates.

Yellow card: Internationally recognized certificate of immunization against diseases such as typhoid, polio, yellow fever and hepatitis A.

Further Reading

*Adventure Trekking: A Handbook for
Independent Travellers*
Robert Strauss
(Mountaineers, 1996)

Backpacker's Pocket Guide
Chris Townsend
(Ragged Mountain Press, 2002)

*Backcountry Bear Basics: The Definitive
Guide to Avoiding Unpleasant
Encounters*
Dave Smith
(Mountaineers, 1997)

Canoeing: A Trailside Guide
Gordon Grant
(Norton, 1997)

Canoeing Handbook
Ray Rowe
(British Canoe Union, 1997)

Complete Walker III (3rd ed. rev.)
Colin Fletcher
(Knopf, 1984)

Culture Shock!: A Traveller's Medical Guide
Paul Zakowich
(Graphic Arts Center Publishing
Company, 1996)

Essential Bushcraft
Ray Mears
(Hodder & Stoughton, 2002)

The Essential Horse Book
Judy Draper
(Lorenz Books, 1999)

First Aid at Sea (4th ed.)
Douglas Justins and Colin Berry
(Paradise Cay Publications, 2003)

*High Summer Backpacking the Canadian
Rockies*
Chris Townsend
(Cloudcap, 1989)

How To Stay Alive in the Woods
Bradford Angier
(Fireside, 1998)

Kayaking: White Water and Touring Basics
Steven M. Krauzer
(Norton, 1995)

Knots for Climbers
Craig Luebben
(Chockstone Press, 1993)

*Medicine for Mountaineering and Other
Wilderness Activities* (5th ed.)
James A. Wilkerson
(Mountaineers, 2001)

Mountain Rope Techniques
Bill March
(Cicerone Press, 1983)

*Packing: A Guide to the Care, Training
and Use of Horses and Mules as
Pack Animals*
United States Army Publication
(Northland Publishing, 1989)

Sea Kayaking
John Dowd
(Douglas & MacIntyre, 1988)

*The Advanced Backpacker: A Handbook
of Year-round, Long-distance Hiking*
Chris Townsend
(Ragged Mountain Press, 2001)

The Alternative Knot Book
Harry Asher
(A. & C. Black, 1989)

*The American Canoe Association's River
Safety Anthology*
Charles Walbridge and Jody Tinsley
(Menasha Ridge Press, 1996)

The Backpacker's Handbook (2nd ed.)
Chris Townsend
(Ragged Mountain Press, 1997)

The Bushcraft Handbooks
Richard H. Graves
(Sydney, 1952)

The Complete Rock Climber
Malcolm Creasey
(Lorenz Books, 1999)

The Great Backpacking Adventure
Chris Townsend
(Oxford Illustrated, 1987)

The Munros and Tops
Chris Townsend
(Mainstream Press, 1997)

*The Practical Guide to Kayaking &
Canoeing*
Bill Mattos

(Lorenz Books, 2002)

*The Ultimate Encyclopedia of Knots &
Ropework*
Geoffrey Budworth
(Lorenz Books, 1999)

*The Ultralight Backpacker: The Complete
Guide to Simplicity and Comfort On
The Trail*
Ryel Kestenbaum
(Ragged Mountain Press, 2001)

The Weather Book (2nd ed. rev.)
Jack Williams
(Vintage, 1997)

*The Weather Sourcebook: Your One-Stop
Resource for Everything You Need to
Feed Your Weather Habit* (2nd ed.)
Ronald L. Wagner and Bill Adler Jr.
(Globe Pequot, 1997)

*The Whole Backpacker's Catalog: Tools
and Resources for the Foot Traveler*
Ed Sobey
(Ragged Mountain Press, 1999)

Tom Brown's Field Guide
Tom Brown Jr. and Brandt Morgan
(Berkley Books, 1983)

Traveller's Healthbook
Nick Beeching and Jonathan Lorie
(Footprint, 2002)

*Treading Lightly with Pack Animals:
A Guide to Low-impact Travel in
the Backcountry*
Dan Aadland
(Mountain Press, 1993)

Weather Forecasting for Sailors
Frank Singleton
(Hodder & Stoughton, 1981)

Wilderness Skiing and Winter Camping
Chris Townsend
(Ragged Mountain Press, 1994)

Useful Addresses

UNITED KINGDOM

Brathay Exploration Group
Brathay Hall
Ambleside
Cumbria LA22 0HP
Tel: (01539) 433942

British Trust for Conservation
    Volunteers
36 St Mary's Street
Wallingford
Oxon OX10 0EU

Earthwatch
57 Woodstock Road
Oxford OX2 6HJ

Foreign & Commonwealth Office
Travel Advice Unit
Old Admiralty Building
Whitehall
London SW1H 9HD
Tel: (0870) 6060 290

Medical Advisory Services for
    Travellers Abroad (MASTA)
Keppel Street
London WC1E 7HT
Tel: (020) 7238 7500

National Trust
36 Queen Anne's Gate
London SW1H 9AS
Tel: (0870) 609 5380

The Commonwealth Youth Exchange
7 Lion Yard
Tremadoc Road
Clapham
London SW4 7NQ
Tel: (020) 7498 6151

The Duke of Edinburgh's Award Scheme
Gulliver House
Windsor
Berks SL4 1EU
Tel: (0131) 556 9097

The Royal Geographical Society
1 Kensington Gore
London SW7 2AR
Tel: (020) 7591 3000

The Young Explorers' Trust
Stretton Cottage
Wellow Road
Newark
Notts NG22 9AX
info@theyet.org

UNITED STATES

Pinkerton Global Intelligence Services
4245 North Fairfax Drive
Suite 725
Arlington
VA 22203

The National Outdoor Leadership
    School
288 Main Street
Lander
WY 82520-3140

The National Park Foundation
11 Dupont Circle NW
Suite 600
Washington
DC 20036

U.S. State Department
Travel Advisory Service
Room 48111
2201 C Street NW
Washington
DC 20520
Tel: (202) 647-4000 (enquiries);
(202) 647-5225 (travellers' hotline)

CANADA

Canadian Tourism Commission
55 Metcalfe Street, Suite 600
Ottawa
Ontario K1P 6L5

Consular Affairs Bureau
Foreign Affairs Canada
125 Sussex Drive
Ottawa
Ontario K1A 0GA
Tel: for enquiries telephone 1-800-
267-6788 (Canada and US only) or
(613) 944-6788; for emergencies
telephone (613) 996-8885.

AUSTRALIA

Department of Foreign Affairs and
    Trade (Consular division)
R.G. Casey Building
John MacEwan Crescent
Barton
ACT 00221
Tel: (2) 6261 1111
For the 24hr Consular Emergency
Centre telephone (2) 6261 3305
or 1300 555 135.

NEW ZEALAND

Ministry of Foreign Affairs and Trade
    (Consular division)
195 Lambton Quay
Wellington
Tel: (4) 439 8000

Useful Websites

Consular services
British Diplomatic Mission
www.fco.gov.uk

Foreign & Commonwealth Office
www.fco.gov.uk

Representatives of foreign states and
    Commonwealth countries in Britain
www.fco.gov.uk

Countryside and environment
British Waterways
www.britishwaterways.co.uk

Countryside Agency
www.countryside.gov.uk

English Nature
www.english-nature.org.uk

The Institute of Public Rights of
    Way Officers
www.iprow.co.uk

The National Trust
www.thenationaltrust.org.uk

Health advice
British Airways Health Advisory Service
www.british-airways.com

BMI Health Service Travel Clinic in
    association with Medical Advisory
    Services for Travellers Abroad (MASTA)
www.bmihs.co.uk

Department of Health
www.dh.gov.uk

London School of Hygiene and
    Tropical Medicine
www.lshtm.ac.uk

National Health Service
www.nhs.uk

Tropical Medicine Bureau
www.tmb.ie

News services
BBC online
www.bbc.co.uk

BBC World Service
www.bbc.co.uk/world service

Tourist information
British Canoe Union
www.britishcanoeunion.co.uk

Cycling and mountain biking
www.thebikezone.org.uk

Driving in Britain
www.dvla.gov.uk

Food imports for pets and livestock
www.defra.gov.uk/animalallowances_eu

General tourist information
www.visitbritain.com
www.UKguide.com

Pet Travel Scheme
www.defra.gov.uk/animals

Weather reports
BBC weather centre
www.bbc.co.uk/weather

Consular services
Official advice on travelling and living
    abroad for US citizens
www.state.gov/travel

United States Embassy – information
    on US embassies abroad and foreign
    embassies inside the US
www.usembassy.state.gov

Countryside and environment
National Parks
www.nationalparksservices.org

US Department of Agriculture
    Forest Service
www.fs.fed.net

Wilderness information and advice
www.wilderness.net
www.wildernessguide.com

Health advice
Traveller's health
www.cdc.gov

Wilderness first-aid kits
www.wildernessmedical.com

Wilderness Medicine, Outdoor
    Leadership and Rescue
www.stoneheath.com

Immigration advice
Government immigration advice
www.state.gov/immigration

News services
CNN online
www.cnn.com

Office of Broadcast Services
www.state.gov

Tourist information
Alaska
www.alaska.net

American Canoe Association
www.aca.net.org

American Camping Association
www.acacamps.org

California Peak to Peak trail and other
    wilderness links
www.peaktopeak.net

Friends of Saguaro National Park,
    Arizona
www.friendsofsaguaro.org

Leadership training courses
www.leadership-training-courses.com

North and South Carolina
www.campcarolina.com

Death Valley National Park
www.death-valley.us

Horse trekking
www.horsevacations.com
www.adventurehandbook.com

Regional wilderness information
www.eco.future.org
www.gorp.com

Trails Wilderness School
www.trailsws.com

Travelling in or out of the US
    with pets
www.cdc.gov/animal

Wilderness Maps and books
www.wildernesspress.com
www.amazon.com

Yosemite National Park
www.yosemite.nationalpark.com

Weather reports
National Weather Service
www.nws.noaa.gov

CANADA

Consular services
Consular Affairs
www.voyage.gc.ca/consular

Health Advice
Government health advisory service
www.canada.gc.ca/health

Immigration advice
Government immigration advice
www.canada.gc.ca/immigration

Tourist information
Canadian Tourism Commission
www.travelcanada.ca

Canada Travel Guide
www.canadatravelguide.info

National parks information service
www.national.parksreserve

Trail expeditions
www.trailcanada.com

Weather reports
Meteorological Service of Canada
www.msc.smc.ec.gc.ca

Weather Warnings
www.weatheroffice.ec.gc.ca

AUSTRALIA

Consular services
Department of Foreign Affairs
    and Trade
www.dfat.gov.au

Health Advice
The Travel Doctor (TMVC)
www.tmvc.com.au

Immigration advice
Department of Immigration
www.immi.gov.au

Australian Immigration Services
www.aust-immigration.com.au

National Parks
Western Australia national parks
www.calm.wa.gov.au

Eastern Australia national parks
www.ea.gov.au

Queensland national parks
www.env.qld.gov.au

National parks in Australia and
    worldwide
www.world-national-parks.net

News services
ABC online
www.abc.net.au

The Australian
www.theaustralian.news.com.au

Tourist information
Department of Environment and
    Heritage
www.ea.gov.au

Information for backpackers
www.backpackers.com.au

Travel advice
Government website for travellers
www.smartraveller.gov.au

Weather reports
Bureau of Meteorology
www.bom.gov.au

NEW ZEALAND

Consular services
Ministry of Foreign Affairs and Trade
www.govt.nz

Health Advice
www.archimedics.com
www.kiwikingdom.co.uk

Immigration advice
www.immigration.govt.nz

National Parks
www.nationalparks.org.nz
www.doc.govt.nz

News services
New Zealand News online
www.newzealandnews.net

Tourist information
www.nzsouth.co.nz
www.nz-tour.net
www.purenz.com
www.tourism.net.nz

Weather reports
Met Service
www.metservice.co.nz

Index

Acknowledgements

The publishers would like to thank the following individuals for their valuable contributions to this book:

Text contributors: Nick Banks for extra navigation text, Colin Drake for help with the section on physical fitness, Beverley Jollands for additional nutrition text, Bill Mattos for kayaking and caonoeing text and Will Patterson for additional cycling text.
Text advisors: Peter Tipling, Dr Bill Turner, J. Evans, Mrs A. Funnel.
Advice and assistance: Malcolm Creasey, Sue Dowson, Andy Middleton, David Williams.
Models for photography: Doncaster Scout Group, Joe O'Brian, Robert Driskel, Mr and Mrs Gibson, Lynn Milner.

With special thanks to Julian McIntosh at Safariquip, The Stones, Castleton, Derbyshire (tel: 01433 620 320) for the loan of camping and walking equipment for photography; and to Holmfirth Cycles, Bradshaw Road, Honley, Huddersfield, Yorkshire (tel: 01484 661672) for the loan of cycles and cycling equipment; and to Andrew Morrison for the loan of additional camping items.

PICTURE CREDITS
All the photography in this book is by Martyn Milner except for the following:
t = top; c = centre; b = bottom;
l = left; r = right

Corbis: p133t, p136t.

Simon Dodd: p11b, p18t, p117tl, p117tm, p117tr, p121b,

Peter G. Drake: p1, p6tr, p7 (both), p10b, p13b, p14b, p16, p18b, p19 (both), p21 (both), p22, p23 (both), p27b, p32, p33 (both), p35b, p36, p37tl, p38/9; p42 (both), p44 (both), p46, p48, p50b, p60t, p62 (both), p63tl, p63tm, p63tr, p64 (both), p65t, p65br, p69 (both), p70bl, p75tl, p75tr, p75ml, p88t, p94t, p101t, p104t, p104br, p105br, p109tl, p109tr, p112 (both), p113tl, p115 (both), 120b,

p128t, p130, p131 (all), p132 (all), p134t, p135 (both), p136b, p137b, p138 (all), p139 (all), p143bm, p143br, p150 (both), p151 (both), p152, p153 (both), p155, p156, p157tl, p157bl, p157br, p158bl, p159tl, p172bl, p173tr, p173br, p178bl, p179br, p180 (both), p181t, p184t, p186t, p191t, p196bl, p202br, p203 (both), p206b, p207tl, p207tm, p209bl, p209br, p211tr, p211bm, p212bl, p212br, p214tr, p214br, p222t, p226/7, p238t, p243, p244/5.

Mick O'Connell: p46br, p47b,

NOTES

NOTES

NOTES

NOTES